Mythology as Metaphor

Recent Titles in
Contributions to the Study of Music and Dance

Mythology as Metaphor

ક⬤ Romantic Irony, Critical Theory, and Wagner's *Ring*

MARY A. CICORA

Contributions to the Study of Music and Dance, Number 46

Greenwood Press
Westport, Connecticut • London

Library of Congress Cataloging-in-Publication Data

Cicora, Mary A., 1957–
   Mythology as metaphor : romantic irony, critical theory, and
Wagner's Ring / Mary A. Cicora.
      p. cm.—(Contributions to the study of music and dance,
ISSN 0193–9041 ; no. 46)
   Includes bibliographical references and index.
   ISBN 0–313–30528–5 (alk. paper)
   1. Wagner, Richard, 1813–1883. Ring des Nibelungen. I. Title.
II. Series.
ML410.W15C53   1998
782.1—DC21   98–9606

British Library Cataloguing in Publication Data is available.

Library of Congress Catalog Card Number: 98–9606
ISBN: 0–313–30528–5
ISSN: 0193–9041

First published in 1998

Greenwood Press, 88 Post Road West, Westport, CT 06881
An imprint of Greenwood Publishing Group, Inc.

Printed in the United States of America

The paper used in this book complies with the
Permanent Paper Standard issued by the National
Information Standards Organization (Z39.48–1984).

10 9 8 7 6 5 4 3 2 1

ે

Contents

Preface

This work is a literary-critical approach to Wagner's *Ring* via the concepts of mythology and Romantic irony. This book grew out of a desire to place both the *Ring* and the drama theory from the second part of *Oper und Drama* within the German tradition of the successive reinterpretations and reworkings of Greek tragedy. This objective in turn necessitated a discussion of mythology and hermeneutics in the *Ring*, and in this manner the book evolved into an argument concerning the essential irony of synthetically refabricating myth in the nineteenth century. The notion that Wagner's dramas have Romantic irony places the *Ring* into the tradition of the Romantic drama, and thus establishes Wagner's affinity to the German Romantic writers in a new way.

The *Ring*, I will argue, exemplifies the theory that Wagner presents in *Oper und Drama* by demonstrating the process of mythological refabrication and reinterpretation on the modern stage of reflection or self-consciousness. The basic concepts of the critical method known as deconstruction or post-structuralism, as represented by the work of Jacques Derrida, prove instrumental in my discussion. Thus my approach is diachronic as well as synchronic. I will examine not only literary theory, but also literary history, in elucidating Wagner's *Ring*. My analysis of the *Ring* will serve not only to place Wagner's work within the context of dramatic and literary history; it will also present a new interpretation of why and how Alberich's ring works the doom of the gods. All translations, unless noted otherwise, are mine. Also, unless noted, I have kept emphasis in the quotations unchanged.

I wrote this book during my stay at Stanford University as a Visiting Scholar with the kind permission of the German Studies Department. I wish to take this opportunity to thank the department for sponsoring my research and thus providing me access to the Stanford library facilities. I am also grateful to the library staff of Green Library for special borrowing arrangements, which not only facilitated my work but also eased the burden of the book renewal process. A special thanks goes to Paul Robinson of the History Department at Stanford, who patiently read the manuscript over and over again in its various versions, giving valuable criticism and advice along the way.

Introduction: Interpreting Wagner's *Ring*

*I*nterpretations of the *Ring* certainly abound. Critics have linked the mythological story told by the *Ring* to various extratextual systems in an attempt to determine and explain what the *Ring* really means. Due to its mythological nature, the work does encourage reductionist interpretations. Wagner's use of mythology as raw material for his music-dramas tempts one to somehow equate the figures, objects, and events portrayed within the *Ring* with extraneous systems of thought or historical, psychological, or sociological progressions. One usually establishes meaning by determining what the *Ring* allegedly represents, and in doing so translates its content into some other ideological or historical structure.

By using this method, the critic, one could say, seeks to uncover a second story or a hidden level of meaning beneath or behind the work itself. This usually entails linking two disciplines: music-drama (the *Ring*) and, for example, world-history or psychology. In addition, to the goal of establishing a consistent interpretation, the critic often has the tendency to explain away details and inconsistencies of the *Ring* in so to speak a genetic way, that is, by referring to its complicated origins and the various sources from which Wagner worked. The two extremes, which I will discuss more extensively in the third chapter of this book, are the political and the psychological interpretations.

Neither interpretation is, in itself, blatantly wrong. Wagner's dramas show that he was a master of depicting human psychology in music and drama; he was also a severe critic of modern society. In fact, both modes of interpretation highlight elements that are essential to an understanding of Wagner's *Ring*; however, neither is adequate in itself. For instance, the psychological mode of interpretation seems to be at odds with the historic-ity of the work, its peculiar nineteenth-century features, and the societal circumstances under which it was composed. Wagner clearly intended his tetralogy as a societal critique, and felt that it portrayed a world-historical process. The psychological interpretation unjustly ignores the world-his-torical progression that the *Ring* (according to Wagner) portrays. The *Ring* clearly contains a strong critique of nineteenth-century society.

The political interpretation is probably the most common mode of explaining the action of the *Ring*, and this is the interpretation with which I will be primarily taking issue in this work. Perhaps to some readers it will seem that, for the sake of arguing the case for my mode of interpretation, I too strongly oppose this political interpretation. That the gold ring is in some way a nineteenth-century critique of capitalism is clear. Wotan is definitely a corrupt ruler, and the *Ring* obviously works on the opposition of nature and society. Furthermore, Wagner's Zurich writings, which are generally acknowledged as the aesthetic counterparts of the *Ring*, embed the theory of the art-work of the future in a framework that dictates the revolution of modern society through art and the destruction of the state through mythological music-drama. Wagner himself was involved in revo-lutionary activities in the mid-nineteenth century.

However, too often it is taken for granted that the *Ring* is a political statement in the guise of a mythological work of art. This interpretation, I would argue, is not as self-evident as it may seem. It would imply that what is depicted in the *Ring* can easily be equated with societal processes. In other words, it poses a sticky interpretative dilemma. The political interpretation must account for just how the *Ring* refers to politics. This is a more complex issue than it may seem at first. Art and politics, especially mythological music-drama and external reality, are two separate spheres entirely. The present study will argue against both the validity of considering the *Ring* a political statement, and the soundness of regarding the world portrayed in the *Ring* as mythological. One can, first of all, debate whether the work is really political. Similarly, its mythological nature is too often accepted at face value.

The mythological nature of the work is not the only quality that encour-ages these extratextual approaches. The ring and other mythological trap-pings of the drama are frequently given some sort of explicit abstract significance or otherwise associated with abstract concepts. For instance, one must renounce love in order to gain the world-dominion that the ring of the title should accord to its wearer. Other details tease the critic into looking for hidden, allegorical meaning under the surface significance of its mythological story. For example, as a dragon Fafner guards the ring and the Nibelung hoard in a cave called "Neidhöhle" (Cave of Envy). Several characters repeat, almost formulaically, that whoever possesses the ring will be consumed by "Sorge" (care) and "Furcht" (fear). Siegfried is immune to

Alberich's curse, for he does not know fear. A scrutiny of such details yields, however, inconsistencies. Often the two levels of significance, the surface and the hidden meaning, the literal and the figural, diverge. The characters of the *Ring* inhabit a strange kind of musical-dramatic modern mythical cosmos.

Beyond hints at some kind of allegory, glimpses into a larger meaning behind the story, one cannot successfully assemble these pieces into an allegorical level of meaning that will encompass the entire work of art. Bringing Wagner's own theory into the picture creates more hermeneutic confusion. These abstract features also give the critic odd glimpses into a parallel of the *Ring* with Wagner's drama theory from the second part of *Oper und Drama*. Here Wagner uses key terms in an abstract sense, giving a modern structural interpretation of the basic forces and themes of Greek tragedy, thus making the use of his tragedy theory to interpret the *Ring* a truly baffling task. When traditionally mythological objects assume metaphorical significance they are no longer mythical, and the various levels upon which a modern myth functions present the scholar with an interpretative quandary. The work simply has too many levels of meaning that do not coincide or work consistently with each other.

The *Ring* somehow defies all interpretative efforts to establish that the tetralogy is somehow trying to convey another story. The parallel always seems to eventually break down. Somehow, something just does not fit right. The *Ring* is a complex, multifaceted, and sometimes contradictory work of art. The following is an attempt to tackle these contradictions and paradoxes head-on. A metaphorical reconstitution of mythology creates problems. This, one could say, is the theme of the *Ring*, as well as the subject of my interpretation of the *Ring* cycle. Critics discuss what the *Ring* means to the exclusion of how the *Ring* means, in other words, how signification is established. Furthermore, the issue of how the *Ring* signifies must be dealt with before one asserts just what the *Ring* means. In this book, I will discuss how the *Ring* creates meaning, and how it establishes its own meaning. These two points are, in a way, synonymous.

Within the plurality of interpretative approaches, the literary-critical one, as I will suggest, though apparently abstruse, can actually serve as some kind of antidote. That no single extratextual system does justice to the artistic complexity of the *Ring* seems self-evident. However, by taking the analysis to a metalevel and investigating just how the *Ring* represents and means—that is, by bringing the apparatus of literary criticism to bear on the *Ring*—I wish to propose an approach to Wagner's tetralogy that is not imposed upon the work from without, but rather arises organically from the work itself. This method therefore approaches the *Ring* on its own terms, with reference to the system of poetics that Wagner presents in *Oper und Drama* and the structures of meaning that the work itself sets up. The accursed ring, for instance, the object that is central to the tetralogy and thus to this analysis of it, has a significance; it carries certain associations for the characters onstage and also for the audience. The various characters in the dramas see it differently. In this study, I will discuss the issue of hermeneutics itself, just how the *Ring* creates and then destroys meaning.

Much has already been written about Wagner's theoretical and practical union of the arts. *Oper und Drama* presents an elaborate theory of how words should be linked with music to form the supreme work of art. In writing such a treatise, Wagner is in actuality formulating a way in which meaning can be created. Each separate medium, modern critical theory would quickly acknowledge, is a kind of language. Wagner, after all, discusses in *Oper und Drama* how in modern times spoken language has "fallen" from its ability to signify properly.[1] One tends to overlook, however, how the *Ring* undermines and even actually thematizes meaning. The discussions about what or how the *Ring* signifies, or the interpretations that link the *Ring* to other systems of thought, fail to acknowledge the fundamentally problematic nature of meaning in the universe of the *Ring*. One writes at length of how words and music are, by Wagner, united. But words and music also at times oppose each other, and their divergence creates nihilistic contradictions within the complex textual fabric of the work itself.

The grandiosity of Wagner's music that can also be described as its "Romantic" nature, or the quality that envelopes the listener or viewer of his music-dramas, seems to mask or obscure the various "layers" of the text at hand, with the term "text" referring, as in modern critical theory, not only to the libretto or the verbal part of the music-drama, but to the work of art as an entire structure of signs and symbols or a system of signification. It is in this sense that this term and its various derivative forms will continue to be used in this book. In this manner, the works under discussion can be analyzed and dismantled with the tools of structuralism, semiotics, and even, I would argue, post-structuralism. Jean-Jacques Nattiez elaborates several schools of literary criticism in proposing "androgynous hermeneutics" as an approach to Wagner's theory and works.[2] I will expand on the idea of doing a post-structuralist (or deconstructionist) analysis of Wagner's works by outlining a way in which the major tenets of this current can be related to the notion of myth, and then applying this literary theory that I have generated directly to *Oper und Drama* and the *Ring*.

That I call the *Ring* a "system of signification" should not mislead the reader into assuming that I am analyzing the *Ring* as I feel that, say, Roland Barthes would. Nor do I propose in this work a complete semiotic analysis of the *Ring* in terms of signs and codes, such as Umberto Eco theoretically outlines.[3] However, terms taken from literary criticism will prove instrumental in my discussion of mythological refabrication in the *Ring*. Without more excursions into its complicated genesis than are necessary, I will take the work under discussion as it stands, analyze it as a finished product, and theorize about how it functions as a whole entity and exemplifies the theory put forward in *Oper und Drama*. In doing so, I will explain what holds the *Ring* together, and how it eventually comes apart.

I am, of course, not the first to analyze Wagner's work with the tools of literary criticism. Claude Lévi-Strauss wrote that Wagner was the originator of the structural analysis of myth. I will, however, propose that he also demonstrates a post-structuralist use of myth as well, and can thus be considered if not the originator, then at least a foreshadowing of what I will describe as the post-structural ironicization of myth. Lévi-Strauss emphasizes that Wagner's structural analysis of myth is carried out by the music. By establishing a link between seemingly dissimilar parts of a drama, the return of a motive prompts one to ask what semantic relationship exists between these passages.[4] I will expand upon this assertion by discussing the self-interpretation of the work that is thus generated, as well as upon Lévi-Strauss' combination of myth and literary criticism. Critics often discuss Wagner's compositional method of mythological synthesis. I will show how the *Ring* almost inevitably invites a hermeneutical analysis along with it. Just as words and music diverge, so does the mythological content of the work.

In her book *Unsung Voices*, Carolyn Abbate has demonstrated the unreliability of narrative and the perspectival nature of knowledge and experience in the world of the *Ring*. Abbate shows that various characters in the *Ring* hear different "voices" in the musical score, and thus the layers of music correspond to what one could call frames of reference of the various characters. Abbate has shown how the *Ring* has various musical levels. I would add that the significance of the sounding of a motive depends on interpretation, that is, whose thoughts the orchestra is depicting, or just what the orchestra is saying with this music. For instance, in her analysis of Wotan's monologue, Abbate argues that Wotan's music is his own fabrication. Abbate's discussion of narrative as performance paves the way for my discussion of a "play within the play" structure that can liken Wagner's tetralogy to a Romantic drama.

Abbate raises some other ideas about the *Ring* that provide further groundwork for my analysis. She proposes the notion of the *Ring* as being somehow a musical-dramatic "stage-world."[5] I would like to extend her ideas to the mythical nature of the work, and investigate the strange kind of musical-dramatic or mythological "stage-world" that the *Ring* comprises. The world of the *Ring* is a complex one indeed, with various layers: verbal, musical, and mythological. I remarked earlier on the frequent divergence of words and music. That they often work together by coming apart presents a major hermeneutical dilemma. The present study will build on, in particular, Abbate's analysis of Wotan's monologue.

In presenting my hermeneutic analysis of the *Ring* tetralogy, I will not only oppose, but also build upon the political aspects of the *Ring*. In doing so, I put the political facet of Wagner's work in what I consider its proper perspective. One is most likely encouraged to give a political interpretation of the *Ring* by the revolutionary nature of Wagner's Zurich writings, which seem to substantiate or conclusively prove this interpretation. However, one could also argue that *Oper und Drama*, the work that deals with the aesthetic theory of the actual art-work of the future, is an aesthetic treatise. The equation of politics and the *Ring* must be mediated by art, theoretically as well as practically. It needs to be taken further and deeper than has previously been the case.

Political interpretations of the *Ring* run the danger of overlooking the fact that, although Wagner wanted to revolutionize nineteenth-century society along with art and by art, he was primarily an artist, and in particular, a musical-dramatist. Furthermore, the *Ring* does not directly portray modern politics. Similarly, though its goal in reality is political, *Oper und Drama* is a theoretical treatise about myth, words, and music. Wagner has reconstituted myth to comment upon history. For this reason, I will be discussing mythology and hermeneutics in Wagner's aesthetics and in the *Ring*. In this book, I will be asking in what way, and to what extent, the *Ring* is political; whether or not it is a truly mythological work of art; how it demonstrates Wagner's reworking of the traditional structure of Greek tragedy outlined in *Oper und Drama*; and precisely how the curse on the ring works the doom of the gods.

ॐ

The following is a hermeneutic approach to the *Ring* in several respects. For one thing, I will discuss the problematics of interpreting the *Ring*, in other words, the problematics of meaning and signification in the world of the *Ring*. Secondly, I will argue that the *Ring* also thematizes the hermeneutic process. In other words, I will discuss not only the meaning *of* the *Ring*, but also meaning *in* the *Ring*. The two points are, of course, interrelated. The refabrication of myth in the nineteenth century causes major inconsistencies in the ontological status of the fictional cosmos that is thus created. Wagner's characters are often seriously confused as to their exact whereabouts.

As the system of signification that I will discuss is made up of mythological elements, I assert that the *Ring* has a basic Romantic irony, for a modern mythical drama will inevitably be a self-conscious product; mythological drama cannot be reborn on the naive level in the nineteenth century. Therefore the *Ring* cannot be justifiably analyzed as a mythological world. A synthetically reconstructed mythological work will not be genuinely mythological. The action of the tetralogy, I will demonstrate, unfolds from its own raw materials. The dramatic impetus is built into the mythological pieces from which it was made, and is latent in its theoretical presuppositions. The *Ring* is, I would argue, self-referential to the end of being political, just as *Oper und Drama* sketches a musical-dramatic work of art that will comment upon and change society and history.

The *Ring* is a modern, synthetic, self-conscious myth, and thus it is by definition simply not folklore. Myth implies consciousness, immortality, and timelessness. History, on the other hand, means self-consciousness, mortality, and temporality. To measure the work by the same tools that are used to discuss its folkloristic sources can run the danger of overlooking the fact that one cannot rightly apply to the *Ring* standards and terms taken from a discipline used to study genuine folklore. A modern myth is self-consciously mythological; for that reason, it is paradoxically *not* mythological. The self-consciousness of a work of art is characteristic of a work of fiction that has Romantic irony, and thus I would suggest that the *Ring* is a Romantic drama rather than a political allegory or parable. Because the *Ring* thematizes its own peculiar fictionality, it belongs, I will propose, in the tradition of the Romantic drama. The *Ring* displays a self-consciousness of its fictionality, in particular, its modern mythical intertextuality. It contains self-reflection and what I would describe as innertextual hermeneutics. It thematizes its own composition, which occurred through a process of mythical synthesis and reinterpretation on a stage of reflection or self-consciousness.

My approach can thus be described as the combination of two very different methods, an historical and an ahistorical one. The historical one is represented by a discussion of Wagner and Romantic irony, and a demonstration of the ways in which the *Ring* is a Romantic drama. Wagner's dramas as mythical works are self-conscious. This is grounded in their aesthetic program. The other side of my thought about the *Ring* concerns a close analysis of the most ahistorical kind. I will apply terms taken from the critical current of deconstruction to the *Ring*. The subtitle of my book unites these two facets of my analysis.

By taking into account the literary-historical context in which the *Ring* was composed, and by discussing the *Ring* as a nineteenth-century synthetic combination of elements taken from mythological raw material and a modern reconstitution of a mythical cosmos, I will show how it both creates and undermines meaning. Thus an application to this tetralogy of terms taken from the literary-critical theory of deconstruction seems to follow inevitably due to the nature of the object of study. Therefore this critical approach is not willfully imposed upon the object of study from without, as a totally unrelated foreign entity; rather, I will show that it evolves necessarily from the analysis I will be presenting and the observations I will be formulating concerning mythology and hermeneutics in the *Ring*.

I would like to propose a new approach to Wagner's tetralogy. It may seem obvious to say that the *Ring* is a set of nineteenth-century music-dramas formed by synthetically refabricating archaic legendary and mythological source materials. Everybody knows that. From this basic fact, however, I would like to present an analysis of the *Ring* that deals with the work on its own terms, and discusses it in relation to its own aesthetic premises as set forth in *Oper und Drama*. The *Ring* demonstrates the theory of *Oper und Drama* by somehow dramatizing mythological reconstitution and self-reflection in nineteenth-century music-drama. In *Oper und Drama*, Wagner discusses the mythological art-work of the future as art. The *Ring*, accordingly, refers to itself. Furthermore, Wagner dictates the use of mythological hermeneutics within his drama by dictating that the art-work of the future should interpret mythology. The *Ring* therefore thematizes its own interpretation.

Any interpretation of the *Ring* that asserts its political aspects must deal with the complexity of *Oper und Drama*, which I feel can indeed be taken as the theoretical counterpart of the tetralogy. *Oper und Drama* is, however, only indirectly political. It proposes the myth of Oedipus as a kind of structural model for both history and the art-work of the future that the treatise theoretically builds. It dictates a mythological drama to be used for political purposes. In dramatizing what is expressed theoretically in *Oper und Drama*, the *Ring* therefore demonstrates the basic paradox in its underlying theory. It contains a dichotomy of myth and history, the ideal and the real, the figural and the literal. In particular, I will discuss the *Ring* in conjunction with Wagner's redefinition of the traditional tragic curse, which he elaborates in his reworking of Greek tragedy in *Oper und Drama*.

A modern myth that is a metaphor for history must have an abstract (or what I will call a metaphorical) level to mediate the equation, as myth such as provided Wagner with the raw material for his dramas does not refer directly to political reality. Archaic Germanic folklore really has nothing to do with nineteenth-century politics. It needs to be redefined for this purpose, and its elements assigned a certain modern significance. The world of the *Ring* is a paradoxical one because, I would argue, its aesthetic theory dictates a synthetic reconstitution of myth to form a metaphor for history. The cosmos of the *Ring* is, accordingly, both mythical and modern, magical and metaphorical. The fact that typically mythical elements assume metaphorical significance wreaks havoc with the order of signification that the work produces and evolves, and in this manner metaphor sets the stage for the final cataclysm.

The *Ring* enacts Wagner's theory of mythological drama as a comment upon history and as a means of changing, that is, revolutionizing history. The *Ring* has a political purpose, but that does not imply that one should give it a political interpretation. I am not contradicting myself here. If there is a contradiction, it is within the work of art itself. *Oper und Drama* sketches a modern revision of Greek tragedy by outlining a process of mythological refabrication. I will discuss the second part of this treatise in the second chapter of this book. The tensions that arise from a work using mythological raw materials on the level of reflection and self-reflection form Wotan's dilemma and thus ultimately bring about the doom of the gods.

In this study, I will argue that the *Ring* takes place on the stage.[6] It is an artistic product. The dramas that comprise the *Ring* cycle are rehearsing their own aesthetic presuppositions. The *Ring* stages its own performance. The *Ring* tetralogy portrays a fake cosmos, a stage-world, and it contains phony mythology and "stage-prop" magic objects. In pointing out how it does so, I will analyze the *Ring* in conjunction with Wagner's redefinition of the traditional tragic curse in *Oper und Drama*, and form a new interpretation of how Alberich's curse on the ring really works the doom of the gods.

Carolyn Abbate's work on the *Ring* is by far not the only research literature that I am building upon. I have also used Stefan Kunze's work on Wagner's theory of art, in particular the function of myth in his theoretical writings and dramas,[7] and Jean-Jacques Nattiez' suggestion of Wagner's thinking and work as somehow being metaphorical.[8] Both have proposed that Wagner's works somehow dramatize his aesthetic theory. I will make the same argument in a different way. In doing so, I will apply literary-critical terms to the *Ring* and open new avenues for Wagner scholarship to explore. Terms such as "deconstruction," "Romantic irony," "metaphor," and "under erasure" will prove instrumental for describing the process by which the *Ring* proceeds and unfolds its action. In this way I will show how the *Ring* fits into the broader German literary, aesthetic, and cultural tradition. The course of the work takes place not as the action in traditional, Classical drama does, but, rather, in a literary-critical way, through innertextual hermeneutics and progressive self-reflection. In this way, the *Ring* exemplifies Friedrich Schlegel's notion of "progressive Universalpoesie."

From Hans Blumenberg's *Arbeit am Mythos* I have taken the idea of myth as metaphor. Blumenberg, like Wagner, explains myth as a means by which primitive man masters his environment. Primitive man, as Blumenberg puts is, "absolutizes reality," for he does not think he himself is in control of his existence. Anxiety is rationalized to fear, and a general anticipation of danger is specified to a particular danger, through telling stories and giving names, that is, by an artistic ability. Anxiety signifies an inability to deal with substitutions or metaphors, and it shows that one cannot "work on myth," forget one's feelings of helplessness, and distance oneself from reality. Overreaction is a symptom that one has problems dealing with metaphor; one either has difficulty producing it or one takes it too literally. It is almost as though Blumenberg were describing Wotan's dilemma.[9]

The problem of defining each of the literary terms that I use could itself be the topic of a full-length study. As soon as one uses a term such as "metaphor," problems and confusions arise, and the issue of defining the term becomes crucial. In the following study, I will use the term "metaphor" in the sense given to it by what is known as the traditional substitution view. This theory states that a metaphor is figural language, as opposed to a literal expression. It often functions upon analogy or similarity. Critics have noted that metaphor raises the problem of interpretation. Paul Ricoeur, for instance, notes that the tension that a metaphorical utterance contains exists between two opposed interpretations of the utterance, not between two terms in the utterance. Ricoeur notes that the literal understanding of metaphor self-destructs in an inherent and a significant contradiction.[10] This almost seems like a discussion of Wotan's textual analysis.

This dichotomy of mythological raw material and its figural interpretation, aesthetics and politics, mythological objects and their abstract significance, as presented in Wagner's theoretical revision of Greek tragedy, actually determines the plot, action, and dramatic conflict of the *Ring* tetralogy. In the third and fourth chapters I will demonstrate my theory, in particular, by analyzing the ring of the title. The paradox of modern mythological refabrication not only makes the *Ring* function; it also ends the cycle. The self-reflection of the *Ring*, which is rooted in its modernity and its second-hand synthetic mythological nature, causes it to self-destruct or, in the terminology of modern critical theory, deconstruct. Wotan's innertextual reflection, which he performs in his monologue, causes the *Ring* to self-destruct from within. He actually dismantles or deconstructs the text of the *Ring*.

Not only does the plot of the *Ring* derive from the mythological raw materials that went into constructing it. The work implicitly anticipates and rehearses its reception. Wagner's conflation of aesthetics and politics in his Zurich writings necessarily produces a work that inherently contains metaphor and Romantic irony. Furthermore, its modernity actually brings the world of the *Ring* to ruin. In the fourth chapter, I will analyze how this happens by discussing Wotan's monologue as a process of "mythological deconstruction." Thus I will reverse the designation that Lévi-Strauss pronounced upon Wagner's mythological synthesis, arguing that he not only proposes a structural analysis of myth, but that the *Ring* also necessarily deconstructs myth.

Many features of the *Ring* do seem to resemble Derrida's theory of deconstruction, thus inviting some kind of an application of the theory of post-structuralism to this work.[11] Derrida suggests that all texts rehearse their grammatological structure, self-deconstructing as they constitute themselves. The *Ring*, I would argue, is an example of this. The music progresses through time, but the tetralogy, after all, is a cycle. It progresses by finally reverting to the beginning. Wotan's monologue shows these two trends beautifully. Derrida argues it is impossible not to deconstruct/be deconstructed. Wotan's demise seems inevitable, and thus the doom of the world over which he rules seems to follow necessarily, as does the end of the cycle of music-dramas.

The authority of the text is taken away by deconstruction, just as Wotan renounces his power as a conventional god and the alleged ruler of the world when he unwittingly deconstructs the metaphoricity of the ring. Derrida writes that deconstruction is a never-ending process. One can deconstruct the deconstruction and thus experience the joy of never being finished. Similarly, the *Ring* portrays an endless, eternal cycle of events, symbolized by the object named in the title. Deconstruction takes the metaphoricity of a text seriously. Similarly, I will discuss the *Ring* as a metaphorical structure of significance that is held together by the title object, and which eventually comes apart because of that same object.

Deconstructionists often discuss the issue of origin. In describing the infinite regress of signification and language, Derrida says that secondarity affects all signifieds in general. Siegfried often raises the question of origin; he is on a futile search for his own origin. The *Ring*, too, seems an infinite regress, just like the activity of a post-structuralist. The work, some have argued, actually begins with a fallen secondarity, for the world it portrays was already corrupt at the start of *Rheingold*. Wotan tore a branch from the World Ash Tree and thus fatally maimed it long ago; the Norns relate this in the first scene of *Götterdämmerung*. Modern directors are fond of staging the opening of *Rheingold* in a way that would indicate this. For instance, the Rhinemaidens are portrayed as prostitutes at a polluted river or a nuclear power plant.

The parallels between Wagner's and Derrida's systems of thought are, however, more than coincidental. I am not merely applying terms and theories as a useless exercise in hermeneutics. Rather, I wish to point out essential parallels in these two systems of thought. Wotan's declaration of the end of the gods, his willing of his own destruction, is a process that, in ways that go far beyond the obvious, can most adequately be described with terms that are taken from the theory of post-structuralism. My analysis is not definitive. I do not intend to show that the *Ring* follows strictly the ideas outlined in Derrida's *Of Grammatology*. But the basic concepts of post-structuralism can prove useful when modified and applied in analyzing the *Ring*.

It is, of course, common knowledge that the *Ring* self-destructs. One commentator has organized his extratextual approach to Wagner's *Ring* around this very concept, demonstrating the various interrelations between Wagner's work and nineteenth-century intellectual and cultural history.[12] I wish to take a different approach to this idea. In doing so, I will take, one could say, the opposite approach. I will show that the *Ring* self-destructs, or deconstructs, in a way that is actually inherent in the work. In other words, I will demonstrate that the self-destruction of Wagner's *Ring* is latent in its aesthetic program, and thus follows inevitably from the theoretical presuppositions upon which the *Ring* is based.

Thus this is not a pointless exercise in hermeneutics, nor an idle deconstruction that serves no useful purpose. It is not contrived; rather, it emerges from the very nature of the work of art under discussion. The basic structure of signification that the *Ring* creates is composed of a mass of mythological pieces. In fact, the image of Siegfried reforging his father's broken sword could be considered representative of how the *Ring* was created. Wagner builds his *Ring* out of mythological fragments, and thus in composing the *Ring*, Wagner does the same thing with myth that Siegfried does with Nothung. As Siegfried melts down the pieces and makes something new from them, Wagner assembles pieces of mythology, and in the process reworks and redefines them.

The *Ring* was synthetically constituted at a point in (historical) time, and as a system of signs or meaning it successively reconstitutes itself at each subsequent hearing or viewing. The mythological universe evolves out of the initial primal chords, and sung language, musical articulation, then proceeds from the nonsense syllables of the Rhinemaidens. The *Ring* is actually a structure of shifting significance that progresses by establishing meaning, and thus it evolves its own interpretation. In doing so, it also recapitulates its own genesis. Derrida discusses the problematic nature of presence. As the *Ring* is performed, it is constantly shifting; it is a dynamic system, rather than a static one. Meaning is therefore never fixed; rather, it is process and absence, not stasis and presence.

Wagner, like Derrida, deconstructs truth and metaphysics. The *Ring* raises the question of signification. Meaning is often problematic in Wagner's modern mythical work. In the world of the *Ring*, there is no transcendental ontology or metaphysics of presence. Wotan is a god, but he is human, too. He has authority, but he has undermined it. Wagner gives us gods that no longer have divine authority; this is an essential point of Wotan's realization in the second part of the tetralogy. The mythical cosmos of the *Ring* exists, I will argue, "under erasure." It is a theater set; phony, artificial, and synthetic.

Thus the self-destruction of the *Ring* is an inevitable consequence of its aesthetic program of revolution through mythological reinterpretation. In this manner, the *Ring* demonstrates its own program and illustrates in various ways the inherent contradiction of refabricating in the nineteenth century a cycle of music-dramas from archaic raw materials, and of re-forming myth to comment on and change history. As a result of Wotan's self-reflection, the mythological nature of the work comes apart. The Romantic irony of the work causes myth to deconstruct. The doom of the gods happens because the *Ring* has undermined, unworked, and dismantled its system of signification.

NOTES

1. For a discussion of Wagner's views on language, see my article, "From Metonymy to Metaphor: Wagner and Nietzsche on Language," *German Life and Letters* 42, no. 1 (1988): pp. 16–31.

2. Jean-Jacques Nattiez, *Wagner Androgyne*, trans. Stewart Spencer (Princeton, NJ: Princeton University Press, 1993), pp. 263–74.

3. See Umberto Eco, *A Theory of Semiotics* (Bloomington: Indiana University Press, 1976); *Semiotics and the Philosophy of Language* (Bloomington: Indiana University Press, 1984). For an application of semiotics to music-drama, see Herta Elisabeth Renk, "Anmerkungen zur Beziehung zwischen Musiktheater und Semiotik," in *Theaterarbeit an Wagners "Ring"*, ed. Dietrich Mack (Munich: Piper, 1978), pp. 275–88.

4. Claude Lévi-Strauss, *The Raw and the Cooked*, trans. John and Doreen Weightman (New York: Harper and Row, 1969), "Overture," pp. 1–32 (esp. pp. 14–30). See discussion by Nattiez, pp. 245–53. See also Carl Dahlhaus, "Musik als strukturale Analyse des Mythos. Claude Lévi-Strauss und 'Der Ring des Nibelungen,' " in *Wege des Mythos in der Moderne. Richard Wagner, "Der Ring des Nibelungen"*, ed. Dieter Borchmeyer (Munich: Deutscher Taschenbuch Verlag, 1987), pp. 64–74.

5. Carolyn Abbate, *Unsung Voices: Opera and Musical Narrative in the Nineteenth Century* (Princeton, NJ: Princeton University Press, 1991). In particular, I am referring to chapter 5, "Wotan's Monologue and the Morality of Musical Narration," pp. 156–205, and chapter 6, "Brünnhilde Walks by Night," pp. 206–49. More specific references will be given in the course of this study when necessary.

6. For a discussion by Götz Friedrich of his *Ring* productions that were based on this general idea, see: Götz Friedrich, "Die Bühne als Welttheater," in *Theaterarbeit an Wagners "Ring"*, ed. Dietrich Mack (Munich: Piper, 1978), pp. 104–10; "Regieprobleme im 'Ring,' " in *In den Trümmern der eignen Welt: Richard Wagners "Der Ring des Nibelungen"*, ed. Udo Bermbach, Hamburger Beiträge zur öffentlichen Wissenschaft, vol. 7 (Berlin: Dietrich Reimer, 1989), pp. 85–102.

7. Stefan Kunze, *Der Kunstbegriff Richard Wagners: Voraussetzungen und Folgerungen* (Regensburg: Gustav Bosse, 1983).

8. Nattiez, pp. 91–96.

9. Hans Blumenberg, *Arbeit am Mythos* (Frankfurt am Main: Suhrkamp, 1979).

10. Paul Ricoeur, *Interpretation Theory: Discourse and the Surplus of Meaning* (Fort Worth: Texas Christian University Press, 1976). On metaphor, see also: I.A. Richards, *The Philosophy of Rhetoric* (New York: Oxford University Press, 1936); Max Black, *Models and Metaphors: Studies in Language and Philosophy* (Ithaca: Cornell University Press, 1962); George Lakoff and Mark Johnson, *Metaphors We Live By* (Chicago: University of Chicago Press, 1980); Mark Johnson, ed., *Philosophical Perspectives on Metaphor* (Minneapolis: University of Minnesota Press, 1981); Wendell V. Harris, *Dictionary of Concepts in Literary Criticism and Theory* (Westport, CT: Greenwood Press, 1992). The amount of literature on the subject is, of course, enormous. Other general works I have consulted regarding the definitions of terms I will use in this study include: Chris Baldick, *The Concise Oxford Dictionary of Literary Terms* (Oxford: Oxford University Press, 1990); Karl Beckson and Arthur Ganz, *Literary Terms: A Dictionary*, 3d ed. (New York: The Noonday Press, 1989); Günther and Irmgard Schweikle, eds., *Metzler Literatur Lexikon. Stichwörter zur Weltliteratur* (Stuttgart: Metzler, 1984).

11. The basic premises of deconstruction are presented in: Jacques Derrida, *Of Grammatology*, trans. Gayatri Chakravorty Spivak (Baltimore: The Johns Hopkins University Press, 1976). It is from this work and its Translator's Preface that I am summarizing.

12. L.J. Rather, *The Dream of Self-Destruction: Wagner's "Ring" and the Modern World* (Baton Rouge: Louisiana State University Press, 1979).

Chapter 1 ❧

Wagner, Romantic Irony, and Mythology

*T*he two main theses of this book are as follows: 1) the *Ring* has Romantic irony; and, 2) the *Ring* is a myth that has been created on the level of reflection. They are complementary statements. Each thesis implies the other. The *Ring* has an essential irony as regards its essence as a mythological work of art. Similarly, the project of reconstituting mythology in the nineteenth century necessarily means refabricating mythology on a stage of reflection and self-consciousness. In this manner, Wagner's work can be considered a response to Friedrich Schlegel's appeal for a "new mythology" and a "progressive Universalpoesie" that proceeds through a process of unending poetic self-reflection.

❧

The subject of Wagner's affinities with the literary current of German Romanticism is by no means a new one. Othmar Fries[1] and Paul Arthur Loos[2] have devoted entire studies to the topic. Although nobody would deny the statement that Wagner's works represent the epitome of Romanticism in music, a discussion of such musical phenomena as tonality and dissonance does a grave injustice to a complex and multifaceted work of art. Wagner's works are not purely music; they are drama. In their themes, texts, and plots, Wagner's dramas invite comparison with the literature of the German Romantics. In addition, the theory that he presents in his aesthetic treatises was obviously influenced by the German literary and philosophical tradition.

Literary scholars, for instance, have noted similarities between Wagner's theories of art and those of the German Romantics. Wagner's theory of the "art-work of the future," the union of the arts or "Gesamtkunstwerk," is

similar to that of Romantic "Poesie." His writings also express a metaphysics of music comparable to that propounded by Tieck and Wackenroder in
their writings on art, though Wagner embeds this metaphysics in a theory
of music-drama by revising Schopenhauer's philosophy to suit his purposes. The concept of "unending melody" has been likened to the Romantic
longing for the endless. Scholars further note the similarity, which I will
examine later, between Wagner's emphasis on myth and Friedrich
Schlegel's appeal for a "new mythology" in his *Gespräch über die Poesie*.

When the discussion turns to how these theories are reflected in works
of fiction, the examples to which Wagner's works are compared are usually
taken from Romantic poetry or, more often, prose. For example, scholars
compare the death-mysticism and "night thoughts" of *Tristan* with the
treatment of these themes in Novalis' *Hymnen an die Nacht* (even though the
work was not in Wagner's library, and thus there is no firm evidence that
he knew it).[3] Other themes link Wagner's works with those of the Romantics—the three-stage model of fall and redemption, the importance of
dreams and nature, the image of the woman (as sinner and saint, destroyer
and mother), the theme of the artist and society, the amalgamation of art
and religion, the use of folk-literature such as the folk-tale ("Märchen") and
the legend ("Sage"), and the portrayal of supernatural phenomena.

The topic of Wagner and Romantic drama, though, seems to have little
or nothing fruitful to offer. The Romantics did campaign for reuniting the
arts, but they favored the novel to the drama. Wagner, in contrast, had only
contempt for the novel. Romantic drama, moreover, is simply not very
dramatic. It seems to hold no points of comparison with Wagnerian music-
drama. Peter Schmidt, in an essay on Romantic drama theory, has even
termed Romantic drama a kind of "anti-theater."[4] The Romantics are noted
for the comedy or "Lustspiel," the prime example of which is usually
considered Ludwig Tieck's *Der gestiefelte Kater*. It is hard to think of a
stronger contrast to Wagner's dramas. Gerhard Kluge also notes that the
dramas of the German Romantics violate the rules of dramatic form and
dramatic presentation.[5] Wagner's theoretical writings clearly indicate that
he considered his works "drama" (as opposed to modern, contemporary
"opera"). In contrast, there are, Gerhard Kluge points out, hardly dramatic
structures in Romantic drama, if one defines the "dramatic" as some
suspenseful plot that progresses to an end. The plays of the Romantics are,
rather, scenically organized. One could say they are just as epic or lyric as
they are dramatic. They were "Lesedramen" (dramas to be read), which
Wagner, influenced by Feuerbachian materialism, detested. He considered
sensual presentation the essence of drama.

The basic themes and goals of Wagnerian and Romantic drama are,
however, comparable. The usual theme of the Romantics, which provides
the framework within which the Romantic comedy should be understood,
was the loss of harmony in the modern world. Romantic comedy was

supposed to illustrate and mend the basic duplicity of existence. This simultaneously regressive and progressive theme of the "fall" and re-establishment of unity with nature, the critique of modern society, and the aim of establishing community, all seem to resemble the *Ring* in both form and content, a similarity that will provide a cornerstone for my arguments.

Nobody, however, even in an age of literary-critical approaches to opera,[6] would mention the notion of Romantic irony, a major element of Romantic literary theory and thus an essential feature of "Poesie," and probably the most prominent stylistic device of Romantic comedy, in connection with Wagner. And this is understandable. The concept of Romantic irony seems directly opposed to the associations that the term "Romantic" has when applied to Wagner's works. There is irony, one would say, in the works of Ludwig Tieck and E.T.A. Hoffmann—definitely not in those of Wagner. The modern directors who "frame" the action onstage to remind the audience that they are in the theater, interpret the whole story as the dream of one figure in the drama and thus internalize and "deconstruct" the work, or, for example, dress Wotan as Wagner are often regarded as heretics who shamelessly distort a work of art for the sake of directorial novelty and theatrical sensation. The scandals have almost become routine nowadays.

Harry Kupfer, for instance, "framed" his 1988 Bayreuth *Ring* production in what one could describe as a kind of socially and ecologically oriented Romantic irony. A pantomime staged before the *Rheingold* prelude showed a dead man lying on the stage. The figures of the evening's performance just stood there and stared the audience down long enough for it to become uncomfortable, apparently demanding something, then finally turned around as if disappointed and walked wearily away down the long street that formed the unit set for the entire cycle. When admiring Valhalla, the gods looked right at the audience, as though the theater in which they sat were the castle of the gods. As Valhalla burned, elegantly dressed men and women (obviously a theater crowd) onstage watched television. I intend to demonstrate in this book that such an approach is totally true to this work of art.

One does not often think of Wagner's works as ironic. In his essays on Wagner, though, Thomas Mann (who has been called "the ironic German") does lay the groundwork for my discussion. Not only does he say (in the essay "Leiden und Grösse Richard Wagners") that Wagner's art, in its ambiguity and "double optic" of the healthy and the sick, the duality that allowed him to appeal to the most banal and at the same time also to the most refined, could be best described as the epitome of Romanticism. He also argues that Wagner's compositions had an essentially literary way of using music. This implies that it is safe and justified to analyze Wagner's works with concepts of literary criticism, including those often applied to Romantic literature in particular. Furthermore, Mann praises Wagner for uniting myth and psychology, and without explicitly using the literary term "irony," notes the contradiction inherent in this undertaking. For myth in its primal, genuine form has little or no interest in the psychic depths of its gods and goddesses, and a psychological internalization of action and conflict seems to contradict and "dematerialize" the outwardly mythological nature of the material.

I will be expanding in a literary-critical way on the work that has previously been done on Wagner and the Romantics by applying the concept of Romantic irony, a central notion of Romantic literary theory, to *Oper und Drama* and the *Ring*. One of my fundamental propositions is that because the *Ring* has Romantic irony, it is a Romantic drama. Wagner's works are essentially ironic. Not only do they contain Romantic irony, but various other kinds of irony as well. Wagner's works, both theoretical and dramatic, show the basic contradictions of his age. They evince a tension between art and politics, the real and the ideal, and Romanticism and Young Germany.

Although the concept of irony might seem inapplicable to Wagner's dramas, the task of defining one's terms does suddenly make this topic a rich one. I do not propose an exhaustive systematization of the various kinds of irony. This in itself can easily be the subject of a full-length study, so my analysis is admittedly a simplified one. However, one must distinguish "Romantic" irony from various other kinds of irony, such as Socratic, rhetorical, or tragic irony.

To speak in broad categories, scholars differentiate verbal irony, that is, dissimulation or classical irony, from literary or fictional irony. When these terms or devices are elucidated, one must confront the seemingly incongruous and apparently unbelievable statement that Wagner's works, despite or even because of their nineteenth-century Romantic nature, are indisputably full of irony. After this survey, which will also serve to further highlight the modernity of Wagner's work and the complexity of the *Ring* as a text, I will define Romantic irony, giving examples from Romantic literature.

When asked to condense and incorporate the various kinds of irony into one overriding general principle that they all share, one would probably do best to say that irony is basically a dialectical structure, and further, that it consists of a contradiction.[7] In the third act of *Walküre*, for instance, it is ironic when the other congregating Valkyries say they have to wait for Brünnhilde because Wotan will be angry if they adjourn to Valhalla without her. When Brünnhilde enters, she relates that she is fleeing from him, and the reception he gives her when they meet is grim indeed, for he is furious with her for defying his command. There is irony, similarly, in *Götterdämmerung* when Siegfried drinks the potion offered to him by the Gibichungs, subjunctively toasting to Brünnhilde on the rhetorical condition that he might forget everything else she taught him. The potion will make him forget her until it is counteracted by its antidote.

The conclusion of *Rheingold* is full of various kinds of ironies. The Entrance of the Gods into Valhalla consists of an essential irony when Wotan exclaims, "So grüss ich die Burg, / sicher vor Bang' und Grau'n!"[8] (I greet the castle, safe from all dangers!) With these words Wotan triumphantly and repressively greets his new castle, which he wants to think is a safe fortress from external cares and dangers. He does not stay free of internal danger, though; he has in fact incurred danger himself as a direct result of building the castle. He will learn that the enemy is really, on the deepest level, within. The building of Valhalla only dramatizes and expedites his downfall. The castle is built on a paradox.

Rhetorical irony occurs only in isolated instances, that is, it usually does not encompass an entire work, and it is usually a tactical maneuver in such things as dialogues. Socratic irony is a specific type of classical irony or dissimulation. Socratic irony is when one (usually for the sake of pedagogy) pretends not to know something. Socrates used this technique for didactic, moral purposes, taking an ironic stance and playing down his talent and knowledge. Socratic irony is essentially a kind of verbal manipulation. In the verbal battle between the godly couple in the second act of *Walküre*, Fricka reproaches Wotan for his "Socratic irony" with the words, "Wie törig und taub du dich stellst" (MD 605). (How unassuming and deaf you pretend to be.) She sees through his ironic stance. Wotan has only superficially pedagogical intentions, and even these are self-serving. He criticizes Fricka with, "Nichts lerntest du, / wollt ich dich lehren" (MD 607). (You have never learned anything, much as I have tried to teach you.) The instances of irony in the *Ring*, in fact, make Nietzsche's pronouncement of the future utopian culture of "Socrates making music" seem to be somehow fulfilled by Wagner and his music-drama, with Socrates embodying irony.

The manipulative aspect of Socratic irony makes one think of Loge in *Rheingold* or Hagen in *Götterdämmerung*, not to mention Wotan between operas and backstage. Characters say things with ulterior motives and as rhetorical gestures or to provoke a reaction in another figure. The moment when Wotan stands there with the ring on his finger and Loge states, knowing that Wotan wants to keep it for himself, that Wotan intends to give it back to the Rhinemaidens is, by this definition, none other than an instance of Socratic irony. The flippant tune of Loge's statement that Wotan's keeping the ring for himself makes Loge look bad, because Loge promised to get it back to the Rhinemaidens, clearly communicates the playful intent of the trickster god who somehow seems to be above it all and "directing" the action, so to speak.

The riddle game between Wotan (the Wanderer) and Mime in the first act of *Siegfried* is an example of Socratic irony for the purpose of exposition. Each of the partners of this riddle game, of course, knows the answer to the riddle he is asking and does not pretend otherwise. In fact, he gloats over his knowledge, hoping to know more than his opponent. One can argue that the scene is more for the education of the audience than for that of the characters onstage. But in its thematization of knowledge, one can see this as a variation on the question and answer device of Socratic irony. Hans Mayer, in arguing that the *Ring* can be understood as an "analytic tragedy," notes that the *Ring*, in several places, thematizes knowledge.[9] Eternal Wisdom (or lack thereof) is a major theme of the *Ring*. The refrain of the Norns, "Weisst du wie das wird?" (MD 754) (Do you know what will happen?), or variations thereof, explicitly concerns the question of knowing.

Another sort of rhetorical (or, interestingly enough, "verbal") irony occurs when the opposite of what is said is meant. In the second act of *Siegfried*, for example, Mime intends to murder Siegfried—he tries to conceal his aim and seem kindly, but the audience (and Siegfried, due to tasting the dragon's blood) hear the real intent. One can consider this a reversal of rhetorical irony, an ironic form of it. In rhetorical irony, one says the opposite of what one means. It is ironic that Mime says exactly what he means, for he does not mean to say it. But in its complexity, one can consider this a Wagnerian version of rhetorical irony, appropriate for the mythological nature of the subject matter and the magical happenings that are taking place onstage.

Peter Wapnewski comments upon the powerful irony of Siegfried's identification of himself to Brünnhilde when he arrives as Gunther to abduct her in the first act of *Götterdämmerung*.[10] Siegfried announces, "Ein Freier kam" (MD 776), unwittingly using word-play to ironic effect. "Ein Freier" means "a suitor," but it also means "a free man." The former is appropriate to the situation; the latter is not. Siegfried, of course, was not aware of the effect that the potion he drank would have, nor does he intend the statement ironically. He honestly means he is coming to court her, that is, take her as a bride. His arrival, however, blatantly shows his lack of free will, as he has been tricked into this plot by Hagen and Gunther. His thinking that he is free, for he has no idea that he is not, merely highlights the fact that he is anything but. His inadvertent statement of his freedom to Brünnhilde is dramatic indeed. The word-play indicates the indeterminacy of verbal meaning in the world of the *Ring*. Musical meaning, furthermore, is sometimes no more secure.

To return to the riddle game in *Siegfried*, when Wotan hails Mime as a "wise smithy" (MD 673) ("weiser Schmied"), this is no doubt ironic. One can, of course, explain the phrase, as Wapnewski does, with reference to the ancient Germanic source materials that Wagner used.[11] Within the context of the work taken by itself, however, the line can only be explained as ironic, as Wotan intends to show Mime how much he does not know. Wotan's words are, as Brünnhilde remarks in the second act of *Walküre*, "zwiespältig" (MD 618) (split). This phenomenon of the "split word" is the essence of verbal irony. Furthermore, Wotan is, as I will show, an essentially ironic figure. Paradoxically, he undoes irony, in an ironic reversal of irony. I will demonstrate how he causes split, ironic, dual textual structures to fall apart and unwind completely.

It is interesting that music, an art that seems incapable of the dissimulation endemic in the form of verbal communication, can be used as verbal irony. Carolyn Abbate, for example, has shown that music can lie, and the *Ring* contains much evidence of this. Not only Loge, but the music, too, casts a cloud over the brilliance of the gods' entry into their new castle at the conclusion of *Rheingold*. Carl Dahlhaus notes that the majestic music that accompanies the Entrance of the Gods into Valhalla is deceptive, for, as Loge comments, they are rushing to their end.[12] In other words, the music does not really mean what it is saying. The simplicity and stationary nature of the music echo that of the start of *Rheingold*, but as Dahlhaus points out, this is also deceptive considering how complex the music has meanwhile become. Dahlhaus notes that the simplicity of the music, which in the prelude to *Rheingold* signified elemental nature and the beginning of all things, seems at the end a reduction and an oversimplification that are not to be trusted. It expresses not solidity, but, rather, the deception, evil, and confusion on which the present condition of the gods is based. In this manner musical meaning shifts.

Repetition (or a mirroring/echoing) can also be used to an ironic end. Dahlhaus explains that the key of C major, which traditionally stands for simplicity and integrity, is the key in which the Rhinegold-motive is initially presented in the first scene of *Rheingold*. The same motive in the same key recurs at the end of Loge's narrative in the second scene, but the key and motive are changed by being cited, and thus the citation indicates Loge's deceptive intent. Loge delivers to Wotan the request of the Rhinemaidens to return the gold to the Rhine, knowing, however, that Wotan does not intend to take his advice. In other words, the good advice is given with full realization that it is virtually useless. Truth is somehow false, and what previously seemed to denote simplicity and veracity becomes somehow suspicious. The advice is given ironically, and the motive and key of C major are thus also used ironically.

Dahlhaus, noting that Wagner uses keys and key relationships allegorically, discusses key relationships in Loge's narrative to show how Wagner makes C major seem the result of chromaticism, and thus what seems to stand for simplicity becomes suspect. In this way, truth and deception merge inextricably. Dahlhaus points out how the significance of keys and motives in a certain instance is dependent on how they were previously used in the work. Wagner, Dahlhaus explains, has a double-edged intention. As the sword-motive is presented, at the end of *Rheingold*, in C major, this key expresses the integrity of the free hero who breaks through the bonds of the gods. But, at the same time, C major expresses the empty grandeur of the gods. From the evidence of the *Ring*, one must agree with Dahlhaus that ambiguity is a central category of Wagner's aesthetics.[13] I will expand on these ideas to show how the mirrorings and echoings can be understood as instances of Romantic irony. The work invites a hermeneutical analysis that likens it to the textual structure of *Oper und Drama* in its self-exegesis and thematization of mythological interpretation.

Not only can the use of keys be, in the *Ring*, at times ironic. Wagner also uses motives ironically. Critics have sometimes been puzzled over Wagner's use of a particular motive when it does not seem appropriate to the present dramatic situation. Such uses can only be explained as ironic. Sometimes a motive can sound to recall one situation when the opposite of what the motive has become associated with is presently happening onstage. The most notable example of this is when the motive usually labelled "renunciation"—for it first sounds when Woglinde tells Alberich that whoever renounces love and forges a ring from the Rhinegold will acquire immeasurable power—sounds right before Siegmund, while singing "Heiligster Minne / höchste Not" (MD 602) (the highest need of the holiest love), pulls Nothung the sword from the tree and frees Sieglinde.[14]

Siegmund is a totally honest and straightforward character; unlike Loge, he has no ironic intent. He is affirming love and in what ensues he even commits incest in a flagrant affirmation of love over conventional morality. Brünnhilde, similarly, sings the words "Die Liebe liesse ich nie, / mir nähmen nie sie die Liebe" (MD 775) (I will not abandon love, they will never take love from me) to this same "renunciation"-motive in the first act of *Götterdämmerung* when she is refusing, despite Waltraute's pleas, to give the ring back to the Rhinemaidens. In other words, she is declaring her intent not to renounce love.

Thus the music helps create a multilayered semiotic and, I will argue, mythological structure. These different textual levels and various mediums sometimes combat each other. For example, the music is an extra layer that can diverge from the words to create meaning. Words and music often work not only with each other, but against each other. Furthermore, each medium can be in itself contradictory, that is, ironic. The entire work is a complex system of signs. The *Ring* is actually full of ironic structures, figures, and situations. The title object, for instance, is an ironic object. In its paradoxical and ironic nature, it represents the work as a whole in a profound way.

Tragic irony, otherwise called irony of fate, is also present in the *Ring*, even though the tetralogy, as I will show, unworks and transcends tragedy. This kind of irony occurs when the hero of a drama is oblivious to what is about to happen to him, but the other characters or the reader/viewer can foresee the tragic outcome of the drama. It can also encompass other instances of the broader contrast between the audience knowing something, and a character onstage not knowing the fact. This can often be a matter of unknown identity. In the traditional Greek drama of Oedipus, the audience knows who murdered the king, but Oedipus doesn't. Siegfried's statement in the first act of *Götterdämmerung*, "Ein Freier kam," which I discussed above, is actually a combination of verbal and tragic irony, as he is totally unaware of the ironic effect and tragic ramifications of the line.

As one would expect from the definition given above, most instances of tragic irony in the *Ring* have to do with Siegfried, and this is only appropriate, for he is naive and unassuming. A chilling and moving example of tragic irony which entails a repetition or echoing occurs at Siegfried's death in *Götterdämmerung*. The Rhinemaidens try to warn him that he will be slain that day, but he merely scoffs at them and refuses to listen, blithely mimicking bird calls from the second act of *Siegfried* as Hagen raises his spear and gets ready to stab him in the back.

Similarly, a tragic irony of unknown identities that seems to recall Greek tragedy occurs in the third act of *Siegfried* when Siegfried meets Wotan the Wanderer but has no idea who he is. Siegfried even accuses Wotan of being his father's enemy, thus unknowingly and ironically touching upon the fact that Wotan was in an indirect way really responsible for Siegmund's death. In a letter to King Ludwig dated 23/24 February 1869, Wagner comments on the scene in which Siegfried, after slaying the dragon, has the ring and the Tarnhelm in his hands but has no idea what they are. The music and drama cinematically pans back to him after showing Alberich and Mime fighting over these magical tokens. The juxtaposition is a strong one. Siegfried's ignorance of what these tokens signify contrasts sharply with the destructive awareness of Mime and Alberich that they are valuable. As I will show, however, their significance is also problematic.

Siegfried, it seems, takes after his father Siegmund in his tragically ironic stance. Despite Brünnhilde's efforts to persuade Wotan that his son should be saved, Siegmund's death has been decided in Wotan's momentous quarrel with Fricka. Siegmund tries to defy his fate, refusing to go to Valhalla when Brünnhilde informs him that he will die, but he has no chance of surviving the fight with Hunding. His fate has already been decided. Interestingly enough, despite his weaknesses, Siegmund is a fully positive figure. One of the reasons Siegmund wins the sympathy of the audience is that he futilely thinks he can decide or deny the inevitable and he is completely and pathetically unaware of the larger cosmic drama within which he has become a pawn.

By far the most interesting kind of irony is Romantic irony, and it is an essential part of the Romantic literature which Wagner's work is often discussed in connection with.[15] This kind of textual structure did not, however, originate in the nineteenth century. Romantic irony existed long before the nineteenth century, but most discussions of Romantic irony start with, or at least concentrate on, the fragments of Friedrich Schlegel. Romantic irony derived from the Transcendental Idealism of Fichte, in which the objective world is posited by the self. In this philosophy, there is a dialectic of subject and object, which is in turn shown by reflection to be a dialectic of the self with itself. Objectivity is thus really subjectivity.

To put the matter simply, Romantic irony is a kind of play with the fictionality of the text. It shows art as art, fiction as fiction. It concerns the relation of the artist to the work of art, which in the case of Romantic irony is, Schlegel writes, alternately creation and destruction, enthusiasm and skepticism. The producer is present and evident in the product. In his creations, the artist portrays himself as well as the fictional world. The artist has distance from the work of art. He has consciousness and freedom to call his creation into question. In this way the artistic creation is relativized. Thus Romantic "Poesie" hovers and vacillates between the real and the ideal. Because the work of art contains within itself reflection, it is comprised of many textual layers that can be picked apart for analysis.

When Friedrich Schlegel, in his famous 116th "Athenäum" Fragment, says, "Die romantische Poesie ist eine progressive Universalpoesie," which should unite "alle getrennte Gattungen der Poesie" (all separate genres of "Poesie"),[16] the link to Wagner's art seems obvious enough. Wagner's music-drama clearly exemplifies Schlegel's notion of "Universalpoesie," for he explicitly intended his work to represent a reuniting of separate art forms in what he termed, in his Zurich writings, the "art-work of the future." However, the ramifications of Schlegel's ideas need to be further explored, for the term "Romantic irony" can be applied to Wagner's works. I would like to take the emphasis off the word "Universalpoesie" and place it, rather, on the preceding word, the adjective "progressive." Schlegel writes of a process of poetic reflection, using the image of an endless hall of mirrors.

Und doch kann auch sie am meisten zwischen dem Dargestellten und dem Darstellenden, frei von allem realen und idealen Interesse auf den Flügeln der poetischen Reflexion in der Mitte schweben, diese Reflexion immer wieder potenzieren und wie in einer endlosen Reihe von Spiegeln vervielfachen. (KFSA 182–83)

Irony can hover in the middle between what is portrayed and the one portraying it, free from all real and ideal interests, on the wings of poetic reflection, and it can also potentiate this reflection repeatedly and multiply it, as in an endless hall of mirrors.

Schlegel's main goal, in fact that of the Romantics in general, was to abolish the basic oppositions of earthly existence and re-establish some kind of primal unity, an objective which the *Ring* shares in both form and content. As Wagner was clearly working within the tradition of German thought, it seems perfectly appropriate to draw such parallels.

In Fragment 238, similarly, Schlegel uses the term "Transzendentalpoesie" in analogy to "Transzendentalphilosophie," clearly showing the affinity of his theory of irony with the thought of Kant and Fichte. Schlegel writes that the essence of "Transzendentalpoesie" is the relationship between the ideal and the real. "Poesie" or "Transzendentalpoesie" should portray itself along with its object in every portrayal, and thus it should also be "Poesie der Poesie" (KFSA 204), that is, "Poesie" on a higher level. It is self-conscious. The poetic representation represents itself; it is reflexive. Romantic "Poesie" is thus a complex process of artistic reflection and self-mirroring ("Selbstbespiegelung"). I will apply these ideas to Wagner's *Ring*. The representative image of Wagner's tetralogy is usually considered to be the ring, to indicate not only the accursed object of the story but also the circular structure of the cycle. As the *Ring*, though, has what I will call a "dual" structure, I would instead suggest the mirror as the key image.

When one discusses Romantic irony, one usually thinks of Romantic narrative literature and Romantic drama.[17] For example, the works of E.T.A. Hoffmann are often taken as prime examples of Romantic irony. In authorial interjections in Hoffmann's stories, the narrator speaks to the reader as such. The narrative is not linear, but, rather, the author plays with the narrative form. This occurs, for example, in Hoffmann's novel *Kater Murr*, which is framed by a "found manuscript" story sketching a bizarre coincidence that produced a seemingly haphazard conglomeration of papers and an arabesque, an intermingling (though not exactly a mirroring) of two narratives. E.T.A. Hoffmann had been Wagner's favorite writer since the composer's childhood.[18] I would propose a similar use of Romantic irony in the works of Wagner and Hoffmann. Wagner's music seems to engulf the listener/viewer of his music-dramas and draw the audience into another realm. Upon close examination, though, Wagner's fictional worlds are really no more homogeneous than those of Hoffmann.

Hoffmann's artistic folk-tales ("Kunstmärchen") are characterized by a two-world structure that depicts the intrusion of a fantasy-world into normal everyday reality.[19] The juxtaposition of these contrasting realms creates irony, the prototype of such a narrative being *Der goldne Topf*. Thus the figures have a sort of "dual" existence, and different explanations for a single occurrence are proposed. The figure of the "double" ("Doppelgänger") is a common theme of Hoffmann scholarship, as this device is often used in his works. In *Der Sandmann*, for instance, Coppola "doubles" as Coppelius, and in *Der goldne Topf*, Veronica and Serpentina are clearly mirrorings of each other.

The simultaneity of various textual levels gives both the reader and the characters opportunity for reflection. The work contains authorial interjections by the narrator, and reflections of the protagonist upon his adventures are presented by means of the narrator and conversations that are reported. Often the work contains, as does *Der goldne Topf*, a mythical-allegorical level of significance, or a folk-tale is somehow placed within the tale as a whole. This mythical-allegorical level often provides a mythological background for the story at hand, which consists in the interpretation and explication of this deeper level of meaning. Thus, in Hoffmann's "Märchen," meaning is constituted through reflection, and as prime examples of Romantic "Poesie," these stories demonstrate the hermeneutical process.

According to Ingrid Strohschneider-Kohrs, irony is the theme of *Prinzessin Brambilla*.[20] The various realms that the work includes consist of the world of bourgeois reality, the theater, the Roman carnival, the plot which revolves around Princess Brambilla, and the myth of the Lake of Urdar, that is, the story of King Ophioch and Queen Liris. The various levels, these narrative strands, develop by playing off of each other and feeding into each other, and in this manner they interpret each other. Through these interconnections and mirrorings the work evolves its own interpretation in a characteristically Romantic and ironic way. Ciarlatano Celionati is, Strohschneider-Kohrs points out, a mirroring of the figure of the omniscient narrator, as he stands above the action and seems to control it. Thus this figure has a kind of ironic significance and function. He has an overview of the story and he "directs" the action of it. Though *Prinzessin Brambilla* seems to have nothing to do with the *Ring*, I am summarizing Strohschneider-Kohrs' analysis of this story because I will propose similar ideas relating to the *Ring*.

Strohschneider-Kohrs discusses the various ways in which the author, via the character of Celionati, toys with the fictionality of his work. There are places in the narrative, Strohschneider-Kohrs explains, in which Celionati refers to himself as a fictional character and shows his consciousness of the fact that the work in which he appears is fictional. For instance, Celionati is the figure who tells the story of the Land of Urdar, which constitutes the deepest level upon which the work thematizes itself. This mythical-allegorical level underlies the action of the entire story. Thus not only does the narrative make the transition from one textual level to another. The narrative is broken in a much more radical way. Through the figure of Celionati the text totally undermines the narrative and negates the fictionality of the work. Within the words of a character in the fiction, the plot and the characters are named as fictional. The author and the reader are also mentioned.

Strohschneider-Kohrs shows how this story, via the image of the Fountain of Urdar, allegorically thematizes the idea of art as a kind of mirroring, that is, as ironic. Form and content consist of reflection. Furthermore, form has somehow become content. In this manner, the story thematizes its own aesthetic premises. I propose that the *Ring* can be analyzed in a similar manner as a Hoffmann story. It is full of mirrorings and dual oppositions, such as that of the Volsung twins reflected in each other's eyes; Fasolt and Fafner; Gunther and Gutrune; and Wotan and Alberich. A similar process to that which Strohschneider-Kohrs outlines in *Prinzessin Brambilla* takes place in the *Ring*, as it thematizes, via Wotan, its own aesthetic program in the form of endless reflections.

Some may object to my likening the *Ring* to a Romantic comedy. However, when one considers that Romantic irony also occurs in drama, and in comedy especially, then the analogy no longer seems out of place. In Tieck's comedy *Der gestiefelte Kater*, which is usually taken to be a prime example of Romantic irony, the dramatic action or subject is obviously the performance of a folk-tale.[21] The work of literature is thus folk-literature, so to speak, at one remove. The audience of this "play within the play" is shown onstage, and thus the dramatized folk-tale and the portrayal of the audience, which is satirized, relativize each other. In this way, various textual levels are played off against each other. Furthermore, the author and various other technicians (who should properly be behind the scenes) appear onstage and speak about their own functions. The collision of the audience and the stage, the play and its technical aspects, becomes a theme of the work as a whole. A tension exists between the various realms that are depicted in the work. I propose that the *Ring*, in a very different way, stages its own performance and thematizes its own fictionality.

The fragments of Novalis, like those of Friedrich Schlegel, also provide crucial (though often cryptic) information concerning Romantic philosophy and the resultant poetics. Scholars debate to what extent the "magical idealism" of Novalis was influenced by Friedrich Schlegel's concept of irony, and they discuss the various affinities and differences between the thoughts of these two men. The "Romantic," according to Novalis, was the marvelous, the otherworldly, into which the poetic imagination would transform the world.[22] When Novalis writes, "Die Welt muss romantisirt werden" (The world must be romanticized),[23] he means that the usual must become mysterious. He is, in other words, propounding a two-world theory and an interrelationship of myth and history, or a mythicization of history. The Romantics saw no strict dichotomy between history and myth. And one can interpret the vacillation between the real and the ideal that defines Romantic irony as some kind of intermingling and the mutual relativization of history and myth.

By linking the terms "irony" and "myth" I will show how the *Ring* has a similar conglomeration of textual levels and thus exemplifies the theory of Romantic irony. The *Ring*, I will show, is a myth about myth. I would argue that the *Ring* has a self-consciousness of its own mythical nature, a self-referentiality concerning its mythical raw material. It refers to itself, just as Novalis' novel *Heinrich von Ofterdingen* is a work of "Poesie" about "Poesie." Novalis' novel tells of the education of a poet, the title figure, by Klingsohr, thus in essence dealing with itself as literature or fiction. *Heinrich von Ofterdingen* gradually moves from the "real world" to a magical, mythical realm, with Klingsohr's "Märchen" forming a text within a text. Similarly, Wagner's *Ring* is self-referential and can be understood as having texts within texts. Furthermore, Wagner's *Ring* presents an amalgamation of history and myth, as the aesthetic theory presented in *Oper und Drama* outlines an interrelationship of history and myth. In the following chapters, I show how the *Ring* thematizes its aesthetic program of mythological refabrication and revolution through music-drama.

Nattiez, in discussing Wagner's works with reference to the theme of androgyny in the writings of the early Romantics, raises the issue of just which works of the Romantics (such as Böhme, Humboldt, Ritter, Baader, Schlegel, and Novalis) Wagner knew.[24] Nattiez points out there is no evidence that Wagner had read the theoretical writings of Friedrich Schlegel and Novalis. Their names (among those of other German Romantics) figure neither in the indexes to the volumes of Wagner's correspondence for the period until 1852 nor in his autobiography. None of their writings was in his Dresden library, though we do know that Wagner borrowed a copy of Schlegel's *Lucinde* from his Uncle Adolf's library in Leipzig and that he read it during the early part of 1828. It is particularly striking, then, that one can find Romantic irony in the *Ring* and, in *Oper und Drama*, a poetics that can be considered the theoretical expression of a revolutionary, subversive kind of Romantic drama. Nattiez discusses how ideas can be in the air at a given historical period, and how ideas of one writer can influence an artist without there being real evidence of this connection. This, I propose, is the case with the *Ring* and *Oper und Drama*. The tetralogy contains an essential Romantic irony, and its corresponding theoretical basis is expressed in *Oper und Drama*.

The *Ring* has, of course, no authorial interjections (or interpolations of the author hiding behind the persona of the narrator) such as one finds in stories by E.T.A. Hoffmann. It does, however, contain self-reflection, which causes, in turn, the progression that Schlegel writes about in the fragments I have discussed. Dahlhaus writes that the web of "Leitmotive" reflects upon the drama and creates a "second drama," and that the orchestra both expresses feeling and makes a commentary upon the drama. Dahlhaus remarks upon the soundness of the analogy that Wagner drew between the orchestra of Wagnerian drama and the chorus of Greek tragedy, as the chorus fulfills the function of distancing the audience from the drama. Thus the orchestra can be considered the voice of the composer/author, speaking in the language of the "orchestral melody" or "Leitmotive."[25] As dissimilar as the *Ring* might superficially seem to a work of Hoffmann, the affinities are, I will show, deep and structural.

Carolyn Abbate discusses a phenomenon analogous to Romantic irony without using the term in her book *Unsung Voices* when she treats songs within music as a kind of "metalayer" of singing within an entirely sung work, or when she analyzes an instance in which an operatic character hears the music that another character within the work is singing. That is, the character perceives the formal structure of the work, which only the audience (but not the fictional characters) should be hearing.[26] She discusses, for instance, how the music of Wotan's monologue "rings false," and

Brünnhilde, in an instance of Romantic irony, hears this. Abbate's theories, as I show in my final chapter, have grave ramifications for the interpretation of the *Ring* dramas. Hearing the formal structure of the work implies knowing that one is in a work of art.

The textual layers of this "total work of art" can work together (or, rather, against each other) to confirm that its Romantic (or artistically synthetic) nature, that is, its encompassing or incorporation of various art forms, *makes* it ironic. The music, which seems to create illusion and emotionally draw the audience in to the drama, actually serves at times to distance the spectator from what is going on; one could say it "alienates" him/her, and thus causes him/her to take a critical stance toward what is happening onstage. Music can express something that the words do not, or it can contradict or subtly undermine the words. The music seems to "potentiate" the drama in many ways, as I will show. The various art forms not only construct the drama as it progresses, but also deconstruct it.

For instance, music can omnisciently communicate something that the character doesn't know, such as the Valhalla-theme when it sounds in Sieglinde's narrative in the first act of *Walküre*. She doesn't know that the old man who stuck the sword into the tree at her wedding feast was Wotan, let alone that Wotan was her (and Siegmund's) father. Music, in this way, complements the words. The musical or motivic repetitions that I discussed earlier, and cited as examples of "verbal" or rhetorical irony in music, can also be considered Romantic irony, for they create a structure of echoings or "mirrorings" that forms the essence of Romantic irony. Dahlhaus notes that Loge's irony at the end of *Rheingold* is a parodistic reflection of Erda's oracular pronouncement about the end of the gods.[27] The lament of the Rhinemaidens over their misfortune distortedly echoes their earlier praise of the Rhinegold.

In defining "fictional irony" and explaining what distinguishes Romantic irony as a specific type of fictional irony, Bernhard Heimrich uses terms and differentiations that will prove useful later in my analysis of the *Ring* as a Romantic drama.[28] A fiction as a whole, he proposes, consists of two levels, a phenomenon of doubling that one can describe as appearance and reality. This creates the fictional level (what happens within the fiction) and the objective level (for example, a play being performed onstage). Fictional irony, according to Heimrich, is the reflection of the fictional nature of a work or text within the fiction itself. For example, the self-reflection of a fictional character would constitute fictional irony. In other words, the fictionality of the text contradicts itself.

Heimrich terms the effect of fictional irony a "reduction," and he theorizes that the means by which this effect is reached is an improvisation. The reduction, Heimrich explains, is a break in the fictionality, an uncalculated moment, and therefore an improvisation. The reduction is a phenomenon in the fictional vehicle, not a mere "framing" device, whereas the improvisation occurs within the fiction. Heimrich terms it a "reduction" when an element of the fictional reality refers to the objective reality. In this manner, fiction reveals itself as fiction.

Heimrich points out that the characteristically Romantic form of fictional irony does not disrupt the illusion, nor does it relativize the fictionality of the work. Rather, it occurs within the work. The reflection does not raise one above the fictionality, but it is, rather, a self-mirroring within the fiction. It is the dialectical phenomenon of a transcendental reflection within the work as a whole, an elevation over the conditionality of the work that takes place without violating this conditionality. This Romantic alternative to the usual kind of fictional irony raises a formal condition to the content of a form. It raises form to its own content. I will show how form has become content (and vice versa) in Wagner's *Ring*, creating a confusion from which Wotan in particular suffers fatal consequences.

In analogy to Schlegel's term "Tranzendentalpoesie," Heimrich calls the specifically Romantic form of drama with an ironic structure the "Transzendentaldrama." He shows that the Romantic form of fictional irony causes progression and reflection, just as the corresponding theory dictates. In the Romantic modification of the traditional "play within a play" device, the whole play, the real drama, is itself conceived and represented as a "play within a play," and the fictional levels are, moreover, multiplied. The actors do not reflect on their roles; rather, the roles reflect on themselves. The roles represent themselves as roles in a play. The reflections do not relativize or potentiate the role; rather, they belong to it. There is no illusion as such to destroy. That is the essence of such a Romantically ironic work. The reflections do not, Heimrich argues, actualize the objective reality. The role is the role of a role.

I will apply these ideas to the *Ring* to demonstrate a structure of Romantic irony that in its progression and reflection actually makes the *Ring* surprisingly similar to a Romantic comedy. The *Ring* contains Romantic irony, instances where it can be interpreted as thematizing itself, places where it seems to refer to its own fictionality. The *Ring* contains moments that can be understood as reductions, where the drama figures seem to be reflecting on their roles or the parts that they are playing in the *Ring*. The characters at times perform the role of literary-musical critic for the drama in which they exist by reflecting upon the work and discoursing upon what it could possibly mean. They seem to be taking the *Ring* apart from below, or looking down on their dramatic situations from above. Thus the *Ring* contains various patterns of shifting meaning. In this manner, the work thematizes its own interpretation.

The notion of improvisation is not totally unknown to Wagner scholarship. Dieter Borchmeyer[29] explains that according to Wagner, improvisation was the first artistic production of the "Volk," and he shows how in Wagner's later aesthetic treatises the concept of improvisation has become the structural principle of music-drama. Borchmeyer points out the paradox of fixed improvisation and calculated spontaneity, and he observes that the idea of improvisation was also present in Romantic aesthetics. Borchmeyer theorizes that Wagner used improvisation as a means to break through and transcend conventional genres and forms. Improvisation is absolute artistic freedom, but free improvisation is really planned and bound by strict rules. Borchmeyer shows how the concept of improvisation is demonstrated by *Meistersinger*. In my third and fourth chapters, I will argue that the concept of improvisation characterizes the aesthetic theory represented by the *Ring* also.

I will bring the notion of improvisation, as represented in Wagner's *Ring*, more directly into relation to the theory of Romantic irony to show how the *Ring* embodies a mythological, ironic, improvisatory paradox to the end of transcending the conventional form of tragedy. The *Ring* contains various textual levels and an implicit "play within the play" structure. The stage directions at the end of the *Ring* do state that men and women onstage watch the catastrophe, implying that the entire drama is some kind of a "play within a play." There are numerous instances in the *Ring* when some characters are manipulating others, or suddenly one seems to know or not know that he or she is in a drama, or on the stage participating in a performance of a music-drama. Some characters may know things, while others do not. Thus I would suggest that the *Ring* is the staging of a staging. In chapters 3 and 4, I will show how the *Ring* both establishes and destroys such structures.

As Rainer Franke points out, Wagner did not want to totally exclude reason or reflection from the production or reception of his work of art. The poetic understanding ("dichtender Verstand") establishes the network of associations. Feeling and imagination are ordered, Wagner felt, by the understanding.[30] The aesthetic system that *Oper und Drama* outlines and that the *Ring* demonstrates represents, with regard to both artistic production and reception, a dialectic of faculties such as that which the German Romantics proposed in their theoretical writings. In fact, it does not seem excessive to assert that Romantic irony is somehow central to Wagner's aesthetics.

ta

Whereas Romantic irony is a fairly new topic for Wagner scholarship, the topic of myth is a common one. Scholars have painstakingly studied which mythological works Wagner was familiar with, and how he used elements of his sources. All agree that Wagner had an original and eclectic way of using what he found. The most frequent pursuit is to ask what changes he made in his raw material, and which features of his work he took from which mythological sources. For example, Deryck Cooke[31] and Elizabeth Magee[32] have written about the relation of the *Ring* to its sources, which include works of Scandinavian mythology (such as the *Edda*s and the

Volsunga Saga), and the nineteenth-century cataloguing effort of Jacob Grimm's *Deutsche Mythologie*. Gerhart von Graevenitz discusses Wagner's mythological syncretism with reference to the mythological theories of Jacob Grimm, Franz Joseph Mone, Friedrich Creuzer, Giordano Bruno, and Giambattista Vico.[33] I will take a more theoretical approach to the topic of myth in Wagner's work by addressing the very concept itself. Wagner refabricated myth to comment on modern history. Comparisons of his works with their sources just outline the basic issue that I would like to treat in more depth.

Wagner's interest in mythology clearly places him within the Romantic tradition. The primal, indigenous products of the Germanic peoples—both history and myth—interested the Romantics. For the German Romantics, the past replaced what was lacking in the present, history faded into myth, and the supernatural intruded into normal reality. The philologists sought medieval songs and epics, "Volkslieder" (folk-songs) and "Volksbücher" (folk-books), to restore the lost fatherland. Dagmar Ingenschay-Goch uses a structural model to explore Wagner's method of mythological syncretism and explains that the Romantics saw an intermingling of history and myth, being interested in an archaic past that took on mythological contours.[34] I will be asking to what extent Wagner's dramas are really mythical, and analyzing them as typically Romantic, that is, self-reflective and ironic, myths.

From the evidence of Wagner's works, it would not be going too far to argue that Romantic irony seems to be an essential element in the use of myth in the nineteenth century. Wagner's works are second-hand myth, historically relativized interpretations of myths. The *Ring* was written in the nineteenth century. It is thus myth on a stage of reflection and self-consciousness. The *Ring* is a synthetic product, not a genuine myth. Thus it cannot be analyzed with the same concepts and standards as one would use for real myth. It works differently. The *Ring*, I would suggest, has an essential irony with regard to its mythological nature. It is self-consciously mythological.

Here Mann circled around but overlooked an important aspect of Wagner's work. He evidently failed to notice that the *Ring* demonstrates a basically ironic use of myth. In the essay "Richard Wagner und der 'Ring des Nibelungen' " he compares Wagner's use of myth to Goethe's ironic use of it in *Faust*. Granted, Wagner is totally serious about myth, as Mann points out. Wagner does not have a humorous or playful intent, Mann correctly notes. Mann writes that Goethe's use of myth in *Faust* lacks the tragic and pathetic accent of Wagner's mythological dramas. I would add, however, that with his distinctly untragic use of myth, Wagner gives his mythological source elements an ironic twist when one understands "irony" to mean a kind of Romantic irony used toward totally earnest purposes.

Most would agree with Thomas Mann that Wagner discovered the use of myth for opera, and commentators frequently discuss Wagner's turn from history to myth for his composition of the *Ring*. His autobiographical essay "Eine Mitteilung an meine Freunde" is the document that is usually cited in such discussions. Here Wagner narrates his abandonment of a drama plan about Friedrich Barbarossa in favor of one about Siegfried, which was, if not a complete about-face, then at least a shift of perspective from history to myth. This use of mythology as raw material for his dramas was not, however, an individual preference, nor is the resultant mythological nature of the *Ring* totally unproblematic. Rather, Wagner's turn from history to myth needs to be understood with reference to Romantic theories of art and the inherent contradictions that these posed. The assertion that Wagner discovered the use of myth for opera is definitely not a simple statement.

Stefan Kunze discusses the interrelationship of the real and the ideal, history and myth, in Romantic aesthetics. He points out the essential contradiction in Wagner's use of myth, and in doing so outlines an approach to Wagner's aesthetics, and by reflection his dramas, that I would like to expand upon.[35] For the Romantics art was considered a sensual revelation or a symbolic representation of the Idea. The dichotomy of the sensual raw material used and the objects portrayed, on the one hand, and the spiritual aspect of art, was formulated in many ways and variations. As art gained in importance, Kunze points out, it was no longer self-explanatory. In the nineteenth century, reflection, the critical capacity, dominated art and was considered the means by which art could attain perfection. Because it tended to the symbolic, myth was the raw material that would raise the real to the ideal and thus legitimate the work of art. But this mythological legitimation of the work of art ultimately, like Wotan, undermines its own authority, as I will later show. Reflection, I will demonstrate, can work against mythology in a decisive way, and the ideal can dangerously dematerialize the real.

The nineteenth-century synthetic reconstitution of mythology was therefore not unproblematic, as it inevitably occurred on the level of reflection and self-consciousness. Kunze cites Waldimir Weidlé as writing that mythical thinking and modern reflexivity (the consciousness of myth) are mutually exclusive. Kunze notes that a synthetic reconstitution of mythology is a sharp contrast to genuine "mythical" thinking. The demand for an artistic reconstruction and re-creation of myth is an implicit admission that a binding mythology, one that would automatically bind the artist with the public, no longer exists.[36] A synthetic myth, one could say, is not really a myth. In discussing Wagner's *Ring* in particular, Herbert Schnädelbach also notes the contradiction of an individual production of myth, since myth is by definition (as Wagner never tired of pointing out) a product of a collective, of the "Volk."[37]

A modern myth created by an individual artist in the nineteenth century is invariably not mythical in a conventional way. Rather, it unmasks itself, as does the *Ring*, as a contradictory and paradoxical work of art. The "new mythology," one could say, was even self-defeating. Helmut G. Meier notes the essential contradiction of the "new mythology" of the nineteenth century, that is, that it was used in opposition to the rationality of the modern age, but was itself a product of the modern, rational age.[38] The *Ring*, I will show, contains a duality of myth and reflection upon myth within the work itself. Heinz Gockel feels that the Romantic project was doomed from the start. He remarks upon the futility of the presumption that myth would obliterate the split of Spirit and Nature, the individual and the collective or species. Just as, according to Gockel, art could not possibly reconcile mankind with the environment, myth was unable to transcend the problematic relationship of mankind to empirical reality.[39]

The appeal to mythology, Kunze points out, though it occurred in the name of Idealism, degrades myth at the same time by using it as a mere material substrate for symbolic revelations. As art was spiritualized, thus being understood as symbolic, its raw material, myth, was dematerialized.[40] The objects portrayed were meant to stand symbolically for Ideas. Similarly, there is, for various idiosyncratic reasons, a tension between the real and the ideal, the simultaneous re-creation and destruction or dematerialization of myth, in the *Ring*. This process is symbolized by the object named in the title. Kunze points out that irony in a work of art is a sign that the artist no longer has a healthy relationship to his art and the materials that have been passed down to him. Accordingly, I will point out an ironic use of myth in the *Ring*. In fact, I will argue that the plot of the *Ring* is formed by the self-consciousness of a modern mythical world. Furthermore, Wagner's tetralogy shows how mythology in modern times negates its own veracity and subtly undermines its own claim to truth value.

Furthermore, nineteenth-century Idealism, despite its emphasis on myth, had a profound awareness of history. According to Kunze, myth was an attempt to escape historicity, at least in the realm of art. Paradoxically, though, history and myth imply each other in Idealistic aesthetics. The flight from history was as futile as Wotan's flight from Alberich's curse. Because real works of art all referred to the ideal concept of art, these individual works were therefore considered manifestations, realizations in history of the idealized concept of art. Accordingly, the nineteenth-century use of myth demonstrates, on the contrary, a profound awareness of its own historicity. Wagner's work shows these dichotomies of the real and the ideal, the objective and the subjective, history and myth, and life and art. Furthermore, it reflects upon them and itself, with catastrophic results.

Greek tragedy, Kunze points out, merely confirmed Wagner's theories of art, which Kunze feels can hardly be derived from Greek tragedy, since Wagner's theories are firmly rooted in nineteenth-century Romantic aesthetics. Wagner's use of myth is much more than the participation in a contemporary trend; rather, it was essential to his theory of art. Myth fulfilled, Kunze explains, two main criteria of Wagner's aesthetics. In this way myth for Wagner guaranteed the comprehensibility of his works. It was abstract, having a distance from normal prosaic temporal reality and being free from conventionality, and therefore it was universal and general, portraying what Wagner called "das Reinmenschliche" (the purely human). However, at the same time it had sensual immediacy.[41] Mythology was a condensed world-view, which made it easily communicated to the senses. Wagner had been influenced in his revolutionary years by the materialism of Ludwig Feuerbach, and thus he felt that art should not appeal to the intellect without addressing the senses as well. Wagner's aesthetics represents the collision of Idealist aesthetics and revolutionary purposes.

When one investigates it closely, one finds that Wagner's *Ring* is a paradoxical work in many respects. Wagner stressed that his work had some relation to "life," but, as Kunze points out, the identification of art and life was deceptive. Art is not life.[42] Wagner's use of myth demonstrates, one could say, the contradiction of Feuerbachian materialism and German Idealism. I will show, though, how his *Ring*, in exhibiting this basic paradox of art and life, bridges the gap in a revolutionary way. It portrays, in itself, its own aesthetic program. Via the device of Romantic irony, that is, by paradoxically referring to itself, art affects life. To show how aesthetics merges with politics in Wagner's theory, I will use the tools of modern critical theory, thus linking literary hermeneutics with the idea of mythological music-drama, writing with music, and the construction and reception of mythological music-drama with the notion of writing "under erasure."

These contradictions make the *Ring* a highly ironic work of art. Perhaps part of its irony resides in its nature as a total work of art, and its intent to unite opposites. Paradoxically, its self-referentiality demonstrates its revolutionary purposes. The mediation between the real and the ideal, the subject and object, that myth was supposed to fulfill according to Idealism is mirrored in the textual structure of Wagner's myth. One can see these two requirements I just mentioned, the abstract nature and sensual immediacy, as somehow contradictory. I will call the former the ideal aspect of myth, and the latter, the real aspect of myth, and show how the *Ring* in its very textual structure mediates between the real and the ideal, and illustrates the clash of the two in its mythological portrayal of history, thus unworking the work of art in the process of depicting its own creation and reception.

Despite the emphasis he placed on myth, Wagner's historical consciousness is pronounced, thus exemplifying a main trait of Romantic aesthetics. The ostensibly mythological nature of the *Ring* dynamically negates its own veracity by virtue of the *Ring* being a nineteenth-century myth that explains history. Wagner saw an interrelationship of myth and history. He subjectively and self-consciously reinterpreted myth to be a metaphor for history. He contradicts himself, defeating his own purpose, creating a paradoxical and multilayered work. The aesthetic program, which is reflected in the structure of the work of art, is highly paradoxical. The *Ring* shows a self-consciousness of its own historicity that reveals its outwardly mythological nature to be a facade and ultimately destroys the mythological cosmos, thus aesthetically demonstrating its own political program. With his political use of aesthetic mythology, Wagner is, unexpectedly enough, a forerunner of Jacques Derrida, demonstrating, via his alter ego Wotan, innertextual deconstruction.

In other words, one can establish a series of analogies that interlink to form a hall of mirrors, a series of endless reflections. One can draw an analogy, for instance, between the dichotomy of history and myth, on the one hand, and that of life versus art. Furthermore, there is a discrepancy between the mythological raw material and the uses to which Wagner has put this material. The *Ring* thus contains a paradox within itself, in its very structure that reflects its aesthetic program. It is, and is not, a mythological work of art. Despite its outwardly mythological nature, the *Ring* is actually in many ways a historical work. Romantic irony is the device through which myth and history collide and the work deconstructs itself.

Kunze explains that there is a contradiction between the atemporality of the mythical raw material and the fact that Wagner uses this material to interpret history. Furthermore, Kunze also notes the tension between the outwardly mythological trappings of the *Ring* and the temporality of the work as an explanation of history.[43] In other words, an equation is established between the mythological work of art and the real events of history, and this is the analogy that I have previously argued must be mediated by abstract concepts. Wagner's mythological work stands in some kind of a relation to history. It is a metaphor for history. I would also add that the Romantic self-reflection of the work makes the antagonism explosive. Tibor Kneif points out that the subject of the *Ring* is history, and that it has a historical consciousness beneath its mythological exterior.[44] A myth, though, cannot be both historical and ahistorical, that is, temporal and mythical, at the same time. This is Wotan's dilemma. Aesthetic self-reflection causes Wotan to acknowledge his lack of ontological status.

Furthermore, Wagner's mythological work of art was intended to change reality. With his *Ring*, Wagner hoped to mediate between life and art. His ultimate goal was political. By mythologizing history, Wagner felt he could historicize myth. Those who interpret the *Ring* as a political myth overlook the fundamental paradox of the use of myth, which was chosen as raw material because it is divorced from reality, as a vehicle for political change. A myth cannot by definition be directly political. A "political myth" is an oxymoron. Wagner's *Ring* can be political only in an indirect way. It refers to itself and demonstrates its own aesthetic program of indirectly affecting external reality. Wagner's *Ring* shows that a modern myth that has political intent will inevitably come apart and, in self-reflexively demonstrating its own nihilistic political-aesthetic program, destroy itself.

The statement that in his use of mythology Wagner is an heir to the Romantics is a complex one indeed. The famous passage of Friedrich Schlegel from his *Gespräch über die Poesie* demonstrates the dilemma beautifully. Dual, ambiguous linguistic usage illustrates the paradox of the "new mythology" of the nineteenth century. He writes, using the fictional persona Ludovico as his mouthpiece,

Es fehlt, behaupte ich, unsrer Poesie an einem Mittelpunkt, wie es die Mythologie für die der Alten war, und alles Wesentliche, worin die moderne Dichtkunst der antiken nachsteht, lässt sich in die Worte zusammenfassen: Wir haben keine Mythologie. Aber setze ich hinzu, wir sind nahe daran eine zu erhalten, oder vielmehr es wird Zeit, dass wir ernsthaft dazu mitwirken sollen, eine hervorzubringen. (KFSA 312)

Our literature lacks a center, such as mythology was for the ancient world, and the basic inferiority of modern literature to ancient literature results from the fact that we do not have a mythology. But I would add that we are close to having one, or, rather, the time is coming when we must seriously work at creating one.

The first use of the term "mythology" is literal, the second, figural, just as in the first instance Schlegel uses the definite article (*die* Mythologie) and in the second sentence the indefinite article (we need *a* mythology). For instance, Schlegel mentions the philosophical system of Idealism as an example of the "new mythology." "Poesie," he further notes, is an "indirect mythology" ("indirekte Mythologie").

The term "myth" can thus be understood in various senses. According to a broad, general definition of the term, any explanatory story can be a myth. The *Ring*, though an explanatory story in itself, uses elements of traditional mythology to form this new myth. Furthermore, these elements, when used in a modern, metaphorical way, somehow make the entire work, if you will, nonmythical. To say that Wagner obeys Schlegel's command and forms a "new mythology" just because his *Ring* uses mythical raw material is thus an oversimplification that ignores a basic paradox and the fundamental complexity of the work. It glosses over the question of in what way the works that somehow formed a "new mythology" for the Romantics are really mythical. The word "myth" must be qualified when applied to such complex works as Wagner's *Ring*. Linguistic ambiguity is often anything but meaningless; it can be, on the contrary, quite significant.

I will explore the paradox of an artistic reconstitution of myth, which is, I propose, illustrated by Wagner's work. Schnädelbach discusses various meanings of the word "Kunst" in the term "Kunstmythos," such as "artistic" or "artificial."[45] In doing so, Schnädelbach seems to neglect the fact that here there is an interrelation of history and myth. I would like to emphasize

the different ways that the *Ring* is mythical. Wagner's "Kunstmythos" has
a duality analogous to that which I outlined in the typical E.T.A. Hoffmann
"Kunstmärchen." This duality results from the contradiction inherent in the
mythical nature of the *Ring*. Thus I am defining an issue that goes far
beyond a mere word-play or a double meaning that one could consider
merely coincidental. Rather, this verbal ambiguity points to a much larger
problem that is firmly rooted in Wagner's aesthetics, as I will later show.

The *Ring* uses conventional mythological raw material, and thus has the
usual trappings of mythology. It is also a myth in that it is an explanatory
story. A myth in the sense of modern critical theory does not necessarily
have to do with gods and goddesses. Roland Barthes, for instance, defines
"myth" as a type of speech, a system of communication, or a mode of
signification, pointing out that everything can be a myth.[46] One could say
that Wagner uses elements of myth to form a new myth. Wagner's works
are thus mythic in two senses. This duality of myth creates a tension in the
work. Wagner was certainly a "bricoleur" of the most complex and intricate
kind. In writing the *Ring*, Wagner performs mythological as well as musical-dramatic "bricolage." The new myth that is thus created is a metaphor
for history and reflects its own aesthetic program via Romantic irony.

Because Wagner's *Ring* is an explanatory story, a myth in the extended
sense, it necessarily uses mythological raw material, the elements of traditional myth that it contains, in a modern way. Therefore the mythological
nature of the *Ring* is, I propose, overdetermined and paradoxical. Because
of the various ambiguities of their mythical nature, Wagner's works, I
would suggest, have layers of myth and are myths in an extended sense
that even seems to work against and negate the literal, more conventional
sense of the term. Unlike traditional mythology, Wagner's myth is modern,
reflective, self-conscious. The tetralogy has gods, magical curses, gold rings
that give the owner world-dominion, dragons, and noxious potions. It even
gives a cosmology of sorts. But despite these features it is not strictly
mythical. It demonstrates, rather, the contradiction inherent in a nineteenth-
century synthetic reconstitution of mythology.

Scholars have, of course, written about the problem of defining the term
"myth." This in itself is no easy task, and it is not my purpose to attempt
an exhaustive survey of the topic, but a superficial examination of Wagner's
Ring with reference to some of the distinguishing features of myth reveals
the dilemma that I am outlining and the paradoxical nature of this "myth."
Walter Burkert proposes four features that distinguish "myth."[47] Firstly, he
explains, myth is a "folk-tale," a narrative that has no author, no authorial
responsibility, and is not a direct mirror of reality. Secondly, it is a structure
of signification that lends itself well to structural analyses that work with
binary oppositions and the relation of the parts to the whole. The content
has, thirdly, to do with gods and events that precede temporality. Fourthly,
myth has a connection to ritual, and is an explanation of reality.

The *Ring* does correspond to some of these specifications. For instance, it is an explanatory story. One could even say that the very performance of it, modelled as it was on Greek tragedy, gives it some connection to ritual. It also lends itself, as I will show, to a structural analysis. In some significant respects, though, it is, by this definition, mythical in a strange, nineteenth-century way. It is a work of art, a "Kunstmythos." As such it embodies its own aesthetic theory in a Romantically self-reflexive way. Through self-consciousness of its own historicity, it dismantles its own textual structure. The cataclysm that occurs in the finale of *Götterdämmerung* is a result of the dual mythical nature of the work, and it merely demonstrates that self-referentiality can be fatal.

I am not meaning to equivocate about the definition of the term "myth." Rather, the terminological imprecision that Schlegel and Wagner demonstrate regarding this word in its various forms points to the very paradox that I am describing. In fact, one could even say that the dilemma of a modern reconstruction of myth, the contradiction inherent in the "new mythology," is somehow represented or expressed by the ambiguity of the term "myth." The various ways in which the *Ring* is mythical or mythological, the literal and/or extended sense of its mythical nature, forms the crux of my argument and creates a multilayered textual structure that can be likened to and analyzed as Romantic irony.

Wagner's irony as regards myth results from his works being a nineteenth-century synthetic reconstitution of myth using mythic material. He has written a myth with a practical, political purpose. Only modern myths ostensibly portray and intend to change history. This myth is thus not genuine. The work is simply not purely mythological in the way that one would expect. Because of its modern, reflective nature, Wagner's myth is not mythical in the way that genuine mythology is. It has other characteristics. The *Ring* shows a modern self-consciousness as concerns its dual mythical nature, and it reflects its own metaphoricity as a quasi-mythical explanation of history. A metaphorical myth, that is, myth used as metaphor, and given metaphorical properties, is an oxymoron of sorts.

Because of this essential contradiction at work in the text of the *Ring*, and because of its multilayered textual structure which is grounded in the theory presented in *Oper und Drama*, the work can be effectively analyzed with concepts taken from the literary theory of post-structuralism. Self-consciousness, on the part of both the artist and the characters within the work, of the metaphorical nature of an artistic myth is simply not viable, as the *Ring* demonstrates. Innertextual self-reflection can prove catastrophic. Metaphor can be quite dangerous when one thinks about it too much, as Wotan demonstrates. A discussion of how the curse on the ring affects Wotan leads to the conclusion that Romantic irony, as I will show, works the doom of the gods.

The mythological self-reflection that somehow obviates mythological consciousness is the problem I will investigate. A modern myth that is supposed to explain and affect history is not really mythical. This is the basic paradox from which the world of the *Ring* suffers. A myth on the level of consciousness or reflection is self-conscious, reflective, that is, ironic. The *Ring* is a modern work; despite its outwardly mythical nature, it was written by a composer in the nineteenth century. By reflecting on itself, a modern myth can reveal its own historicity and therefore destroy itself by undermining its basic premises. Thus, in Wagner's aesthetic system, mythological reconstruction leads, via Romantic irony, to mythological deconstruction.

In the next chapter I will discuss *Oper und Drama* as a Romantic treatise that shows the basic dichotomies and even discourses on the issue that I have discussed in this chapter. I will then demonstrate how the *Ring* dramatizes the contradictions inherent in the nineteenth-century aesthetics I have outlined in this chapter. It dramatizes, in particular, Wagner's theory of tragedy as a rebirth of myth. It demonstrates the basic irony and the paradox in its mythological nature, for this essentially forms the plot and determines the action of the work.

NOTES

1. Othmar Fries, *Richard Wagner und die deutsche Romantik: Versuch einer Einordnung* (Zurich: Atlantis, 1952).

2. Paul Arthur Loos, *Richard Wagner: Vollendung und Tragik der deutschen Romantik* (Munich: Leo Lehnen, 1952).

3. Dieter Borchmeyer, *Das Theater Richard Wagners: Idee, Dichtung, Wirkung* (Stuttgart: Reclam, 1982), pp. 261–62.

4. Peter Schmidt, "Romantisches Drama: Zur Theorie eines Paradoxons," in *Deutsche Dramentheorien. Beiträge zu einer historischen Poetik des Dramas in Deutschland,* ed. Reinhold Grimm (Frankfurt am Main: Athenäum, 1971), vol. 1, pp. 245–69.

5. Gerhard Kluge, "Das romantische Drama," in *Handbuch des deutschen Dramas,* ed. Walter Hinck (Düsseldorf: August Bagel, 1980), pp. 186–99.

6. For recent examples of these approaches, see, for example, the following collections: Arthur Groos and Roger Parker, eds., *Reading Opera* (Princeton, NJ: Princeton University Press, 1988); David J. Levin, ed., *Opera Through Other Eyes* (Stanford, CA: Stanford University Press, 1994).

7. On the various different kinds of irony, see: Uwe Japp, *Theorie der Ironie* (Frankfurt am Main: Vittorio Klostermann, 1983); Ernst Behler, *Klassische Ironie, Romantische Ironie, Tragische Ironie. Zum Ursprung dieser Begriffe* (Darmstadt: Wissenschaftliche Buchgesellschaft, 1972).

8. Richard Wagner, *Die Musikdramen,* ed. Joachim Kaiser (Hamburg: Hoffmann und Campe, 1971; Munich: Deutscher Taschenbuch Verlag, 1978, 1981), p. 576. Subsequent references to this edition of the *Ring* text will be given in my text by page numbers, preceded by the abbreviation "MD."

9. Hans Mayer, "Der 'Ring' und die Zweideutigkeit des Wissens," in *Richard Wagner: Mitwelt und Nachwelt* (Stuttgart: Belser, 1978), pp. 230–35.

10. Peter Wapnewski, "Die Oper Richard Wagners als Dichtung," in *Richard-Wagner-Handbuch*, ed. Ulrich Müller and Peter Wapnewski (Stuttgart: Alfred Kröner, 1986), p. 299.

11. See: Peter Wapnewski, *Der traurige Gott. Richard Wagner in seinen Helden* (Munich: C.H. Beck, 1978; Deutscher Taschenbuch Verlag, 1982), pp. 160–64.

12. Carl Dahlhaus, *Richard Wagners Musikdramen* (Velber: Friedrich, 1971), pp. 108–9.

13. Dahlhaus, *Richard Wagners Musikdramen*, pp. 109–10.

14. On Wagner's use of this motive and the interpretative dilemma of this musical phrase, see: Deryck Cooke, *I Saw the World End: A Study of Wagner's "Ring"* (London: Oxford University Press, 1979), pp. 2–10.

15. On Romantic irony in particular, see: Helmut Prang, *Die Romantische Ironie*, *Erträge der Forschung*, vol. 12 (Darmstadt: Wissenschaftliche Buchgesellschaft, 1972); Ingrid Strohschneider-Kohrs, *Die romantische Ironie in Theorie und Gestaltung*, Hermaea, Germanistische Forschungen, Neue Folge, vol. 6, rev. ed. (Tübingen: Max Niemeyer, 1977); Strohschneider-Kohrs, "Zur Poetik der deutschen Romantik II: Die romantische Ironie," in *Die Deutsche Romantik: Poetik, Formen, und Motive*, ed. Hans Steffen (Göttingen: Vandenhoeck und Ruprecht, 1967), pp. 75–97; Peter Szondi, "Friedrich Schlegel und die romantische Ironie," in *Schriften II*, ed. Wolfgang Fietkau (Frankfurt am Main: Suhrkamp, 1978), pp. 11–31.

16. Friedrich Schlegel, *Charakteristiken und Kritiken I (1796–1801)*, ed. Hans Eichner, vol. 2 of *Kritische Friedrich-Schlegel-Ausgabe*, ed. Ernst Behler et al. (Munich, Paderborn, Vienna: Verlag Ferdinand Schöningh, 1967), p. 182. References to this volume of Schlegel's works will hereafter be given within my text by page numbers, preceded by the abbreviation "KFSA."

17. See, for instance, Ralf Schnell, *Die verkehrte Welt. Literarische Ironie im 19. Jahrhundert* (Stuttgart: Metzler, 1989).

18. See: Linda Siegel, "Wagner and the Romanticism of E.T.A. Hoffmann," *The Musical Quarterly* 51 (1965), pp. 597–613.

19. See: Strohschneider-Kohrs, *Die romantische Ironie*, pp. 352–62.

20. Strohschneider-Kohrs, *Die romantische Ironie*, pp. 362–420.

21. For a discussion of Tieck's comedies, see: Strohschneider-Kohrs, *Die romantische Ironie*, pp. 283–336.

22. See: Strohschneider-Kohrs, *Die romantische Ironie*, pp. 100–112.

23. Novalis, *Das philosophisch-theoretische Werk*, ed. Hans-Joachim Mähl, vol. 2 of *Werke, Tagebücher und Briefe Friedrich von Hardenbergs*, ed. Hans-Joachim Mähl and Richard Samuel (Munich and Vienna: Carl Hanser, 1978), p. 334.

24. Jean-Jacques Nattiez, *Wagner Androgyne*, trans. Stewart Spencer (Princeton, NJ: Princeton University Press, 1993), p. 117.

25. Carl Dahlhaus, *Wagners Konzeption des musikalischen Dramas* (Regensburg: Gustav Bosse, 1971), p. 22.

26. Carolyn Abbate, *Unsung Voices: Opera and Musical Narrative in the Nineteenth Century* (Princeton, NJ: Princeton University Press, 1991).

27. Dahlhaus, *Wagners Konzeption des musikalischen Dramas*, p. 26.

28. Bernhard Heimrich, *Fiktion und Fiktionsironie in Theorie und Dichtung der deutschen Romantik* (Tübingen: Max Niemeyer, 1968).

29. Borchmeyer, *Das Theater Richard Wagners*, pp. 57–63. For his *Meistersinger* discussion, see pp. 206–30 of the same work.

30. Rainer Franke, *Richard Wagners Zürcher Kunstschriften: Politische und ästhetische Entwürfe auf seinem Weg zum "Ring des Nibelungen"*, Hamburger Beiträge zur Musikwissenschaft, vol. 26 (Hamburg: Verlag der Musikalienhandlung Karl Dieter Wagner, 1983), pp. 199–226 (see esp. pp. 214–18).

31. Cooke, *I Saw the World End* (see note 14 above).

32. Elizabeth Magee, *Richard Wagner and the Nibelungs* (New York: Oxford University Press, 1990).

33. Gerhart von Graevenitz, *Mythos: Zur Geschichte einer Denkgewohnheit* (Stuttgart: Metzler, 1987), pp. 261–89.

34. Dagmar Ingenschay-Goch, *Richard Wagners neu erfundener Mythos: Zur Rezeption und Reproduktion des germanischen Mythos in seinen Operntexten*, Abhandlungen zur Kunst-, Musik- und Literaturwissenschaft, vol. 311 (Bonn: Bouvier Verlag Herbert Grundmann, 1982).

35. The following discussion is based on: Stefan Kunze, *Der Kunstbegriff Richard Wagners: Voraussetzungen und Folgerungen* (Regensburg: Gustav Bosse, 1983), pp. 65–78, 178–87. More specific references will be given when appropriate.

36. The material in this and the preceding paragraph has been summarized from: Kunze, pp. 65–70.

37. Herbert Schnädelbach, " 'Ring' und Mythos," in *In den Trümmern der eignen Welt: Richard Wagners "Der Ring des Nibelungen"*, ed. Udo Bermbach, Hamburger Beiträge zur öffentlichen Wissenschaft, vol. 7 (Berlin and Hamburg: Dietrich Reimer, 1989), pp. 145–61. Here cited from p. 145.

38. Helmut G. Meier, "Orte neuer Mythen. Von der Universalpoesie zum Gesamtkunstwerk," in *Philosophie und Mythos. Ein Kolloquium*, ed. Hans Poser (Berlin: Walter de Gruyter, 1979), pp. 154–73.

39. Heinz Gockel, "Mythologie als Ontologie: Zum Mythosbegriff im 19. Jahrhundert," in *Mythos und Mythologie in der Literatur des 19. Jahrhunderts*, ed. Helmut Koopmann, Studien zur Philosophie und Literatur des neunzehnten Jahrhunderts, vol. 36 (Frankfurt am Main: Vittorio Klostermann, 1979), pp. 25–58.

40. This and the following paragraph are based on: Kunze, pp. 69–70.

41. Kunze, pp. 181–82.

42. Kunze, pp. 75–77.

43. Kunze, p. 70.

44. Tibor Kneif, "Wagner: eine Rekapitulation. Mythos und Geschichte im *Ring des Nibelungen*," in *Das Drama Richard Wagners als musikalisches Kunstwerk*, ed. Carl Dahlhaus, Studien zur Musikgeschichte des 19. Jahrhunderts, vol. 23 (Regensburg: Gustav Bosse, 1970), pp. 213–21.

45. Schnädelbach, pp. 145–46.

46. Roland Barthes, *Mythologies*, trans. Annette Lavers (New York: Hill and Wang, 1972), pp. 109–11.

47. Walter Burkert, "Mythisches Denken. Versuch einer Definition an Hand des griechischen Befundes," in *Philosophie und Mythos. Ein Kolloquium*, ed. Hans Poser (Berlin: Walter de Gruyter, 1979), pp. 16–39.

Chapter 2

Mythology and Tragedy in *Oper und Drama*

*T*he early nineteenth century saw a confusion of aesthetics and politics.[1] The theater of such playwrights as Laube and Gutzkow, both of whom were Wagner's contemporaries, became an instrument for social change. Furthermore, in this time period there was not only a prevalent desire to change reality for the sake of art. The critics had the opposite wish, too. They felt that art should be changed so as to better influence reality. After 1830 at the latest, all seemed to agree that political conditions as well as drama desperately needed to be reformed. The movement toward theater reform was widespread in the age of Young Germany. The idea of Wagner as a political dramatist does, however, seem highly incongruous. The issue is not that simple. Although the affinities of Wagner's aesthetics with those of the Romantics have already been investigated, they warrant further attention.

Wagner, of course, was influenced by political trends. For instance, his essays on theater reform, many of which he wrote during the 1840s, show his political interests. They express his Socialistic, democratic, anti-aristocratic ideas. He advocates the financial independence of the theater, the establishment of a collective of artists, and the change from a "Hoftheater" to a "Nationaltheater." Conversely, his political views, whether revolutionary or reactionary, were decisively influenced by his art. The later, more conservative essays, such as those written during the 1860s, show the influence of Schopenhauer's philosophy of the will, a Romantic glorification of the position of king, and an Idealistic view of what the term "German" really refers to, all of which are notions that might more properly belong to aesthetics rather than politics.

Wagner's Zurich writings, of which *Oper und Drama* is the third and last, definitely reflect these various concerns. In the first one especially, "Die Kunst und die Revolution," he makes the link between art and society clear, stating the interrelationship between art and political and social conditions. Whereas Greek art was conservative, he proclaims, art should be revolutionary in the modern era. Wagner, as he wrote in a letter to Minna (14 May 1849), became a revolutionary for the sake of his art. Furthermore, he intended his art to revolutionize society. But did he really, to that end, write what one could consider political dramas?

In this chapter, I wish to explore the complex interaction of art and politics in Wagner's theory, by investigating just how the art-work of the future was to revolutionize society. My conclusion, incongruous as it may sound, is that despite his political sympathies and his ties with the Young Germany movement, Wagner needs to be situated more closely to Friedrich Schlegel, Ludwig Tieck, and E.T.A. Hoffmann. Wagner, I would argue, really belongs more appropriately within the context of Romantic aesthetics, rather than within the theater reform movement of Young Germany. In fact, taking this approach would even help explain how, in Wagner's theory, aesthetics can affect politics.

Social and political considerations certainly form the framework for the aesthetic theory that Wagner presents in *Oper und Drama*, but they are refracted into this last of the Zurich treatises in a very complex way. "Die Kunst und die Revolution" is the essay that forms a political "frame" for *Oper und Drama*. This last of the Zurich writings, most critics would agree, deals primarily with words and music, myth and tragedy, history and psychology. Thus it reflects various dual concerns in a way that is much deeper and more intricate than is evident upon first reading or superficial analysis. Wagner was influenced not only by the movement of Young Germany, but also by Romanticism as well. The notion of a dialectic between the inner and the outer seems to recall the theory of Romantic irony and place Wagner firmly within the series of Romantic theoreticians.

Accordingly, within the framework that links *Oper und Drama* to the outside world, Wagner has embedded a very intricate drama theory that I will analyze by discussing the concepts of tragedy, myth, and Romantic irony. I defined some of these concepts in the previous chapter. The treatise under discussion, which itself has various textual levels that I will point out, outlines a drama that has Romantic irony. Here Wagner sketches a drama that in its dual mythological nature is a highly ironic product indeed. In fact, to the end of changing reality, *Oper und Drama* is a distinctively Romantic treatise. In this chapter, I will dissect both the content as well as the textual structure of this treatise. The two elements, content and structure, are inseparably linked; they reflect each other.

Even in its rough outlines, the treatise resembles the theoretical works of the Schlegels. For the Romantics, literary theory meant literary history. An example of this would be the section "Epochen der Dichtkunst" from Friedrich Schlegel's *Gespräch über die Poesie*. In *Oper und Drama*, however, Wagner presents two historical aesthetic surveys, for he is dealing primarily with two basic art forms—music and literature, notes and words. They would be synthesized, he felt, in the art-work of the future. What the Schlegels say about modern literature being in a state of decay is exactly what Wagner also says about music and drama. He surveys an art form to show that according to its proper definition it simply does not exist.

Furthermore, Wagner sketches in *Oper und Drama* the three-stage model of fall and redemption that characterized the theoretical writings of the Romantics. Its typical expression is the "Marionettentheater" essay of Heinrich von Kleist, which presents a dialogue in which one of the partners proposes the notion that consciousness can be pushed to its limits and thus mankind, by eating from the Tree of Knowledge a second time, can achieve a new state of immediacy and unconsciousness and re-enter Paradise through the back door. The essay combines aesthetics with a speculative philosophy of history, and couches it within a metaphorical texture.[2] Wagner's *Oper und Drama* forms a musical-dramatic counterpart to this essay, and I propose that it shares these points of comparison with the Kleist essay, placing Wagner clearly within the Romantic tradition.

Whereas the concepts of Romantic irony and mythology have been discussed and defined in the previous chapter, the present chapter will focus on just what tragedy, for Wagner, really means and entails. The impact of Greek drama and mythology on Wagner has been well documented by, among others, Wolfgang Schadewaldt.[3] Like the Romantics, Wagner glorified the Greek age as the first stage in his theoretical historical progression. Wagner's idea of music-drama as a rebirth of Greek tragedy was based on the notion of Greek tragedy being a religious celebration, the raw material of Greek tragedy being folk-literature, and Greek tragedy being a "Gesamtkunstwerk," a union of the arts of poetry, music, and dance (mime). It is the second point that I would like to consider central, and I will argue that it entails the other two. Wagner's theory of tragedy is a theory of mythological drama, as he saw the two forms as inseparable.

In this chapter, I will present what I will call Wagner's theory of tragedy, concentrating on the second part of *Oper und Drama*. Wagner's extensive discussion in *Oper und Drama* of myth, his retelling and exegesis of the Greek myth of Oedipus, and his frequent statements concerning "fate" and the traditional tragic curse lead one to firmly assert that if Wagner has any theory of tragedy, it is here to be found. Analyzing the drama theory of *Oper und Drama* with reference to the main features of traditional tragedy theory is much more than a heuristic device or a convenient interpretative schema, an arbitrary checklist of sorts. It will also help place this treatise more firmly within the context of the German tradition by considering it as primarily a nineteenth-century reworking of traditional tragedy theory. This method thus serves an important literary-historical purpose.

In *Oper und Drama*, tragedy is not only politicized by Wagner, but also psychologized as well, as I will show. My main theses are that, firstly, *Oper und Drama* fits more suitably into the Romantic tradition than in the tradition of Young Germany. Furthermore, the treatise is essentially a theory of tragedy, the most basic element of which is its mythological subject matter. Lastly, just as tragedy implies myth, in Wagner's theory myth, in turn, implies Romantic irony. In this chapter, I will discuss how Wagner revises the dramatic form of tragedy, and how he thus gives mythological music-drama its revolutionary potential through the use of historical consciousness and mythological self-reflection, in other words, via Romantic irony.

Wagner was certainly a multifaceted talent, and *Oper und Drama*, in uniting many dual concerns in a series of dichotomies that lends itself to a structural analysis, clearly shows the various influences upon his thought. Wagner's theory of drama, which entails a discussion of his theory of art, since he saw drama as the supreme work of art and a synthesis of the arts, is full of contradictions. The treatise *Oper und Drama* seems an amalgam of Feuerbach and Hegel, Kant and Schiller, Friedrich Schlegel and Wackenroder. It appears to synthesize aesthetics and politics, literary history and metaphysics. Wagner seems to attribute some kind of priority to music, but the larger framework of his theory has major tenets of Feuerbachian materialism as its main principle. He holds that the separate arts are deficient, that music is a means and not an end in itself, and that only the total work of art would appeal to the senses as well as the intellect and thus unite these various faculties in the artistic experience. These dichotomies, which are expressions of Wagner's dual concerns, bring to mind the dialectical structure that is a distinguishing feature of Romantic irony, and they actually make the work of art an ironic one, as I will show.

Furthermore, while the works that he theoretically constructs in this treatise are performed in opera houses, for they consist of words, music, and onstage action, he takes special care to place them outside of the operatic tradition, and sooner in that of perhaps German drama, or better still, of the symphony. While he theoretically preferred a union of the arts to purely instrumental music, in the Zurich writings he actually evolves music-drama out of the symphony, thus showing how his own art necessarily and inevitably follows Beethoven's Ninth Symphony in his theoretical teleology of music history. The treatise *Oper und Drama* is both regressive and progressive. The art-work of the future is a rebirth of Greek tragedy. Wagner analyzes history (or, rather, construes and interprets it) as a metaphysical teleology, with a utopian goal. A sick society produces inferior art, but the supreme work of art will revolutionize society. Accordingly, Wagner's theories of tragedy are ambiguous; he revives and unworks it at the same time.

While there can be no doubt that Wagner saw his work within the tradition of Greek tragedy, one must also remember that he saw his dramas as in some way modern versions of Greek tragedy, perhaps one could say the corresponding equivalent for German lands. What makes this investigation so interesting is the qualification—the time differences cannot and should not, he felt, be overlooked. He never advocated a simple return to Greek tragedy; he felt this would be totally inappropriate for the modern age and the German lands. Rather, he wished to revive it on, so to speak, another level. Form was, for Wagner, historically relative. The question of how Wagner defines "tragedy" is therefore not simple to answer. In *Oper und Drama*, Wagner explains how he interprets Greek tragedy, and thus he presents a complex structure. The critic analyzing *Oper und Drama* must then determine in what ways the music-drama that he is building in the treatise differs from this "interpreted" Greek tragedy. Wagnerian tragedy is appropriate for the modern age. Similarly, *Oper und Drama* sketches a theory that in many ways is an unworking of the traditional theory of Greek tragedy.

Scholars would agree that in his preoccupation with tragedy, Wagner clearly belongs within the tradition of nineteenth-century drama. Scholars see tragedy as a unifying theme of nineteenth-century drama. Edward McInnes argues that the developments in drama during the entire century are unified by a common concern, that is, they can be considered in some way as deriving from the form of tragedy and dealing with the fact that the form had become problematic.[4] The age, most agree, saw a redefinition of tragedy. The traditional ideals of humanism and heroism became problematic.[5] Wagner in particular was definitely concerned with revising and redefining traditional forms. I will take the redefinition of tragedy as an example.

In his reworking of tragedy, too, Wagner is clearly a Romantic. He transcends the form in *Oper und Drama* and the *Ring*. The element of tragedy was not entirely lacking from Romantic drama. In particular, the concept of fate appealed to the Romantics and assumed a dark, mysterious, inscrutable quality. The "Schicksalstragödie" (tragedy of fate) became popular during the first two decades of the nineteenth century. The Romantics were especially concerned with the notions of fate, guilt, and reconciliation. But built into the Romantic world-view, and by extension what one could generalize as the Romantic theory of drama, was also the inherent unworking of tragedy.

The Romantics were intent on not only portraying but also fixing the dissonance of existence. George Steiner points out that Romanticism is characterized by an evasion of the tragic.[6] In the Romantic vision, crime leads not to punishment, but, rather, to redemption. Steiner mentions *Götterdämmerung* as an example. Though tragedies have an aspect of reconciliation, a renewal of society, they leave some questions unanswered. Tragedies, as Steiner explains, end badly. The tragic conflict is never fully resolved. Redemption and utopian notions seem to obviate tragedy.

Otto Mann explains that the Romantics wanted to either overcome tragedy altogether in Romantic "Poesie" or write tragedies that ended in some kind of satisfying reconciliation.[7] The Romantics had a new version, a new conception, of tragedy. For the Romantics, it was not some eternal possibility for mankind to suffer and fall. Up until the time of the Romantics, tragedy was a form or a goal of art. With the Romantics, though, tragedy became more an expression of a problematic human condition that was to be overcome. They used it only to show its ultimate destruction. They were intent rather on reconciliation. Otto Mann uses the adjective "übertragisch" when discussing the Romantics and tragedy. They used tragedy to transcend it. Wagner's *Ring* can in this way be considered, as I will show, the epitome of Romantic drama. Accordingly, I will show how Siegfried is, as hero, superseded by Brünnhilde and Wotan in the *Ring*.

Furthermore, *Oper und Drama* exemplifies in many ways what Bryan Magee refers to as Wagner's incessant historicism, the constant desire to show where each phenomenon under discussion originated, and what function and significance it has within the teleology of history.[8] I previously remarked on the similarity between Wagner's treatise and the theoretical literary histories of the Schlegels. In *Oper und Drama*, Wagner is not presenting a normative theory of drama that outlines the proper choice of characters, plots, and the like, as one would expect from a more traditional and conventional aesthetic treatise. In *Oper und Drama*, Wagner gives an interpretation of myths and a theoretical reflection upon the use of myth in drama. Wagner actually redefines tragedy by writing of the origin and synthetic reconstitution of myth.

In this chapter, I will outline Wagner's theory of tragedy by discussing his theory of mythological refabrication, his exegesis of the Greek myth of Oedipus, and his reinterpretation of various traditional elements of Greek tragedy, such as the tragic curse. In subsequent chapters, I will analyze how his mythical music-drama portrays his interpretation of Greek tragedy. Furthermore, I will show how *Oper und Drama* theoretically outlines the paradox of myth and history that Kunze discusses, and that I outlined in the previous chapter. *Oper und Drama* sketches a theory of mythological refabrication and reinterpretation, but it also shows Wagner's historical consciousness. *Oper und Drama* tells and interprets myths, as do Wagner's dramas.

Furthermore, *Oper und Drama* clearly illustrates that Wagner's thinking was essentially metaphorical, a feature of Wagner's thought to which Nattiez has already pointed. I would like to expand on this idea. *Oper und Drama* outlines what I would call, building on the work of Nattiez, an aesthetics of myth as metaphor. Myth, for Wagner, is to be used as a metaphor for history. Just as *Oper und Drama* exemplifies nineteenth-century historicism, it also shows the interpenetration of myth and history that was essential to the Romantic idea of history. Furthermore, it explicates this outlook theoretically, proposing a reflection on the interrelationship of myth and history. From the evidence of *Oper und Drama*, a theoretical dialectic of history and myth dominated the composition of the *Ring* and its reception theory. In the next chapter, I will discuss how this dialectic of myth and history is expressed in the world depicted in the *Ring* itself.

In this manner, both *Oper und Drama* and the *Ring* express the dichotomies of nineteenth-century aesthetics as Kunze has discussed them. Furthermore, it is just this reflection between myth and history that throws the world of the *Ring* into disarray. The theory of *Oper und Drama* sketches an interrelationship between history and myth and a theory of endless mirrorings. This treatise therefore implicitly outlines a kind of drama that necessarily has Romantic irony, that is, internal self-reflection. Therefore, *Oper und Drama* contains an appropriate theoretical expression of Wagner's Romantic transcendence of tragedy.

The treatise under discussion presents a theoretical reflection on the form of Greek tragedy that unworks it in the process, for it describes a dramatic form that uses myth on the stage of reflection or self-consciousness, and thus relativizes and ultimately undermines itself. Thus Wagner's theory is what I would consider a deconstruction of Greek tragedy. Wagner, one could say, deconstructs myth to transcend tragedy. It is Romantic irony, furthermore, that gives myth its revolutionary potential. According to Wagner's theory of art as he expounded it in his Zurich treatises, history can be mythologized, and life can be changed, through the artistic experience in the theater.

๛

Appropriately enough, as his treatise deals primarily with the theory of art in particular, Wagner states his three-stage model in aesthetic terms. The treatise presents a series of analogies. Wagner links art and history, aesthetics and politics. He writes,

Die *Tonsprache* ist Anfang und Ende der Wortsprache, wie das *Gefühl* Anfang und Ende des Verstandes, der *Mythos* Anfang und Ende der Geschichte, die *Lyrik* Anfang und Ende der Dichtkunst ist.[9]

Tone-speech is the beginning and end of word-speech, as *feeling* is the beginning and end of understanding, *myth* is the beginning and end of history, and the *lyric* the beginning and end of poetry.

In the next paragraph Wagner states that the process he is describing should not be understood as a regression, but, rather, a progression toward the achievement of the highest possible human capacities. It takes place, he

notes, in mankind in general and in each individual. Ontogeny recapitulates phylogeny. Individual development mirrors collective history.

This is only one example of the many mirrorings that this treatise
presents. *Oper und Drama* resembles a hall of mirrors that all interlock and
dynamically affect each other, centering on the work of art and the aesthetic
experience. Wagner parallels myth with history, and one historical progression with another. Wagner uses a three-stage model in which a previous
unity, represented by Greek drama and Greek society in general, that is, the
whole Greek world, has been lost and should be re-established by the
art-work of the future. Wagner's three-stage model has a reflective structure
and thus resembles a mirror in that the third stage in some way, on a higher
level, reflects the first stage. Art, furthermore, functions as a mirror in
several ways, for it reverses this process within itself and, by being experienced in history, it reverses history, too.

Formally, the art-work of the future is a return to a Greek model of drama.
Greek tragedy was a union of the arts. It consisted of words, music, and
acting (mime). According to Wagner, each of the separate arts was by itself
insufficient. The adjective "absolute," such as in the term "absolute music,"
had pejorative connotations when used by Wagner.[10] That the union of the
arts had broken up into disparate art forms, that words had become
separated from music and opera dominated by what Wagner disparagingly
called "melody," were just symptoms of the fragmentation of modern
society.

With regard to its subject matter or raw material, too, the art-work of the
future would be in some way a return to a Greek model of art, if not an exact
rebirth or a literal imitation of Greek art. Anette Ingenhoff observes that
Wagner considers form in the light of content—he defines "tragedy" (form)
by its mythological subject matter.[11] According to Wagner, Greek tragedy
was first and foremost a mythological work of art. Wagner writes,

Nur der griechischen Weltanschauung konnte bis heute noch das wirkliche
Kunstwerk des Dramas entblühen. Der Stoff dieses Dramas war aber der *Mythos*,
und aus seinem Wesen können wir allein das höchste griechische Kunstwerk und
seine uns berückende Form begreifen. (OuD 161)

Only from the Greek world-view could up until today the true work of art, the
drama, flourish. The raw material of this drama was *mythology*, and from its essence
alone can we grasp the supreme Greek work of art and its form, which enchants us.

Greek tragedy was, according to Wagner, the artistic realization of Greek
mythology, but myth, as Wagner understands it, is not to be taken too
literally. The meaning of myth is, for Wagner, historically relative.

Wagner seems to echo the Romantics in criticizing the Enlightenment
and the rise of the modern world-view, the scientific, rational outlook on
life, for demythologizing the world, and he voices the need for what

Friedrich Schlegel termed in his *Gespräch über die Poesie* a "new mythology." Furthermore, just as Schlegel's "new mythology" does not necessarily mean using mythological raw material, Wagner's appeal for a "new mythology" outlines a work of art that is not a literal portrayal of mythological source materials. Wagner's treatise sketches a dialectic of myth and history. Furthermore, art is a crucial element in this process. It can cause the mythicization of history and the historicization of myth.

Wagner argues for an innate poetic capacity of mankind. Wagner writes,

Der Mensch ist auf zwiefache Weise Dichter: in der *Anschauung* und in der *Mitteilung*.
Die *natürliche* Dichtungsgabe ist die Fähigkeit, die seinen Sinnen von aussen sich kundgebenden Erscheinungen zu einem inneren Bilde von ihnen sich zu verdichten; die *künstlerische*, dieses Bild nach aussen wieder mitzuteilen. (OuD 159)

A human being is a poet in two ways: in *perception* and in *communication*.
The *natural* poetic gift is the ability to condense the appearances that present themselves to the senses from outside to an inner image of them; the *artistic* one is, to communicate this image back outside.

The capacity of "Phantasie" condenses the appearances it perceives in the external world into images. The condensed image, though, can only be properly understood by one who perceives the world in the same way, that is, with the same proportion of condensation, this condensation being necessary for the limited capacity of the human mind to grasp the disparate, manifold appearances presented to it by the external world.

The above quotation, which makes a distinction analogous to that of Friedrich Schlegel in his 116th Fragment between "Naturpoesie" and "Kunstpoesie," is the first example of a kind of "double vision" that I will be pointing out in Wagner's theoretical writings and in his *Ring*. In these works there is, I will argue, a duality of perception and communication, nature (life) and art, history and myth, and a basic phenomenon of seeing things as existing on two levels. This dual optic also encompasses two senses of myth, a literal and a more figural one. This duality proves the ruin of the fictional world that the *Ring* depicts.

Wagner's treatise sketches a complex interplay between the objective and the subjective, external reality and interpretation, history and myth, that one can thus see as analogous to the dialectic that is the distinguishing characteristic of Romantic irony. Wagner theorizes that myth is a shared world-view and a product of the "Volk." The understanding cannot grasp the actual connections among appearances, so the "Phantasie," that is, the poetic imagination, establishes these in its own way. Myth is a poetic creation. Wagner wrote that myth reflected how one perceived the world, not how the world is in itself. He considers mythology a way of making sense of the appearances of the external world. One establishes connections and correspondences in what one perceives. Myth is an explanatory system. That is, one sees reality—history if you will—with reference to myth.

In this way mankind establishes causes, reasons, and explanations for what is perceived in the external world. Wagner adopted Feuerbach's idea that man creates gods in his own image. Wagner writes,

Gott und Götter sind die ersten Schöpfungen der menschlichen Dichtungskraft: in ihnen stellt sich der Mensch das Wesen der natürlichen Erscheinungen als von einer Ursache hergeleitet dar; als diese Ursache begreift er aber unwillkürlich nichts anderes als sein eigenes menschliches Wesen, in welchem diese gedichtete Ursache auch einzig nur begründet ist. (OuD 161)

A god and the gods are the first creations of the human poetic talent: in them a person depicts the essence of natural phenomena as being derived from a cause; as this cause he grasps involuntarily nothing else than his own human essence, in which this condensed cause is alone founded.

In theorizing that gods are nothing other than Feuerbachian projections, Wagner has thus intellectually begun to undermine the metaphysical aspect, the belief in the Absolute, that critics theorize is necessary to Greek tragedy.[12] The *Ring*, as I will show, demonstrates this process dynamically in the figure of Wotan. It is no contradiction that Wagner still portrays gods in the *Ring*. Wotan comes to realize the limits of his power, for he is not really divine even in the sense that the Greek gods were. Wagner deconstructs the gods in his *Ring* cycle.

Furthermore, myth is, for Wagner, a kind of unconscious self-recognition. Art, when based on mythological raw material, "potentiates" myth and thus brings the process of self-recognition to consciousness. Wagner shares with Friedrich Schlegel and the rest of the Romantics (in fact, the nineteenth century in general) the idea of mythology as a shared world-view, a common way of viewing reality. It should be noted, however, that Wagner both shows and acknowledges a historical relativism as regards myth, and that he is, furthermore, proposing a mythological drama that is a private, an individual and synthetic reconstitution of myth. In his theory and use of myth, Wagner does not transcend his historical conditionality any more than his contemporaries. He shows, however, a consciousness of his own subjectivity. For Wagner, myth is a subjective ontology.

Dagmar Ingenschay-Goch observes that Wagner distinguishes between the structure and manifestation of myths.[13] That is, depending on historical circumstances, myths appear different. Furthermore, in what seems to be a contradiction to (or a mirror-image reversal of) this, he reinterprets the Oedipus myth to represent the conflict between the individual and the state, rather than interpreting the myth of Oedipus as the product of the historical age and the Greek world in which it was created. That is, he projects modern ideas, or at least ideas which one knows he associated primarily with his contemporary world, into the ancient myth. Thus, the distinction between history and myth was not a strict dichotomy for Wagner, but, rather, a complex interrelationship. This was true for the Romantic writers, too. In fact, Wagner's interpretation of Greek mythology and his projections of modern conditions into them somehow anachronistically negate their own historicity as products of the age in which they were created. In exemplifying the drama theory that Wagner outlines in *Oper und Drama*, the *Ring* reflects the interplay between history and myth, the outer and the inner, the objective and the subjective, that Wagner sketches in *Oper und Drama*.

Ingenschay-Goch notes that Wagner scholarship generally assumes that he takes myth to be eternally true and "allgemeinmenschlich." However, this viewpoint overlooks Wagner's historical relativism as regards myth. She points out that in *Oper und Drama* Wagner is writing about the fabrication and artistic refabrication of myth. He interprets the myth of Oedipus from the perspective of a nineteenth-century artist. Whereas in his later "Lebensbericht" (1879) Wagner sees myth in opposition to history, in the "Mitteilung" (1851) he establishes an interrelationship between history and myth. He interprets, for instance, the myth of Zeus and Semele and the myth or legend of the Flying Dutchman, thus explicating their metaphorical significance and their applicability to modern life or contemporary history. Similarly, in the "Wibelungen" essay, written at about the same time of his life as the Zurich treatises, Wagner derives world-history from mythology. Even in his late essay "Religion und Kunst," Wagner writes of using Christian (or, in another "extended" sense, mythical) symbols as symbols, thus severing them from their original context and belief system.

Jean-Jacques Nattiez rightly points out that Wagner's thinking is essentially metaphorical.[14] Wagner frequently finds images to illustrate his points, and this reasoning by analogy is, Nattiez observes, omnipresent. *Oper und Drama* is full of such imagery. Similarly, Wagner tells and retells myths, not only showing that he sees myth as metaphorical, but also explicating the metaphorical significance of myth. It stands for something else. The *Ring* illustrates this process of mythological refabrication and psychological reflection upon it in a complex way. In *Oper und Drama*, Wagner is writing about, and in doing so demonstrating, a process of mythological reinterpretation and refabrication. This metaphoricity of Wagner's thinking creates a series of doublings in *Oper und Drama* and the *Ring*. I will take Nattiez' ideas further and show that just as *Oper und Drama* reflects upon tragedy as mythological drama, unworking it in the process, Wagner's *Ring*, by demonstrating the theory of *Oper und Drama*, portrays myth on the stage of reflection, unworking its own textual structure and overcoming tragedy as it does so.

By interpreting mythology, Wagner, because of his nineteenth-century historical consciousness, in essence deconstructs his very purpose of using myth as raw material. Wagner writes, in *Oper und Drama*:

Das Unvergleichliche des Mythos ist, dass er jederzeit wahr und sein Inhalt, bei dichtester Gedrängtheit, für alle Zeiten unerschöpflich ist. Die Aufgabe des Dichters war es nur, ihn zu deuten. (OuD 199)

The unique quality of myth is that it is true for all time and its content is concise and inexhaustible. The task of the poet has always been to interpret it.

Borchmeyer cites this definition of myth to take issue with modern productions of Wagner's dramas, such as those staged by Patrice Chéreau, Joachim Herz, or Harry Kupfer, who he feels violate the mythical nature of Wagner's music-dramas.[15] However, he thereby emphasizes the phrase "true for all time" and neglects Wagner's assertion of the historical relativism of myth. When used in Wagner's music-drama, myth becomes strangely altered. The poet, one should note, is instructed by Wagner to *interpret* myth, and thus present a work that is one step removed from actual myth.

In other words, if myth, according to Wagner, can be true for all time, it is mainly because Wagner's theory of mythological refabrication is distinctively and significantly vague, allowing the poet to interpret myth as befits historical circumstances. Thus Wagner gives the dramatist interpretative freedom. This, one could argue, is the necessary consequence of what Wagner considers the task of the poet. The synthetic reconstruction of myth consists in genuine myth being filtered through the consciousness of the artist and then being re-produced. The finished product will thus inevitably differ from the mythological source material upon which the work of art is based.

Andrea Mork notes how Wagner's theory of mythology serves a regressive tendency.[16] His exhortation to the poet to use the products of the "Volk" represents some kind of return from civilization to nature. One must distinguish, however, between what Wagner writes about myth in its "pure," primal form and when he discusses his work of art as being mythical. Wagner's art is "Kunstpoesie," not "Naturpoesie." What Wagner writes about myth in *Oper und Drama* is not identical to a description of his music-drama, which is based on myth or, one could say, is a second-hand, synthetic myth. Wagner's myth is progressive as well as regressive. It appeals not only to feeling, but to understanding as well. It is a myth on the level of reflection, a new myth using elements of traditional myth.

The mythical nature of Wagner's art is thus multilayered and complex. In *Oper und Drama*, Wagner is not writing about a strict portrayal of myth, as though there could ever be such a thing in the modern era. He sketches a theory of the reconstitution of myth, the rebirth of myth on the stage of reflection, or, as I would call it, an aesthetics of myth as metaphor. As used in the art-work of the future, myth becomes a metaphor for history. Furthermore, *Oper und Drama* presents an aesthetics of mythological refabrication and reinterpretation. Self-conscious myth is a contradiction in terms. A modern myth is not really mythical. It would be unreasonable, especially considering Wagner's admission of the historical relativism of myth, to expect a modern, self-conscious, and ironic myth to be strictly mythical. In the *Ring*, as I will show, Wagner's assertion of the historical relativism of myth turns against his work of art. A modern, self-conscious myth that portrays history as well as its own fictionality will inevitably deconstruct itself.

Wagner even acknowledges his modern mythological works as a conscious and self-conscious use of myth, just as *Oper und Drama* is a theoretical reflection on the use of myth in drama. He writes,

Wollen wir nun das Werk des Dichters nach dessen höchstem denkbaren Vermögen genau bezeichnen, so müssen wir es *den aus dem klarsten menschlichen Bewusstsein gerechtfertigten, der Anschauung des immer gegenwärtigen Lebens entsprechend neu erfundenen und im Drama zur verständlichsten Darstellung gebrachten Mythos* nennen. (OuD 227)

If we were to describe the highest possible task of the poet, we would have to say that it is *to clearly and consciously re-create myth to suit the needs and the world-view of the present day and bring this modern myth to an understandable presentation in drama.*

The long adjectival qualification and specification of the word "Mythos" indicates that Wagner's theory does not dictate a strict and literal portrayal of traditional myths. Wagner states that in music-drama, myth is to be re-created ("neu erfunden") for the present day. The phrase "justified by the clearest human consciousness" ("aus dem klarsten menschlichen Bewusstsein gerechtfertigt") designates music-drama as also a rational product, a form of art that is consciously and self-consciously produced. It should, moreover, be easily comprehended. *Oper und Drama* is thus the theoretical expression of the paradox that I discussed in my first chapter. It describes a self-conscious kind of art. Myth is interpreted in the music-drama, which gives a modern myth, the myth of modern times. Interpretation implies reflection and consciousness. Wagner is not writing about mere mythological dramatization, but, rather, mythological refabrication.

Modern mythological drama reconstitutes myth on the level of reflection. Wagner's music-drama is a self-referential myth. It shows its self-consciousness and reflects, with Romantic irony, upon itself. Wagner theorizes that myth is in itself an artistic product, a kind of artistic art, as opposed to natural art, and thus Greek drama was a higher level of, a "potentiated" kind of, artistic art. The mythological art-work of the future is no simple product indeed. As Greek tragedy was a mythological work of art, the artistic realization of Greek mythology, so would the new kind of drama that Wagner envisioned be a mythological drama, but it would use a new kind of mythology, and in another way. The *Ring* contains all these stages within itself, as I will show.

Wagner's historical consciousness also concerns the history of myth. Wagner grounds his theory of mythological refabrication in history by recounting the fragmentation of myth through history. In doing so, he sketches a history of myth. Greek tragedy drew on a pre-existing set of myths that were common knowledge, known to the common people. The Greek world represented, for Wagner, a unity of art with public, political life ("Öffentlichkeit").[17] In the modern world, though, according to Wagner, mythology is in a precarious, messy state. He recounts the collision of various kinds of mythologies. The modern world, according to Wagner, has suffered from a process of demythologization. He writes that the characteristic form of the modern age is not the drama, but, rather, the novel. Drama portrays "das Reinmenschliche" ("the purely human"), whereas the novel depicts society and politics. Myth has yielded to the historical chronicle.[18] Thus Wagner embeds his theory of mythological drama in a historical schema.

The modern world, Wagner felt, was characterized by two different mythologies.[19] Firstly, he discusses the Christian myth, in which mankind is a stranger to himself. Wagner gives a political interpretation of Christianity. In this mythology, according to Wagner, martyrdom is the external justification of the law and the state. The individual is freed through redemption by God. This myth glorifies death, rather than life. The other myth is comprised by the indigenous legends of the newer European peoples, especially the Germans, in which natural phenomena were depicted as people. Wagner recounts how these two strands of mythology collided, and the former fragmented the latter. The confused state of mythology in the modern world reflects the fragmentation of modern society.

Wagner sketches a structural model for tragedy that seems to, in its abstract nature and bipolar structure, invite some kind of structural analysis. Wagner bases his notion of tragedy on the opposition between the political state and the free self-determination of the individual.[20] The customs and morals dictated by the state, according to Wagner, conflict with the right of the individual to determine the course of his own life. Wagner was influenced, in his revolutionary years during which *Oper und Drama* was written, by the materialistic philosophy of Ludwig Feuerbach. Wagner, accordingly, felt that life was (or at least should be) spontaneous necessity and material reality. Wagner contrasts the "natural morals" ("natürliche Sitte") of Greek society with the "arbitrary laws" ("willkürlich vertragenes Gesetz") of modern society. The foundation of modern society is custom ("Gewohnheit"). It is based on tradition.

The poet, Wagner felt, should, in reviving tragedy on the modern level, portray the conflict between the individual and political or religious dogma. Thus Wagner (from the standpoint of modern history) derives a structural schema from Greek tragedy (which is based, he argues, on mythology). Ingenhoff notes that Wagner makes no distinction between the rules of tragedy and the structure of mythology. He believes that mythology contains within itself the structure of tragedy. Conversely, he feels that Greek tragedy is a "myth" that Greek society has devised for political purposes. Perhaps, I would conjecture, his hypothetical postulation of this conservative origin of Greek tragedy, that is, why Wagner says that myth contains within itself the rules of tragedy, is because both are products of a conservative order.

To assert, however, merely that Wagner gives a political interpretation of Greek tragedy is an oversimplification. It overlooks the fact that Wagner not only gives his own interpretation of Greek tragedy, but also explains or interprets Greek tragedy as itself resulting from an interpretation. The interaction of the state and the individual in Greek tragedy is, as Wagner sees it, a complex one. It involves the subjective and the objective, both art and life. Wagner's theory of Greek tragedy consists of interlocking or overlapping interpretations, layers of myth, different views of myth, or various mythologies. That is, Wagner interprets what he interprets as in itself an interpretation.

According to Wagner, the Greeks viewed the rebellious impulse of the individual from the standpoint of society, and thus they saw it as something negative, for it disrupted the societal order. They therefore in essence rewrote the individual's story, devised a myth, and imagined such an individual as being influenced by powers that robbed him of his free will; for, so the reasoning was, if he were free, he would do what custom dictated. Through his deed, the individual lost the esteem of society. With consciousness of the deed, the individual could re-enter society insofar as he denounced himself according to its laws and therefore in accord with its viewpoint, which he internalized. Thus Wagner indicates both the perspectival nature and the political purpose of myth

In Greek tragedy, then, according to Wagner, an act of unconscious transgression was explained by a curse, which rested upon an individual without his having personally incurred it. In Greek mythology, the curse was portrayed as divine punishment for an ancient crime or misdeed ("Urfreveltat"), and it was viewed as permanently resting upon or hanging over the particular race or family until its decline. The tragic dialectic, according to Wagner, was that the individual unconsciously becomes guilty.[21] In Greek tragedy, according to Wagner, consciousness affirms the societal order. Wagner's interpretational schema, which underlies the artwork of the future, functions differently. When modern music-drama brings one to consciousness, this kind of consciousness is revolutionary.

While he feels that the tragic curse originates with society, Wagner in actuality explains the curse in Greek drama as something psychological, thus explicitly demythologizing it. He writes, similarly, about the concept of "fate,"

Das *Fatum* der Griechen ist *die innere Naturnotwendigkeit,* aus der sich der Grieche—
weil er sie nicht verstand—in den willkürlichen politischen Staat zu befreien suchte.
Unser Fatum ist der willkürliche politische Staat, der sich uns *als äussere Not-
wendigkeit* für das Bestehen der Gesellschaft darstellt, und aus dem wir uns in die
Naturnotwendigkeit zu befreien suchen, weil wir sie verstehen gelernt und als die
Bedingung unseres Daseins und seiner Gestaltungen erkannt haben. (OuD 187)

The fate of the Greeks is the *inner natural necessity,* from which the Greek—*because
he did not understand it*—sought to free himself in the arbitrary political state. *Our
fate* is the arbitrary political state, which presents itself to us *as an external necessity*
for the endurance of society, and from which we seek to free ourselves in natural
necessity, because we have learned to understand it and have recognized it as the
condition for our existence and its organization.

Thus fate in the Greek world was, according to Wagner, nothing metaphysical, but, rather, mere inner necessity. It was interpreted as aberrant from the
standpoint of society. Thus Wagner explains the ancient dramatic idea of
fate as a kind of rationalization or projection for political ends, an instrument of brainwashing with which society can manipulate a nonconformist
into more compliant behavior. That the fate of the modern world, that is,
the modern equivalent of what the Greeks considered fate, is the state may
very well be because modern society accords the state the power that the
Greeks attributed to a metaphysical fate. Attaining a consciousness of the
power of the state over us, according to Wagner, will destroy it.

Greek tragedy (art) and modern life (history) are, as far as Wagner is
concerned, mirror-images of each other. Wagner interprets traditional
mythological elements in a nonmythological, modern, psychological way.
Wagner writes,

Die Griechen missverstanden im Fatum die Natur der Individualität, weil sie die
sittliche Gewohnheit der Gesellschaft störte: um dies Fatum zu bekämpfen,
waffneten sie sich mit dem politischen Staat. Unser Fatum ist nun der politische
Staat, in welchem die freie Individualität ihr verneinendes Schicksal erkennt. (OuD
201–2)

The Greeks misunderstood as fate the nature of individuality, because it disrupted
the customary ways of society: to fight this fate, they armed themselves with the
political state. Our fate is the political state, in which free individuality recognizes
the fate that negates it.

In the above quotation, Wagner uses two different terms, both of which can
mean "fate": "Fatum" and "Schicksal." The former he applies to the Greek
world, explicitly unworking its metaphysical connotations. However,
when he applies them to the modern world toward the end of the quote, he
uses the two words in a clearly figural or metaphorical way. Wagner
deconstructs the Greek concept of "fate" in a political and a hermeneutic

way, arguing that it depends on interpretation. Furthermore, when Wagner applies the concept of "fate" to the modern world, arguing that in the contemporary world, the state denies the free self-determination of the individual, he completely severs "fate" from its original, objective, mythological context and meaning.

Wagner's theory of tragedy has elements of various approaches, as befits the nature of his art as a modern, cross-disciplinary, synthetic one. His extensive discussions of the free individual versus the state, Wagner's revolutionary sympathies at the time at which he wrote *Oper und Drama*, and the subversive interpretations of fate and the Oedipus myth that he presents might lead one to assert that his theory of tragedy is a political one. Rainer Franke, for instance, writes of Wagner's theory of fate as a political one, describing it as "Wagners eminent politische Interpretation des antiken Dramenmoments des 'Fatums.' "[22] Franke is certainly correct in saying that Wagner interprets fate as something that comes out of human deeds themselves, from the limitation of human knowledge, and not from above as retribution for having violated the laws of the gods.[23] This interpretation, however, does not go far enough. It does an injustice to the complexity of Wagner's theory, and the sophistication of his ideas.

Wagner did, after all, write that Greek drama was conservative, whereas modern art should be revolutionary. However, though Wagner's ultimate aim was a revolutionary one, his theory of tragedy is, upon close analysis, not directly political. It entails a subtle interaction between the outer and the inner, the internalization of a representation imposed upon one from without, and the interplay of history and myth. According to Wagner, mythological music-drama should portray "das Reinmenschliche," not the state per se. Wagner felt that the drama should portray not so much the conflict of the individual with the state, but, rather, that of free self-determination and custom. Wagner writes of the conflict of the free individual versus the state in terms of the abstract concepts that characterize each. Furthermore, the objective interacts with the subjective, in his theory, in a complex way. Fate, he feels, is subjective. Thinking it is so makes it so. Wagner theorizes that fate in Greek tragedy is an imaginary force. According to Wagner, fate for the Greeks was really just a projection for political purposes, which was internalized by the victim.

Wagner's theory of tragedy in *Oper und Drama* is not so much a political one as it is a psychological one. The treatise is a reflection upon myth, and (ironically) thereby a theoretical demythologization of myth. Wagner has unworked metaphysics by explaining the gods and the Greek portrayal of the curse as regulative fictions, projections, or rationalizations. Thus he explains these things with a Nietzschean acknowledgement of their relativity. Fate is, for Wagner, nothing metaphysical. Wagner's theory about the concept of "fate" clearly shows his modern interpretation of an ancient dramatic form. He interprets an ancient tragedy, a "tragedy of fate"

("Schicksalstragödie"), from a modern viewpoint, as a modern work, as a "tragedy of character" ("Charaktertragödie").[24] Wagner's modern reflection upon myth robs it of its metaphysical nature. Mythological music-drama is not so much a rebirth as a deconstruction of Greek tragedy. In interpreting myth, Wagner demythologizes it.

Morality thus becomes relativized, and thereby Wagner demonstrates how, in general, the nineteenth century saw a dissipation of fixed values. The question of the guilt of the tragic hero implies conventional moral standards against which the tragic hero is measured. These are interpreted, in *Oper und Drama*, as false guidelines and psychological weapons that Wagner was intent on unmasking and thereby destroying. In this respect, the modernity of Wagner's theory is evident. By being a modern rebirth of Greek tragedy, the work he sketches in this treatise shows a dialectic of unconsciousness and consciousness much more complex than that of ancient tragedy, both within the work of art and in the function of the work of art as a tool with which to change reality.

Many psychological interpretations of Wagner's works have been written. The fact that Freud was the most famous interpreter of the Oedipus myth invites the comparison of Freud with Wagner. One cannot, of course, describe Wagner's theory of myth as a psychological theory of myth in the sense that myth for him, as for Freud or Jung, embodied patterns that are universal in the human psyche. For Freud, myths, like dreams, portrayed wish-fulfillment, while for Jung myths portrayed archetypes. Wagner has a psychological theory all his own, for he sketches an idiosyncratic interaction of the psychological and political. He has, though, not only politicized, but also psychologized, to a certain extent, the motive of fate. Wagner is writing about the formation of (natural and more artistic) myths (or explanatory stories) and the internalization of myths that have been imposed upon one by society.

Similarly, Rolf Breuer discusses tragedy with reference to what he considers "tragic" situations in everyday life.[25] Taking his inspiration from theories of schizophrenia, tragedy, he writes, is purely subjective, resulting from what is objectively "false consciousness." Tragedy, he feels, is a phenomenon on the level of the superstructure; it is tied to how one explains the world. He interprets the Greek notion of the family curse as a metaphor for family constellations, behavior disturbances, or other problems such as character dispositions, all of which seem to in some way "predestine" a person. In modern times, he writes, the motive of fate assumes a psychological significance. This theory is remarkably similar to Wagner's, which is usually considered a political one. For Wagner, the outer obviously cannot be separated from the inner. To discuss one without discussing the other is somehow inadequate.

❧

Wagner exemplifies his theory with (his interpretation of) the myth of Oedipus, thus creating more textual levels and further complicating the metaphorical structure of both his own text and yet another text, the art-work of the future. The myth of Oedipus (in its pure form, that is) actually forms a major subtext to Wagner's *Oper und Drama*. In this treatise, Wagner retells and in doing so interprets this myth, thereby showing the relevance of this myth to the modern world. Ingenhoff notes that myth becomes, for Wagner, a mirror of history and of contemporary problems. He sees a contemporary conflict, that of love versus power, in the myth of Oedipus, and he thereby builds a structural model for his own dramas. With the notion of a mythical portrayal of contemporary history, Ingenhoff notes, Wagner is fully within the Romantic tradition, and thus he answers Schlegel's appeal for a "new mythology."

However, the issue is much more complex than this. The myth of Oedipus, or, rather, Wagner's exegesis of it, is a complex product indeed. It not only exemplifies Wagner's theory of the tragic curse, as I will subsequently show. More deeply than that, it becomes a model of the metaphorization of myth and the interplay between history and myth that Wagner outlines in *Oper und Drama* and practices in the *Ring* cycle. Wagner raises the myth of Oedipus to some kind of mythical-historical eschatological significance.

Den *Oidipusmythos* brauchen wir auch heute nur seinem innersten Wesen nach getreu zu deuten, so gewinnen wir an ihm ein verständliches Bild der ganzen Geschichte der Menschheit vom Anfange der Gesellschaft bis zum notwendigen Untergange des Staates. Die Notwendigkeit dieses Unterganges ist im Mythos vorausempfunden; an der wirklichen Geschichte ist es, ihn auszuführen. (OuD 200)

Today we only need to interpret the *Oedipus myth* in a way that is true to its innermost essence, and thus we attain from it a comprehensible image of the whole history of mankind from the beginning of society up to the inevitable fall of the state. The necessity of this fall is prefigured in the myth; it is up to history to carry it out.

Wagner raises this myth to eschatological significance in a hermeneutical way. In other words, the appeal of this myth is mediated by and dependent upon interpretation. Furthermore, it portrays the destruction of the "state" only in an extended sense. That Wagner appeals to the musical-dramatist to interpret myth somehow seems to imply that the myth of Oedipus is not strictly portrayed, but, rather, interpreted in the art-work of the future. Wagner's theory is clearly an aesthetics of mythological reinterpretation.

Thus a derivative, second-hand mythological pattern underlies the drama that Wagner's theory is describing. Just as his dramas have been called mythological palimpsests,[26] so is his theory formed of interpretation upon interpretation. The drama that Wagner sketches is a few steps removed from standing in any strict parallel to the myth of Oedipus. They are, rather, related only in a loose structural way. An interpretation of the myth of Oedipus underlies the drama Wagner is sketching. Furthermore, Wagner not only projects modern ideas, in particular the situation of modern history, into the myth of Oedipus. He also sees the myth as portraying all of world-history. Here again one can discern a doubling of art and life; the latter should reflect and put into practice what is in some way portrayed in the former. The former foreshadows the latter, and there is, furthermore and very importantly, a causal connection between the two. The mythological music-drama forms a crucial link in the process.

The mythological content of the drama that has come to define form (tragedy) thus has a content of its own that dynamically portrays the destruction of the state. Not any myth, but the myth of Oedipus, in particular, underlies the music-drama that Wagner is theoretically outlining, and this myth, at least in Wagner's interpretation of it, portrays the destruction of the state. Wagner's music-drama is comprised of layers upon layers of myth, or a hall of mirrors. Furthermore, history should follow this mythological pattern (which is itself an interpretation of what Wagner interprets as an interpretation). The myth of Oedipus becomes an emblem for the simultaneous mythologization of history and historicization of myth.

That the interpreted myth of Oedipus portrays the destruction of the state, and that music-drama should portray an interpretation of this myth and cause the destruction of the state, implies that if the Oedipus myth underlies the art-work of the future, then music-drama portrays both its own interpretation and its own reception, too. Thus one can form a pyramid from Wagner's theory of history and the myth of Oedipus, with the drama—a miniature interpretation of the myth of Oedipus—at the peak of the pyramid, portraying and causing the destruction of the state; thus a "hall of mirrors" effect is created by Wagner's theory. That the Oedipus myth contains the fall of the state and all of world-history means that the work of art stages its own reception. This is why, I would argue, the *Ring* deconstructs.

Just as the myth of Oedipus portrays past, present, and future history, having the structure of a mirror or a pyramid, so will the mythological drama that Wagner outlines in this treatise, by mirroring the myth of Oedipus on another stage of reflection, function as a mirror. The drama is a mythological reflection upon the course of history. It will, through being experienced, reverse both ontogeny and phylogeny. Modern mythological music-drama should, in various ways, reverse history. Art is both a mirror-image and a mirror that reverses something. Ironically, holding the mirror up to history does not reinforce the status quo, but instead changes history. A mirror reverses the image that it reflects. When the art-work of the future stages its own reception, it reverses history.

Drama, Wagner feels, should portray the conflict of the free individual and society, the clash of free self-determination with political and religious dogma. Wagner sanctions the incest of Oedipus with his mother. Traditionally, Wagner explains, sexual love is supposed to enlarge the family by linking it to other families. Custom dictates that we see sexual love and familial love as opposites. Wagner argues that Oedipus did not violate nature by marrying his mother. According to Wagner, the fact that the union produced children was proof that it was fully natural. Wagner uses this myth to illustrate his theory of the tragic curse when he writes that "der unabwendbare Fluch dieser Gesellschaft" (OuD 191) (the inescapable curse of Greek society) rested upon Oedipus and Jocasta. Here Wagner seems to clearly state that to him the traditional tragic curse is not a literal, but, rather, a metaphorical one.

Furthermore, according to Wagner, the myth of Oedipus portrays all of world-history. Modern society, according to Wagner, suffers from lovelessness. Wagner describes a societal progression from love to lovelessness and custom. Upon a first reading the treatise seems to ramble and wander, but despite his verbosity and terminological imprecision, Wagner has definite systematic intentions. What seems an anthropological digression helps place the course of the drama in some relation to the course of history. Wagner establishes a series of oppositions, including individual and collective life, youth and age, instinct and consciousness, activity and contemplation. Society, Wagner explains, evolves its first moral principles from the family. Respect for age was at one time motivated by love; the father loved the son.

As society evolved and lovelessness began to pervade, respect was transferred from persons to mere representations, that is, nonhuman, unreal forms that could not return the respect with love and thus take the fear out of it. Whereas reverence for authority was once inspired by love, in the course of history the paternal authority that the father represented was later portrayed as the decree of a god. Parental advice is seen as law, as the family has been replaced by the state. In mythological drama, as I will show, the historical progression of these projections is reversed as in a mirror. I will argue that in the *Ring* the god becomes a father when the state is destroyed and consciousness is achieved.

This development, too, is epitomized for Wagner by the myth of Oedipus. In his explication of the myth, Wagner describes a progression from love to lovelessness. The rule of Laius, Wagner explains, is the root of all evil. For the sake of possessions, according to Wagner, Laius became an unnatural father. However, in Wagner's version, the myth of Oedipus illustrates not only past and present history. It also portrays the future destruction of the state. Creon is, according to Wagner, the personified state, while Antigone symbolizes the necessary destruction of the state. Antigone's love was fully conscious. In Wagner's interpretation, Creon's decree to leave the body of Polynices unburied was a political decision for the purpose of securing his power. Morality ("Sittlichkeit") must of necessity oppose the order of the state.

Critics have noted that with his interpretation of the Oedipus myth Wagner actually does an injustice to Greek mythology. In Greek society, the individual was integrated into the community, and one suffered by being excluded. Wagner anachronistically projects into the Greek myth his anarchic ideas that the state needs to be destroyed, seeing in the individual suffering of the tragic hero only the martyrdom of the revolutionary hero who opposes the state.[27] Furthermore, a basic feature of the Antigone myth is not the destruction of the state, which in Wagner's eyes it exemplifies, but the purification of the ruler, a notion for which Wagner in his revolutionary years obviously would have no use.[28]

Antigone's love for Polynices, in Wagner's version of the story, causes the destruction of the state. Significantly enough, Wagner again uses the terms "curse" and "state" metaphorically when writing of Antigone's indirect destruction of the state. The "love-curse" ("Liebesfluch") of Antigone destroys the state by violating Creon's ban. Wagner writes,

Antigone sagte den gottseligen Bürgern von Theben: Ihr habt mir Vater und Mutter verdammt, weil sie unbewusst sich liebten; ihr habt den bewussten Sohnesmörder Laios aber nicht verdammt und den Bruderfeind Eteokles beschützt: nun verdammt *mich*, die ich aus reiner Menschenliebe handle—so ist das Mass eurer Frevel voll!— Und siehe! *der Liebesfluch Antigones vernichtete den Staat!* (OuD 198)

Antigone said to the pious citizens of Thebes: You have damned my father and mother, because they unconsciously loved each other; but you did not damn Laius, who consciously killed his son, and you protected Eteocles, who was his brother's enemy: so now damn *me*, for acting out of pure human love—then your wicked crime will be complete!—And look! *the love-curse of Antigone destroyed the state!*

Creon's son loved her, begged for Creon's pardon of her, and killed himself out of love for her after she was buried alive. Wagner writes,

Vor dem Anblicke der Leiche des Sohnes, der aus Liebe seinem Vater hatte fluchen müssen, ward der Herrscher wieder Vater. Das Liebesschwert des Sohnes drang furchtbar schneidend in sein Herz: tief im Innersten verwundet stürzte *der Staat* zusammen, um im Tode *Mensch* zu werden. (OuD 198–99)

At the sight of the corpse of his son, who cursed his father out of love, the ruler became a father. The love-sword of the son cut into his heart: deeply wounded the *state* collapsed, to become a *human being* in death.

In Wagner's interpretation, the "state" is destroyed when the ruler (Creon) becomes a father.

Wagner's terms "love-curse" and "love-sword" clearly indicate his metaphorization of traditionally literal mythological requisites. The curse and the sword are, in Wagner's interpretation, merely figural. Similarly, the destruction of the state is a psychological process. Whereas Greek art is conservative, modern art is revolutionary, that is, it mirrors the myth of Oedipus on another level. It parallels Wagner's analysis of the Oedipus myth, but through self-reflection it undoes itself, thereby showing the revolutionary potential of consciousness and self-consciousness.

However, Wagner's music-drama is, in several ways, intimately connected with the demise of the existing order. Not only does the mythological subject matter harken back to the previous age, and thus forward to some kind of a return to this unity with nature, though on the stage of reflection, what Carl Dahlhaus termed a "second immediacy" ("zweite Unmittelbarkeit").[29] The work of art that Wagner envisions in this treatise should both demonstrate and in some way cause the overthrow of the existing order, that is, the state, by communicating to the audience the necessity of the overthrow of the state. As it unites various art forms within itself and appeals to all the faculties of mankind, the work of art is to ultimately synthesize the dualities of existence. Furthermore, it portrays its own aesthetic program by depicting its own reception, demonstrating how art can affect life and thereby enable myth to change history.

Mythological music-drama portrays the past, present, and future. That it portrays the future also implies that it portrays its own reception. Moreover, the anticipated future reflects the past on another level. The drama has the structure of a mirror-image, a reflective structure. Furthermore, the experience of this drama has revolutionary potential. Wagner presents a mythological solution to modern political problems. Not only does the drama portray the future destruction of the state, thus reversing history within itself. Consciousness can work its reversal. Romantic irony can become revolutionary. Wagner's mythological drama is very different from the myth that the hypothetical Greek society of which he writes projected upon the unsuspecting populace as a tool of political power.

In Wagner's theory, mythology via ironic mythological self-interpretation has some political significance, and political upheaval, in turn, can be brought about through mythological music-drama. The nature of the raw material (which defines the tragic form for Wagner) mirrors the content. Just as the raw material of the drama, mythology, is regressive, but is used on a stage of reflection, the course of the drama spirals to a new state of innocence, and shows the present societal order being destroyed and mankind entering a new state of conscious unconsciousness. The drama, furthermore, should not only portray the destruction of the state, but should cause societal overthrow by doubling the raw material (which has come to define the form) and the content, and instigating this last decisive dialectic of history and myth. Mirrorings or doublings can become explosive. Thus

Wagner clearly shows that his music-drama is the decisive factor in his dialectic of history and myth.

In explaining just how the art-work of the future can revolutionize society, that is, in grounding his ideas concerning the audience reception of the drama, Wagner constructs a theoretical apparatus from the concepts of understanding ("Verstand"), reason ("Vernunft"), feeling ("Gefühl"), and consciousness ("Bewusstsein") that sounds at times vaguely Kantian, though these concepts remain in Wagner's treatise imprecise, since he was an artist and not a systematic philosopher. The imagery that Wagner uses to define the mental capacities I have just mentioned is that of the stages that a person's life goes through. The goal is a synthesis of these various capacities.

Understanding is "das bewusste Anschauungsvermögen des Erfahrenen" (the conscious capacity of perception that the experienced one has). It is "der Ermahnende" (the warner). Feeling is "das zu Ermahnende" (that which is to be warned) or "der unbewusste Tätigkeitstrieb des Erfahrenden" (the unconscious instinctive activity of the experienced one). Understanding justifies feeling, and reason ("Vernunft") is "der aus dem Gefühle gerechtfertigte, nicht mehr im Gefühle dieses einzelnen befangene, sondern gegen das Gefühl überhaupt gerechte Verstand" (understanding which has been justified by feeling, and is no longer engrossed in feeling, but is, rather, just to feeling) (OuD 213–14).

In the drama that Wagner is outlining, the world-view of the adult is communicated. Wagner writes, "Nur im vollendetsten Kunstwerk, im *Drama*, vermag sich daher die Anschauung des Erfahrenen vollkommen erfolgreich mitzuteilen" (OuD 215). (Only in the supreme work of art, in *drama*, can the perception of the experienced one be adequately communicated.) Only myth on the stage of reflection—the supreme drama of the modern era that appeals to the various faculties of mankind and portrays the course of history—can lead mankind to a second state of innocence. By appealing to all human faculties, the art-work of the future will formally represent all stages of human history, both individual and collective.

Mythology is the appropriate vehicle for the art-work of the future because it is easily comprehended. Mythology is a condensed world-view. Mythological drama appeals to the immediacy of feeling. Wagner writes, "Im Drama müssen wir *Wissende* werden durch *das Gefühl*" (OuD 216). (In drama we must become *wise* through *feeling*.) Wagner is describing a sort of circular progression from understanding and rational capacities, that is, through feeling to some sort of new, second state of innocence. The experience of (mythological) drama reverses previous history (both ontogeny and phylogeny). The art-work of the future will return mankind to its childhood. Progression is at the same time regression.

One can structurally envision Wagner's theory consisting of various textual levels, with mental and emotional faculties simultaneously existing in analogy to different stages of life, history parallelling myth, art reflecting life, and all these elements and realms feeding into each other and finally colliding. The art-work of the future is the nodal point that contains everything in miniature, the apex of the pyramid, and the catalyst for a powerful reaction. When the apex of the pyramid is reached—at the point of individual and collective development at which the drama (which thus incestuously portrays its own reception) is experienced—the slide down the right side mirrors the ascent up the left side and returns one to ground level. The experience of the drama will reverse individual and collective development. The reception of the work of art, with the audience becoming conscious through feeling, mirrors the process of artistic creation, which Wagner describes as "Gefühlswerdung des Verstandes" (OuD 215) (understanding becoming feeling).

Furthermore, just as the drama appeals to different mental faculties that are represented by different stages of phylogenetic and ontogenetic development, the tragic hero of this drama unites various historical ages within himself. Wagner felt that the tragic conflict should be internalized in the main character. The tragic hero is the epitome of mythological condensation. The conflict of free will and destiny, which is essential to the tragic genre, is, in Wagner's theory, an inner conflict, a psychological one. The tragic hero of modern mythological drama should have the decisive conflict within himself.

Das verschiedenen Menschen zu verschiedenen Zeiten und unter verschiedenen Umständen eigene und je nach diesen Verschiedenheiten sich besonders gestaltende Interesse soll—sobald diese Menschen, Zeiten und Umstände im Grunde von typischer Ähnlichkeit sind und an sich eine Wesenheit der menschlichen Natur dem beschauenden Bewusstsein deutlich machen—zu dem Interesse *eines* Menschen zu einer bestimmten Zeit und unter bestimmten Umständen gemacht werden. (OuD 228–29)

The various interests of various human beings of various times and under various conditions—so far as these human beings, times, and conditions are basically typical and show the essence of human nature—should be made into the interest of *one* human being at a particular time, under specific conditions.

The mythological drama encompasses various ages, thus transcending history. The modern mythological tragic hero is himself a historical montage. The temporal progression that the drama represents is, in the figure of the tragic hero, frozen to simultaneity. The drama somehow mythologically stops history within itself, thus in real-life slinging it back to a future utopia.

Accordingly, I will show how Wotan is the exemplification of mythological reconstruction. Wotan is Oedipus, Antigone, and Creon at the same time, the accursed one and the suicidal destroyer of the state. Like Oedipus, he has a tragic insight, a self-recognition. And like Antigone, he causes the destruction of the state. The condensation of modern mythological drama that simultaneously portrays its own creation and reception can become explosive when consciousness becomes self-consciousness. Just as mythological drama must reverse history by being experienced, it deconstructs itself by portraying its own aesthetic program and depicting within itself its own audience reception.

Wagner's theory of drama and thus its revolutionary potential is based on the identification of the audience with the dramatic figures. The mirroring of the audience in the work of art can revolutionize society. This is a special kind of doubling; the self is doubled when one sees oneself or one's own reflection as in a mirror.

Die Kunst ist ihrer Bedeutung nach nichts anderes als die Erfüllung des Verlangens, in einem dargestellten bewunderten oder geliebten Gegenstande sich selbst zu erkennen, sich in den durch ihre Darstellung bewältigten Erscheinungen der Aussenwelt wiederzufinden. Der Künstler sagt sich in dem von ihm dargestellten Gegenstande: "So bist du, so fühlst und denkst du, und so würdest du handeln, wenn du, frei von der zwingenden Unwillkür der äusseren Lebenseindrücke, nach der Wahl deines Wunsches handeln könntest." So stellte das Volk im Mythos sich *Gott*, so den *Helden* und so endlich den *Menschen* dar. (OuD 163)

Art is by definition nothing else than the fulfillment of the desire to recognize oneself in a depicted object, to find oneself in the appearances of the external world, which have been mastered by being depicted. The artist says to himself in the object he has depicted: "Thus you are, thus you feel and think, and this is how you would act, if you, free from the compelling necessity of external impressions, could involuntarily act according to your choices and wishes." In this way mankind depicted *God* in mythology, the *hero*, and finally *mankind*.

Earlier I cited a passage from *Oper und Drama* in which Wagner explains myth as unconscious self-recognition. Art brings the process of self-recognition to consciousness. The mythological pattern that is transposed into the modern mythological music-drama will be duplicated in real-life through the experience of the work of art. History will follow myth. The audience reception of such a complex mythological work of art will, in real-life, overcome tragedy and mythologize history.

Not only is the conflict internalized within the drama. The destruction of the state that the work of art will cause is also an inner process, with the audience coming to consciousness through the experience of the drama. One could say that the performance of the drama will project its structure and the internalization of action that it represents outward, to the audience, just as a mirror throws an image back at a person. The dialectic of consciousness that Wagner sees as occurring within the tragedy, exemplified by the dialectic of consciousness that Wagner points to in the myth of Oedipus, is to be mirrored, on another level, at a higher stage by the experience of the audience at the performance of the art-work of the future. The false, conservative consciousness that Oedipus attains contrasts with the revolutionary self-consciousness and insight into the falsity of the state that the audience of the art-work of the future will achieve.

Wagner describes a progression from unconsciousness to consciousness. Similarly, in a quote I cited earlier, he explains Greek tragedy as resulting from unconsciousness of internal necessity, whereas modern life is characterized by the consciousness (at least on the part of the artist) of how the state deprives human beings of freedom. This modern consciousness is revolutionary. It mediates between history and myth. The work of art that portrays this dialectic of consciousness in a self-conscious way forms the crucial link in this process. Myth on the level of reflection reverses history. The "potentiation" of myth can, ironically, bring forth a societal overthrow.

Both individual life and history, ontogeny and phylogeny, show a progression, in this treatise, from unconsciousness to consciousness. Paradoxically, consciousness is paired with unconsciousness. Regression is at the same time progression, just as Kleist theorized that mankind should re-enter Paradise through the back door by eating from the Tree of Knowledge a second time. The audience reception of the work of art mirrors the content of the drama. The progression, in both cases, is from history to myth. The drama that Wagner describes portrays this in a complex way within mythological material. In doing so, it portrays itself in a Romantically ironic, reflexive way. The drama, however, must deconstruct itself when it portrays its own reception.

The destruction of the state consists of bringing what is unconscious to consciousness. True knowledge, Wagner writes, is knowledge of what is really known but unconscious. Cognition is ideally recognition (Wagner uses the terms "Erkenntnis" and "Wiedererkenntnis.") Wagner writes,

Der Untergang des Staates kann vernünftigerweise nichts anderes heissen als *das sich verwirklichende religiöse Bewusstsein der Gesellschaft vor ihrem rein menschlichen Wesen.* (OuD 208)

The destruction of the state can reasonably mean nothing else than that *the consciousness of society has fully realized its purely human essence.*

The destruction of the state consists in a reflexive act of self-consciousness. One recognizes oneself in the modern-day reworking of an interpretation of the myth of Oedipus. Recognition, as the prefix implies, connotes reversal. Furthermore, self-recognition can have societal consequences. Paradoxically, one can change external reality by turning inward. Art can, in an indirect way, by being self-reflective and thus apolitical, have profoundly political repercussions.

Wagner writes, "In der freien Selbstbestimmung der Individualität liegt daher der Grund der gesellschaftlichen Religion der Zukunft" (OuD 209). (The free self-determination of the individual characterizes the societal religion of the future.) Wagner uses the term "religion" in a loose sense that possibly reflects his interest in Feuerbach, who, one could say, deconstructed the metaphysics of religion in the nineteenth century. Wagner later specifies (OuD 209) that religious consciousness is a collective consciousness. Individual progress will lead to collective progress. The mirroring will be a telescopic enlargement that mirrors and thus reverses the process of condensation that gave rise to the art-work of the future.

However, Wagner presents an inner, an individual, a psychological solution to external societal problems. Wagner describes a dialectic of unconsciousness and consciousness.

Das Unbewusste der menschlichen Natur *in der Gesellschaft zum Bewusstsein bringen,* und in diesem Bewusstsein nichts anderes zu wissen als eben *die allen Gliedern der Gesellschaft gemeinsame Notwendigkeit der freien Selbstbestimmung des Individuums,* heisst aber soviel, als—*den Staat vernichten;* denn der Staat schritt durch die Gesellschaft zur Verneinung der freien Selbstbestimmung des Individuums vor—von ihrem Tode lebte er. (OuD 202)

To bring *what is unconscious* in human nature *to consciousness,* and to recognize in this consciousness nothing other than *the common and basic human necessity of the free self-determination of every individual,* means *to destroy the state;* for the state denies the free self-determination of the individual; it thrives on this denial.

The destruction of the state is an inner upheaval, a psychological revolution, a mental progression from unconsciousness to consciousness. Wagner continually describes the phenomenon with abstract terms. The "state," it seems, exists, according to Wagner, only when its dictates have been internalized, and when one thinks it is real and binding. In other words, it is in power as long as one thinks it is. In his mythological drama, Wagner seems to have deconstructed politics just as he undermined metaphysics. Even his political writings are notorious for their impracticality and idealism, as he was an artist, and not a reality-oriented politician. When one attains a consciousness of the necessity of the free self-determination of the individual, then the destruction of the state, according to Wagner, has been achieved.

Collective progress, that is, the ultimate revolution, will ensue upon individual progress and reverse history, that is, as in a mirror. Internalization leads, as though in a slingshot reaction, to externalization. In reflecting the myth of Oedipus on another level, the drama will reverse previous history both within itself and in reality.

Der Untergang des Staates heisst daher so viel als der Hinwegfall der Schranke, welche durch die egoistische Eitelkeit der Erfahrung als Vorurteil gegen die Unwillkür des individuellen Handelns sich errichtet hat. Diese Schranke nimmt gegenwärtig die Stellung ein, die naturgemäss der *Liebe* gebührt, und sie ist nach ihrem Wesen die *Lieblosigkeit*. (OuD 212)

The destruction of the state means the falling down of the barrier, which has established itself through egoistical vanity as prejudice against the instinct of individual action. This barrier presently takes the place that would naturally belong to *love*, and is in its essence *lovelessness*.

Wagner's version of tragedy has little to do with cataclysmic endings or cosmic debacles. The external overthrow of a political system is not the center of Wagner's attention. Rather, he seems to feel that this will follow inevitably upon the inner progress that his drama will induce. Wagner writes of the conflict of the free individual and the state in terms of the abstract concepts that characterize each. It even seems that Wagner might also be using the term "state" in a figurative, rather than a literal, sense. It exists when one thinks it has power over one's actions, or when one gives it such control. The destruction of the state will overcome the lovelessness of modern society.

The experience of the drama can reverse history. Collective progress will follow upon individual progress. The process of ontogeny recapitulating phylogeny is reversed when the art-work of the future has become a thing of the immediate past and the reversal of individual development is mirrored by that of collective history. The inner changes the outer. Art transforms history. The mythological nature of the drama should be ultimately mirrored in history through the very experience of this drama, by the mythologization of history. As the modern tragic hero represents anachronistically various historical ages at once, the mirroring of the mythological essence of the drama in history will produce a new Golden Age, a timeless realm of existence, a second Paradise of unconscious consciousness.

The *Ring* reflects not only Wagner's interpretation of the myth of Oedipus, but also the broader structure and various levels of the second part of *Oper und Drama*, and its nature as an *aesthetic* treatise (with, of course, some political ramifications at the fringes). The *Ring*, I will show, demonstrates the theory of mythological narration and interpretation presented in *Oper und Drama* not in a static, but, rather, in a dynamic way. It thematizes myth (in the various senses of the term) and proceeds through Romantic irony or innertextual reflection and interpretation, folding in upon itself, unfolding itself, and ultimately crumpling completely.

As a mythological drama, the *Ring* deconstructs itself due to its historical, perspectival nature. Schnädelbach points out that the *Ring* is not true for all time. It represents not "das Reinmenschliche," but what an artist of the nineteenth century took to be "das Reinmenschliche." It is a modernized myth, the myth of modern times, with myth standing for, that is, being a metaphor for, history. This metaphoricity of the work, when coupled with a Romantic kind of self-referentiality or reflexivity, proves both catastrophic and redemptive in its revolutionary potential. Wagner's own assertion of the historical relativism of myth proves self-destructive at the end of the *Ring*. It works against the fictional world he has established when self-consciousness of the synthetic nature of the mythical world in the *Ring* destroys the gods. This process is exemplified most strikingly by Wotan in particular.

NOTES

1. See: Horst Denkler, "Politische Dramaturgie. Zur Theorie des Dramas und des Theaters zwischen den Revolutionen von 1830 und 1848," in *Deutsche Dramentheorien. Beiträge zu einer historischen Poetik des Dramas in Deutschland*, ed. Reinhold Grimm (Frankfurt am Main: Athenäum, 1971), vol. 2, pp. 345–73.

2. On the Kleist essay, see: Bettina Schulte, *Unmittelbarkeit und Vermittlung im Werk Heinrich von Kleists* (Göttingen and Zurich: Vandenhoeck und Ruprecht, 1988), pp. 70–84.

3. Wolfgang Schadewaldt, "Richard Wagner und die Griechen," in *Richard Wagner und das neue Bayreuth*, ed. Wieland Wagner (Munich: Paul List, 1962), pp. 149–74. See also: Dieter Bremer, "Vom Mythos zum Musikdrama. Wagner, Nietzsche und die griechische Tragödie," in *Wege des Mythos in der Moderne. Richard Wagner, "Der Ring des Nibelungen"*, ed. Dieter Borchmeyer (Munich: Deutscher Taschenbuch Verlag, 1987), pp. 41–63; Ulrich Müller, "Richard Wagner und die Antike," in *Richard-Wagner-Handbuch*, ed. Ulrich Müller and Peter Wapnewski (Stuttgart: Alfred Kröner, 1986), pp. 7–18; Dieter Borchmeyer, *Das Theater Richard Wagners: Idee, Dichtung, Wirkung* (Stuttgart: Reclam, 1982), pp. 76–85.

4. Edward McInnes, *Das deutsche Drama des 19. Jahrhunderts*, Grundlagen der Germanistik, 26 (Berlin: Erich Schmidt, 1983). On German drama in the nineteenth century, see also: Helmut Schanze, *Drama im Bürgerlichen Realismus (1850–1890): Theorie und Praxis*, Studien zur Philosophie und Literatur des neunzehnten Jahrhunderts, vol. 21 (Frankfurt am Main: Vittorio Klostermann, 1973).

5. Benno von Wiese, *Die Deutsche Tragödie von Lessing bis Hebbel*, 6th ed. (Hamburg: Hoffmann und Campe, 1948, 1964), pp. 535–71; "Probleme der deutschen Tragödie im 19. Jahrhundert," *Wirkendes Wort* 1 (1950/51), pp. 32–38.

6. George Steiner, *The Death of Tragedy* (New York: Alfred A. Knopf, 1961), pp. 106–50.

7. Otto Mann, *Geschichte des deutschen Dramas*, 3d ed., Kröners Taschenausgabe, vol. 296 (Stuttgart: Alfred Kröner, 1969), pp. 322–27.

8. Bryan Magee, *Aspects of Wagner*, rev. ed. (Oxford: Oxford University Press, 1988), p. 14.

9. Richard Wagner, *Oper und Drama*, ed. Klaus Kropfinger (Stuttgart: Reclam, 1984), p. 230. References to this work will hereafter be given within my text by page numbers, preceded by the abbreviation "OuD."

10. On the idea of "absolute music," see: Borchmeyer, *Das Theater Richard Wagners*, pp. 102–25 (here cited from p. 102); Dahlhaus, *Die Idee der absoluten Musik* (Munich and Kassel: Deutscher Taschenbuch Verlag and Bärenreiter Verlag, 1978).

11. Anette Ingenhoff, *Drama oder Epos? Richard Wagners Gattungstheorie des musikalischen Dramas*, Untersuchungen zur deutschen Literaturgeschichte, vol. 41 (Tübingen: Max Niemeyer, 1987), pp. 103–12. All subsequent references to Ingenhoff in this chapter will be to this reference.

12. Friedrich Sengle, "Vom Absoluten in der Tragödie," *Deutsche Vierteljahrsschrift für Literaturwissenschaft und Geistesgeschichte* 20, no. 3 (1942), pp. 265–72.

13. In this and the following paragraph, I am citing: Dagmar Ingenschay-Goch, *Richard Wagners neu erfundener Mythos: Zur Rezeption und Reproduktion des germanischen Mythos in seinen Operntexten*, Abhandlungen zur Kunst-, Musik- und Literaturwissenschaft, vol. 311 (Bonn: Bouvier Verlag Herbert Grundmann, 1982), pp. 17–20.

14. Jean-Jacques Nattiez, *Wagner Androgyne*, trans. Stewart Spencer (Princeton, NJ: Princeton University Press, 1993), pp. 91–96.

15. Dieter Borchmeyer, "Vom Anfang und Ende der Geschichte. Richard Wagners mythisches Drama. Idee und Inszenierung," in *Macht des Mythos—Ohnmacht der Vernunft?*, ed. Peter Kemper (Frankfurt am Main: Fischer, 1989), pp. 176–200.

16. Andrea Mork, *Richard Wagner als politischer Schriftsteller: Weltanschauung und Wirkungsgeschichte* (Frankfurt: Campus, 1990), pp. 27–35, 45–76.

17. See the section entitled " 'Schöne Öffentlichkeit': Die Griechen und *Das Kunstwerk der Zukunft*," in Borchmeyer, *Das Theater Richard Wagners*, pp. 63–74.

18. For discussions of Wagner on the novel, see: Borchmeyer, *Das Theater Richard Wagners*, pp. 125–51 ("Die 'Erlösung' des Romans im musikalischen Drama"); Ingenhoff, pp. 80–100.

19. For an application of Wagner's theoretical mythological schema to *Tannhäuser* and an analysis of this early opera as a rudimentary foreshadowing of Wagner's later quasi-political reworking of traditional tragedy theory, see my book, *From History to Myth: Wagner's "Tannhäuser" and its Literary Sources*, Germanic Studies in America, 63 (Bern: Peter Lang, 1992).

20. In preparing this section, I have consulted: Rainer Franke, *Richard Wagners Zürcher Kunstschriften: Politische und ästhetische Entwürfe auf seinem Weg zum "Ring des Nibelungen"*, Hamburger Beiträge zur Musikwissenschaft, vol. 26 (Hamburg: Verlag der Musikalienhandlung Karl Dieter Wagner, 1983), pp. 273–312. All subsequent references to Rainer Franke in this chapter will be to this discussion, which I am both using and revising.

21. See: Franke, pp. 292–302.

22. Franke, pp. 273–92 (cited from p. 275).

23. Franke, p. 276.

24. For a catalogue of these various forms, see: Paul Kluckhohn, "Die Arten des Dramas," *Deutsche Vierteljahrsschrift für Literaturwissenschaft und Geistesgeschichte* 19, no. 3 (1941), pp. 241–68.

25. Rolf Breuer, *Tragische Handlungsstrukturen. Eine Theorie der Tragödie* (Munich: Wilhelm Fink, 1988).

26. Schadewaldt, "Richard Wagner und die Griechen," p. 167.

27. Ingenhoff, p. 108.

28. Franke, p. 309.

29. Dahlhaus, *Richard Wagners Musikdramen*, p. 84.

Chapter 3

Mythology and Hermeneutics: The *Ring* as Romantic Drama

*W*agner's *Ring*, to which *Oper und Drama* is usually considered the theoretical counterpart, is likewise a contradictory, multifaceted work. Its conception goes back to 1848, and its composition was finished in 1874. With a genesis of about twenty-six years, it synthesizes material from Norse and Middle High German sources (with, of course, significant changes). In it one finds revolutionary, Feuerbachian, Hegelian, and Socialist ideas. Wagner even retrospectively explains Wotan with reference to Schopenhauer's philosophy, and some critics still discuss what they consider the influence of Schopenhauer on the *Ring*. Others point out that Schopenhauer's philosophy had no bearing on the main body of the *Ring*, and thus insist scholarship has disproven and discounted this notion of a so-called break in the *Ring*, relegating it to the many myths of Wagner scholarship.

The complexity of the *Ring* defies any kind of ultimate, definitive classification of its dramatic structure. Like *Oper und Drama*, the *Ring* contains elements that correspond to many different kinds of tragedy theories, like the faces of a prism. The multifaceted nature of the work reflects its complicated genesis—the numerous sources from which Wagner freely drew and elements of which he combined in a very eclectic way; the various philosophical and political ideas with which Wagner was acquainted and which could not but find some reflection in the *Ring*; the length of time during which Wagner worked on the *Ring*; and the many revisions and changes in his conception, resulting in inconsistencies which are not noticeable in performance but which, as in many great works of art, defy rational analysis.

In this chapter I will discuss how to interpret the *Ring*. I will, first of all, summarize and critique two extratextual interpretative methods, the psychological and the political. As a compromise between them, I suggest that one can apply the theory of tragedy (which is a theory of myth) contained in *Oper und Drama* to the *Ring*. I have generated an apparatus that outlines how in Wagner's theory of tragedy the psychological interacts with the political, the inner with the outer, and I have pointed to the historical relativity of mythological interpretation in the treatise. In applying Wagner's theory to his tetralogy, I will show how the *Ring* is actually a Romantic drama that bears comparison with those of Tieck who is known, significantly enough, for his untragic comedies. The *Ring* is, I will demonstrate, a mythological work in the most profound way. It thematizes not only its own mythological raw material, but also its extended mythical nature, in the form of endless self-reflection.

Referring to how I defined the concepts of "Romantic irony" and "myth" in chapter 1, I will also point to how the *Ring*, because it is a Wagnerian tragedy (that is, an unworking of tragedy), has an ironic use of myth. To this end, I will discuss, in particular, the ring named in the title, which is a microcosmic structure that represents the work as a whole. The *Ring*, I will argue, demonstrates the aesthetics of myth as metaphor that Wagner outlines in *Oper und Drama*. Thus, the tetralogy contains layers of myth, a self-consciousness of its own dual mythical nature, and a conglomeration of history and myth that befits its self-reflection of its own extended mythical nature as a nineteenth-century metaphorical explanation of history. In other words, the *Ring* reflects the endless self-reflections and dialectical political-aesthetic program of *Oper und Drama* in a complex way.

る

The richness of the work is reflected by the various schools of interpretation that have been devised to explain it. The two extremes of interpretation, which I will present following the example of Deryck Cooke, are the societal or political approach and the psychological approach. The former is epitomized by George Bernard Shaw's *The Perfect Wagnerite*.[1] Shaw interprets the *Ring* with reference to his own political orientation, that of Socialism. For example, he likens Nibelheim to a factory and the Nibelungs to factory workers. Alberich is, to Shaw, a plutocrat, and Siegfried is an anarchist. Shaw blatantly states, despite the mythological raw material, that the *Ring* deals with events of the second half of the nineteenth century, and he therefore recounts Wagner's revolutionary activities. For Shaw, the *Ring* is a political allegory. Wotan, according to Shaw, is Godhead and Kingship, Loge is Logic and Imagination, and Fricka is State Law.

The social, political aspect, however, falls short of adequately explaining the work. Deryck Cooke[2] points out that social critique was only one of Wagner's intentions. Love is also an important theme in the *Ring*, one which

Shaw cannot deal with. Wagner ended the work with different intentions from those with which he started it. Shaw's interpretation cannot possibly encompass the complexity of the *Ring*. Shaw can only continue his allegorical explanation by the dubious maneuver of arguing that the allegory eventually collapses, and that love is a panacea. Politics, it seems, cannot explain everything.

Shaw's *Ring* interpretation is, of course, an extreme example of the political mode of interpretation, which in its mechanical equation of figures with abstractions really warrants the term "allegory" rather than "parable." The former term connotes a work that has one definitive and exhaustive interpretation that arises from the mechanical substitution of abstractions for figures in the drama. The deficiencies of Shaw's interpretation of the *Ring* are much more severe than are the shortcomings of the critics, such as Mayer, Bermbach, and Franke, whose work I will discuss in this chapter and who also stress the political aspects of the *Ring*. For their work, "parable," implying a story told in lieu of a second story to illustrate a moral lesson, would be a more apt designation. "Parable" is, after all, the term that Mayer and Bermbach use to describe the *Ring*.[3] Just as hyperbole can be useful for rhetorical effect, however, so does a consideration of Shaw's views blatantly show the fallacy of trying to reduce the *Ring* to a political statement. Such interpretations falter on a disregard for, or a failure to differentiate, the various textual levels of Wagner's tetralogy and the literal versus the figural use of terms in *Oper und Drama*.

Robert Donington's work represents the other extreme, the psychological, and in particular, Jungian interpretation.[4] Analyzing the *Ring* in accordance with Jungian psychology dictates that the characters in the *Ring* are each interpreted as a fragmentary part or a single aspect of one psyche. The events of the tetralogy, accordingly, represent phases of psychic development. For instance, Donington discusses Wotan as the self or ego consciousness, Alberich is the shadow, and the Rhinemaidens, Freia, Erda, and the Valkyries are all representations of the Eternal Feminine. The objective requisites become, in this interpretation, likewise psychologized. The Tarnhelm, according to Donington, is a symbol of unconscious fantasy, and the ring is a symbol of the self. When Wotan casts Brünnhilde out of Valhalla, he is, Donington argues, casting off his anima.

The Jungian interpretation, however, does an injustice to the psychic depths of the characters, which Wagner, as he wrote in *Oper und Drama*, felt should not be reductions to one side of a personality, but, rather, incorporations of many personalities at many times of history. Wagner's figures are, despite the mythological scenario, very complex and very human, and thus, I will argue, very unlike mythological figures, a difference that indicates a basic paradox of the work as a whole. Their feelings resemble our own, even if the situations in which they find themselves do not.

Nattiez even argues that the Jungian interpretation explains nothing, since for Jung all figures of myth are interchangeable. In reducing the multiplicity of symbolic manifestations to a single set of archetypes, according to Nattiez, one deprives oneself of the chance to interpret each individual symbol once it is incorporated into the syntax of a narrative. Nattiez sees this as the essential problem from a semiological point of view. Jung's symbol, Nattiez explains, is asyntactical. One cannot be certain that two mythologems are identical to each other if one has not first studied their meaning in the context in which they appear.[5] Thus the inner interpretation, the internal extreme, also suffers from an inadequacy, just as does the external, political interpretation. Both are reductive in different ways. The truth seems to lie somewhere in the middle.

Wagner, however, often interpreted his own works, and Wagner himself referred to the *Ring* as a tragedy. For instance, in a letter to Theodor Uhlig of 12 November 1851, he calls the combination of elements he has sketched out "eine Tragödie von der erschütterndsten Wirkung"[6] (a tragedy that will have the most moving effect). In a quotation from Cosima's diaries, Wagner terms *Siegfried* "eine Art Intermezzo" (a sort of intermezzo), and then adds, "die Tragödie sei die Götterdämmerung" (the real tragedy is *Götterdämmerung*).[7] It is not that he always used words, especially artistic terms, in a precise way, or that his aesthetic theory was perfectly systematic. His aesthetic judgements are usually controversial. And, of course, special caution is in order when Wagner is discussing his own works. But this term, this concept of tragedy, is important enough to warrant some investigation.

On 6 September 1875, Cosima reported in her diary, "Wir sprechen von Siegfried und Brünnhilde's Liebe, die keine erlösende Welttat vollbringt" (We talk of the love between Siegfried and Brünnhilde, which achieves no universal deed of redemption). Shortly thereafter, she continues, "die Götterdämmerung das tragischste, dafür aber sieht man vorher das höchste Glück durch die Verbindung zweier vollendeter Wesen" (CT I, 435). (*Götterdämmerung* is the most tragic work of all, but before that one sees the great happiness arising from the union of two complete beings) (D I, 410). Nobody would debate that *Götterdämmerung* is "tragic." However, by mentioning the love of Siegfried and Brünnhilde both before and after the statement that *Götterdämmerung* is the most tragic of his works, Cosima seems to imply that tragedy in the *Ring* resides in the failure of a love relationship rather than any huge cataclysm, and is thus more of a personal, inner process than one usually finds in the "tragic" aspect of *Götterdämmerung*.

But not only was the last part of the tetralogy a "tragedy." So was the second. On 31 August 1873, Wagner identified *Walküre* as "das pathetischste, tragischste seiner Werke" (CT II, 720) (the most emotional, most tragic of all his works) (D I, 669), a quotation that might seem strange when one thinks of the cataclysmic ending of *Götterdämmerung*. This quotation, I would argue, indicates that he is referring to a specifically Wagnerian concept of tragedy. For Wagner, tragedy is an inner process. The *Ring*, I will argue, is a specifically Wagnerian tragedy, which means that it unworks traditional tragedy theory according to the corresponding model presented in *Oper und Drama*.

ॐ

It is, of course, common knowledge that Wagner placed his dramas within the tradition of Greek tragedy, and many scholars have discussed his dramas in this regard. Various attempts have been made to discuss Wagner's *Ring* with reference to Greek tragedy. Wolfgang Schadewaldt has termed Wagner's dramas "mythical palimpsests," arguing that the Greek model is usually evident under the surface. Wagner's "Mitteilung an meine Freunde" shows that he saw his dramas as transparencies for Greek mythical models. For instance, he likens Lohengrin and Elsa to Zeus and Semele, and the Dutchman and Tannhäuser to Odysseus. Accordingly, Schadewaldt parallels the *Ring* with the Prometheus trilogy of Aeschylus.[8]

Stressing the similarities between Wagner's works and Greek tragedies, though, overlooks the inevitable differences between the ancient and the nineteenth-century works. There are valid parallels, but Wagner, one should remember, unworks and interprets Greek tragedy in *Oper und Drama*. Michael Ewans parallels the *Ring* with the *Oresteia*.[9] His work, however, has been criticized for being too one-sided, the affinities of Wagner's work with aspects of numerous Greek tragedies rendering a restriction to parallels with the *Oresteia* somehow dissatisfying.[10]

The *Ring* does, of course, have an outward resemblance to tragedy. The mythological nature of the subject matter, the fact that the work deals with gods and heroes, clearly gives it a mythological aura. The fate-motive resounds frequently,[11] Erda and the Rhinemaidens make prophecies, and Siegfried and Siegmund seem to be heroic figures who try to assert their freedom but fall anyway. However, an analysis of how these various elements and themes function within the *Ring* shows that in his tetralogy Wagner, in ways that go far beyond the obvious, far beyond a mere politicization of the dramatic form, has unworked what critics discern as the traditional, basic structure and essence of tragedy.

When it comes to content, it is, beyond such surface similarities as I have just mentioned, not easy to analyze the *Ring* with regard to traditional theory of tragedy. The traditional elements of tragedy, such as oracles and mythological objects such as magical rings that are cursed, are present, but they do not function as they traditionally should. These apparently "tragic" elements are deceptive. One also looks in vain for a tragic hero of the traditional type. The question of who the tragic hero is proves to be a difficult one, the answer to which seems to defy the outward appearance of the work and the expectations of the audience. Several of the figures qualify in various ways, but the nature of each of them as "tragic hero" is at the same time strange and unconventional. The criteria that one should use when discussing the *Ring* as a tragedy must be sought elsewhere than in traditional tragedy theory. Wagner, one must remember, defines tragedy by its content or raw material, that is, as a mythological work of art.

Wagner, it seems safe to assert, did not and could not write simple revivals of Greek tragedies. The *Ring* is a modern tragedy, a strange kind of mythological drama in which gods discourse at length about their own weaknesses, their inevitable fates, and their lack of free will. Tragedy, like the *Ring*, leaves some questions unanswered. Tragedy portrays a metaphysical conception of the world that can never be fully penetrated by mankind, and one can say that the *Ring*, in a very different way, does the same. However, whether the conflicts that the *Ring* presents are really unresolvable, and whether Wagner's world-view is tragic, are, after all, double-edged questions. The *Ring* presents two worlds. It all depends on which world one is referring to, the one within the *Ring* or the one that encompasses what exists after the *Ring*.

Wagner certainly would not have approved of regarding his dramas as a simple modern-day imitation of Greek drama. He would have felt that was anachronistic. For this reason he took special pains to rework the structure of Greek tragedy in *Oper und Drama*. He places his work in the tradition of Greek tragedy solely by virtue of its mythological subject matter, in other ways explicitly redefining Greek tragedy for modern times and for a revolutionary era. Thus a basic contradiction exists between Wagner's redefinition of tragedy and reinterpretation of its traditional elements in *Oper und Drama*, on the one hand, and any analysis of his work with regard to traditional definitions and qualities of tragedy. Accordingly, these analyses that I have just mentioned raise as many problems as they solve. Questions arise as to what the nature of the dramatic conflict is, and just what the mythological trappings of the *Ring* really mean if the work reverses traditional notions of tragedy. Why have mythological "props" in a modern, synthetic myth?

Hans Mayer likens the *Ring* to a Greek tragedy, and he discusses the *Ring* as an "analytic tragedy," arguing that Wotan's ancient crime at the World Ash Tree is gradually revealed through the course of the drama.[12] This interpretation is, however, reductionist. How can one say that what transpires during the whole four evenings results from one ancient deed? One must discuss how and why events follow. That Wotan tore a branch from the World Ash Tree, as revealed in the Prologue to *Götterdämmerung*, is a symptom of his underlying corruption, which determines the events which set the scene for his self-realization. One must take into account the anachronistic discrepancy between the mythological trappings of the *Ring* and the modern influences that helped shape the work, and the dichotomy of the external objective supernatural elements and the psychological internalization of the decisive dramatic action.

Furthermore, Mayer's thesis ignores what Wagner does to traditional patterns in *Oper und Drama*. The *Ring* contains some props of tragedy, but *Oper und Drama* discusses the concept of fate and the gods of tragedy in a modern way, reflecting upon them and unworking or demythologizing them in the process. Similarly, Dieter Borchmeyer writes that fate is embodied in Erda and the Norns.[13] But why do the prophecies come true in such a genuinely tragic way? Do Erda and the Norns actually cause fate, and make the future happen as it does, or do they just comment on it? Is it their expression of fate that is important, or is it important whether or not, extending the interpretation of Abbate to this issue, one hears it? Or must one, as I would propose, interpret it properly? These mythological entities establish the modern reflexivity of the *Ring*. Furthermore, Erda and the Norns, like Wotan, are not omnipotent. Erda and the Norns do not really know what is going on or what will happen. Moreover, Wagner's explanation of the traditional ancient curse undermines conventional, accepted, magical notions of what a curse is. How does the curse on the ring work the doom of the gods, anyway? For that matter, does it, really?

The ancient concept of fate, which Wagner discusses in *Oper und Drama*, is not unambiguous in the *Ring*. In his passages about "fate" in *Oper und Drama*, Wagner sketches a complex interaction between the real and the ideal. For this reason, Wagner's explanation of this concept seems appropriate to the *Ring*, for here it has a "dual" significance. To discuss how the concept of fate functions in the *Ring* entails a deceptively simple problem, the question of why the gods end. To answer this, one must take into account the interplay between the inner and outer causes of the end of the gods. It is caused by both the curse on the ring (directly or indirectly) and the crime at the World Ash Tree. Furthermore, Wotan wills the end, and everything was going to end anyway. Brünnhilde actually causes the end in the Immolation Scene. The end of the gods is thus overdetermined in a multiple way. The two texts are apparently comparable in their ambiguities. In *Oper und Drama*, by demythologizing the concept of "fate," Wagner causes the problem of how to reconcile his metaphorical interpretation of "fate" with an interpretation of his tetralogy that can explain the outwardly mythological elements of the *Ring*.

Most attempts to interpret the *Ring* with regard to the theory of *Oper und Drama* focus on the political aspect of the treatise. Similar problems and complications therefore beset these interpretations. Rainer Franke writes of the conflict of the free individual with the state, parallelling Brünnhilde with Antigone. He argues that fate is political, and that it results from the ancient crime at the World Ash Tree and the fight for power. This argument weakens, though, when one considers that the gods would have ended regardless of these events. Erda pronounces the inevitability of the end. Is fate, in the *Ring*, really political?

The structuralist schema that Wagner abstracts from Greek drama does seem to invite such a political interpretation. That the temptation is great to analyze the *Ring* as a political allegory derives from Wagner himself. Of course, Wotan is definitely corrupt, allowing himself to be ruled by the desire for power and material goods, which for Wagner was the weakness from which the modern capitalist state suffered. It would be much too simplistic and schematic to say, however, that Wotan represents the modern state, or that the conflict between the state and the free individual, of which Wagner writes in *Oper und Drama*, is portrayed by the opposition of Wotan versus Siegfried. According to Wagner, the novel portrays society and politics; his drama conveys "das Reinmenschliche."

The ideas of love versus power, and the notion of the greed for gold (which characterizes modern capitalistic society) as being evil, are indeed at work in the *Ring*. However, Wagner's mythological music-drama is, by definition and tautologically, a nonrealistic genre. Rainer Franke constantly refers to Wotan's rule as a "state."[14] Wotan is, according to Franke, a personified politician.[15] However, "the state" as such does not exist in the *Ring* (and Wagner is far from offering mere personifications—this would be far too simplistic). Similarly, Peter Wapnewski discusses Wotan as a "political god."[16] But a "political god" is a contradiction in terms, an anachronism (if considerations of temporality can at all be applied to a god).

The political interpretation suffers from a fundamental fallacy that overlooks the mythological nature of the work of art. In fact, it ignores the very artistic nature of the work of art. Myth is not realistic. The *Ring* is not a political pamphlet any more than *Oper und Drama* is. Interpreting the gods of the *Ring* as projections of human political actions seems to do a huge injustice to Wagner's own intentions as presented in *Oper und Drama*. If Wotan is a politician, he's a bad one at that. Politicians rarely show the introspection and reflection that Wotan does. Politicians usually lack depth and psychic conflict. They also do not *will* their own destruction. Wotan, however, does.

Udo Bermbach interprets the *Ring* as a political parable, arguing that the gods are projections of political action, and the world of the *Ring* has been ruined by politics, thus mirroring bourgeois society.[17] Bermbach, however, fails to explain why one would need a lengthy cycle of music-dramas merely to demonstrate a "political parable" and, in addition, an accompanying aesthetic treatise. Bermbach neglects aesthetics in favor of politics, thus reversing Wagner's own priorities. It also seems contradictory and anachronistic to discuss, as he does, Wotan's contracts as though the god were in the guise of a nineteenth-century politician. The incongruity of this Shavian image expresses the paradox that I am pointing to.

Mythological worlds typically lack such moral and ethical responsibilities. According to Bermbach, the *Ring* works on the opposition between the state of nature and the political order. These concepts, I would argue, are not applicable to mythological subject matter, for gods are by definition uncivilized, and mythology represents in itself a state of nature, a kind of "folk-literature." One must analyze the *Ring* from without, as a work of art, and take its various mediums and subject matter into account. I would propose a deeper duality of history and myth in the *Ring*. Furthermore, one should not speak of mutually exclusive dualities, but of conditions which are, in the *Ring*, simultaneous.

Schnädelbach terms Wagner's "Kunstmythos" a "Sozialmythos." It tells of the origin of society and of power. Wagner, he relates, wanted to tell the story behind history. This led him into the realm of myth.[18] Schnädelbach both does and does not take the mythical nature of the *Ring* into consideration. Schnädelbach, by calling Wagner's myth a "Sozialmythos," puts Wagner in a class with Rousseau, Nietzsche, Marx and Engels, Spengler, Freud, Horkheimer, and Adorno. But this reduces and seems to violate the artistic nature of the work of art. Why have an aesthetic treatise to accompany a political work? What does the aesthetic theory that Wagner outlines at length in *Oper und Drama* mean for the *Ring* then?

Borchmeyer draws the analogy between the *Ring* and *Oper und Drama* by working from abstract principles, such as custom ("Gewohnheit"), lovelessness ("Lieblosigkeit"), and the like, in analyzing the use of the incest motive in the *Ring*. He takes as his cue the fact that Wagner, in *Oper und Drama*, proposes the story of Oedipus as the outline or model of the history of mankind. The *Ring*, after all, tells, as Wagner wrote in a letter to Franz Liszt (11 February 1853), the story of the beginning of the world and its destruction.[19] In making this analogy, however, Borchmeyer overlooks the larger perspective, interpreting the *Ring* with regard to one facet of *Oper und Drama*, and thereby neglecting the various textual levels that the treatise contains.

To draw simple parallels (such as Brünnhilde and Antigone) violates Wagner's intentions. He puts the art-work of the future at an interpretative remove from the myth of Oedipus. Furthermore, the parallels are there, such as the theme of incest, the dichotomy of custom and nature, the ancient dramatic curse, and the element of fate. But one needs, even when working from these abstract principles, to stress the function of these elements in Wagner's drama as embodying a modern interpretation of the Oedipus myth. Wagner's interpretation of the Oedipus myth is a text within a text, that is, Wagner embeds it in a larger aesthetic perspective, and argues for the historical relativism of myth. One encounters a curious reflexive intertextuality between the *Ring* and *Oper und Drama* when one considers that Wotan and Fricka helplessly discourse and debate about custom and free will, key terms in *Oper und Drama*, as though they had read the treatise.

The *Ring* needs to be more consistently interpreted as a reflection of Wagner's conscious and self-conscious interpretation of the Oedipus myth. Franke feels the "state" of Wotan is destroyed when Brünnhilde throws the firebrand into Valhalla.[20] Borchmeyer, however, is correct in using the term "Chiffre" (symbol) to designate the analogous relationship between the finale of *Götterdämmerung* and the end of the tragedy by Sophocles (mediated by Wagner's interpretation).[21] The term implies only a loose connection. The equation must be carefully qualified. The end of the *Ring* as the destruction of the "state" is (at least) twice removed from reality. Neither the *Ring* nor *Oper und Drama*, that is, neither the story of Wotan nor that of Oedipus (as retold and interpreted by Wagner) should be too strictly equated with reality. Both are mythical; because they both stand for things other than themselves, they are both metaphors.

The ultimate goal in reality is, of course, a political one. Wagner wrote the *Ring* with a revolutionary intent, just as *Oper und Drama* shows a subversive purpose. But what does this have to do with the mythological work of art? Wagner did say that the state was always in decline—but so is everything. Erda tells us that. One must take into account, though, the role of the political aspect in the drama theory of the second part of *Oper und Drama*. The *Ring* is not a political pamphlet any more than is *Oper und Drama*. The treatise, as I have shown, is only indirectly political. The analysis of the Oedipus myth that Wagner proposes has different perspectives. He discusses myth and history, the interaction of inner and outer causes. Similarly, I would argue, the *Ring* has different "layers" and more "textuality" than these critics acknowledge.

Furthermore, the essentially metaphorical nature of how Wagner presents his ideas in *Oper und Drama* and the complex interaction that the treatise sketches between the internal and the external, the objective and the subjective, are clues that the destruction of the state need not be necessarily portrayed literally in the art-work of the future. On the contrary, indications are that there is another level, an extended sense of things, at work in Wagner's aesthetics. Moreover, Wagner wrote in *Oper und Drama* that the conflict of the individual with society must be within the hero. In fact, I will even argue that the political interpretation does a grave injustice to the complex dimensions of both *Oper und Drama* and the *Ring*. That the gods (and everything else) must end has clearly been determined before the curtain has risen on *Das Rheingold*. How this end is brought about, just *how* the four dramas show the story progressing to its end, is another matter entirely.

The *Ring* does need to be understood, first of all, in the context in which it was written and with regard to the circumstances under which it arose. Wagner saw the theater as an instrument of political change, and it is common knowledge that he had revolutionary sympathies at the time when he wrote the *Ring*. Furthermore, there is no doubt that Wagner took part in revolutionary activities. When Udo Bermbach, however, recounts Wagner's revolutionary activities to support his political interpretation of the *Ring*, biographical information and a discussion of contemporary currents of political ideas, however informative and interesting they may be, fall short of an interpretation of the *Ring* as a drama. I am not denying that these connections need to be taken into consideration, but it is not a matter of mutually exclusive alternatives for the interpretation. They need to be qualified and put into perspective.

The debate about Wagner's role in the revolution is, though interesting and informative, pointless for any analysis of the *Ring*, for such questions concern history, and not a mythological work of art. Wagner was an artist, and to this end a revolutionary.[22] In his emphasis on the "purely human," that is, the timeless, eternal, and general, Wagner resembles not the political current of "Vormärz" as much as he does the withdrawal from direct political action characteristic of late nineteenth-century Realism, or early nineteenth-century Romanticism. A discussion of the *Ring* must account for its mythological nature. I will therefore apply Wagner's theory of mythological refabrication and reinterpretation to an analysis of the *Ring*.

Neither the purely psychological approach nor the political approach works. I wish to follow Wagner's theory in *Oper und Drama* and propose a compromise approach, one that takes into account both the outer and inner extremes, the psychological and the social-political aspects. Furthermore, this can be seen as in accordance with the theory presented in *Oper und Drama*. The *Ring* is not a political allegory or a political parable. In *Oper und Drama*, Wagner is concerned with the process of becoming conscious. This, he feels, is the decisive factor in the course of the drama, the reception of the drama, and the destruction of the state. The *Ring*, I will argue, exemplifies Wagner's unworking of tragedy in *Oper und Drama*.

The *Ring*, like *Oper und Drama*, is only indirectly political. Commentators have stressed the political aspect to the detriment of the psychological, or what can also be described as the textual, self-referential, or theoretical aspects. The comparison of the *Ring* with Wagner's version of the story of Oedipus and Antigone, which he presents in *Oper und Drama*, should not be taken too literally. The metaphorical structure of *Oper und Drama* seems to forbid this. Neither the *Ring* nor Wagner's retelling of the Oedipus legend is a strictly political story. Wotan demonstrates most of the phenomena of communication disturbance that Rolf Breuer discusses: the "escalation" structure, the "solution as problem" (which includes "self-fulfilling prophecy" and "utopia-syndrome"), "norm conflicts," and "means-end contradiction." These sound astoundingly like a description of Wotan's performance. Wotan writes his own ticket, and makes his own fate.

The crucial processes within the drama are internal ones. In his letter to August Röckel (25/26 January 1854) Wagner explained his nonrevolutionary revision of Erda's warning to his revolutionary friend, telling him that whereas Erda's warning previously stated that the end of the gods would take place unless Wotan returns the ring to the Rhine (implying, I would add, that the end of the gods can be averted), his new version of Erda's proclamation simply states that the gods will end, and that Wotan should give up the ring. Wagner wrote to Röckel, "Wir müssen *sterben* lernen, und zwar *sterben*, im vollständigsten Sinne des Wortes; die Furcht vor dem Ende ist der Quell aller Lieblosigkeit, und sie erzeugt sich nur da, wo selbst bereits die Liebe erbleicht."[23] (We must learn *to die*, and *to die* in the fullest sense of the word; fear of the end is the source of all lovelessness, and it flourishes where love is already lacking). This is the essence of Wotan's tragedy. In the same letter, Wagner also explains,

Wodan schwingt sich bis zu der tragischen Höhe, seinen Untergang—zu *wollen*. Diess ist Alles, was wir aus der Geschichte der Menschheit zu lernen haben: *das Nothwendige zu wollen* und selbst zu vollbringen.[24]

Wotan rises to the tragic dignity of *willing* his own destruction. This is what we have to learn from the history of mankind: *to will what is necessary* and then accomplish it ourselves.

Tragedy consists in a kind of Schillerian, sublime acceptance of destiny. The objective and the subjective must converge in order for a Wagnerian tragedy to take place.

Furthermore, in writing that this is what we need to learn from the history of mankind, Wagner is saying in essence that the world-historical or eschatological dimension of the *Ring* is not really a political one. It is a more "purely human" one. Though the ring of the title is forged from gold, and Wagner was interested in Utopian Socialism at the time he wrote the work, one has to agree that a character's coming to terms with his own mortality has little to do with politics. Wotan self-destructs in a way that matches not Wagner's political views as much as his aesthetic ones. *Oper und Drama* deals with mythological interpretation and shows the interrelationship of myth and history, thus theoretically instigating the revolutionary interaction of aesthetics and politics. The gold ring, which can be considered representative of the evils of capitalism, sets the stage for Wotan's inner drama.

The conflict of the *Ring* is internalized. The two textual layers or interpretative possibilities that I have discerned seem, upon analysis, to work against each other. The internalization of the action and the idea of some kind of political allegory seem contradictory. In *Oper und Drama*, Wagner presents an interpretation of "fate." He writes that for the Greeks the inherited curse was merely an explanation by (a conservative) society to, so to speak, explain away and thus indirectly control what was seen as deviant or nonconformist behavior. The viewpoint of society is then internalized by the victim. For Wagner, then, one incurs the fictional or metaphorical curse oneself, through one's own behavior. Moreover, the accursed one eventually knows he/she has brought the curse on himself/herself. In other words, he or she comes to consciousness of it, as Wagner's interpretation of Greek tragedy would explain. The drama shows the act of becoming conscious of how the curse is acquired.

Interpreting the *Ring* as a political allegory or parable neglects its nature as a work of art, that is, what holds it together as a music-drama, to establish extratextual associations, such as the terms "allegory" or "parable" indicate. I wish to propose an artistic approach, an aesthetic approach to what goes on within the *Ring* as a work of art. The analysis that I will present will explore what Gregor-Dellin describes as the interaction of deterministic and voluntaristic elements in the *Ring*,[25] and I will propose that this phenomenon is similar to how these forces function in the structural model that Wagner outlines in *Oper und Drama*. I will discuss the *Ring* with regard to the interaction of aesthetics and politics, psychological motivations and societal-political concerns, in Wagner's unworking of Greek tragedy in *Oper und Drama*.

୧

In *Oper und Drama*, Wagner discusses the formation of myth as an explanatory system, a way of making sense of the external world. That is, he discusses mythology as a way of interpreting and understanding the world. In doing so, Wagner gives a conscious or even self-conscious *interpretation* of Greek mythology, saying that the mythology underlying Greek tragedy also results from an interpretation. Similarly, the *Ring* deals with interpretation. One could say that it demonstrates the perspectivism of interpretation and thematizes the hermeneutic process. It shows the figures struggling to understand the world in which they find themselves. Beneath or within the mythological material (which I would like to disregard for the moment) one could say that the *Ring* is about mythology as a world-view. In other words, the *Ring* dramatizes and demonstrates the process of mythological fabrication.

Abbate discusses the unreliability of narrative in the *Ring*, and the epistemological dilemmas that thereby arise. I would like to build on this idea and concentrate on the subjective facet of the problem. Within the work, I would suggest, myth is thematized. Wagner wrote about myths as explanatory stories in *Oper und Drama*. The characters in the *Ring* tell stories in trying to understand the world in which they find themselves. Thus the narratives on which the work of Abbate and others has focussed critical attention demonstrate mythological fabrication. Moreover, each narrative in the *Ring* somehow expresses that character's version, that is, his or her interpretation, of an event.

Insofar as the narratives show different versions of events and varying interpretations of the world in which these figures live, the *Ring* demonstrates the shifting perspectives that Wagner outlines in the theory of aesthetic/political mythological self-reflection of *Oper und Drama*. Part of the paradoxical nature of the *Ring* as a mythological work, then, is how it constructs and deconstructs myth at the same time, according to Wagner's model in *Oper und Drama*. Myths are constantly created and then relativized. When one defines "myth" as an explanatory story, one could say that the *Ring* is a synthetic myth about myth.

Whereas the stories that Wotan tells concern the ring (as in his monologue) or other events of *Rheingold* (as in the riddle game in *Siegfried*), Brünnhilde repeatedly tells the story of how she disobeyed Wotan and he punished her. She tells her story, for instance, to Siegfried when he awakens her in the last act of *Siegfried*, and to Waltraute in *Götterdämmerung*. In fact, upon Waltraute's arrival, the first thing that Brünnhilde asks her is whether Wotan has forgiven her. The music expresses the interpretative, hermeneutic aspect of Brünnhilde's textual dilemma. Dahlhaus wrote that the music of this drama embeds the events into the "Göttertragödie."[26] Accordingly, Brünnhilde interprets the events of the present tragedy with reference to Wotan's tragedy, at the same time misinterpreting them.

When about to be abducted, for instance, she screams, "Wotan! Ergrimmter, / grausamer Gott! / Weh! Nun erseh ich! / der Strafe Sinn! / Zu Hohn und Jammer / jagst du mich hin!" (MD 777) (Wotan! Furious, horrible god! Now I see the sense of the punishment! You are condemning me to mockery and misery!) She interprets the abduction as his punishment. In the previous scene she had just told Waltraute the whole story of her betrayal of Wotan and her banishment from Valhalla, thus glorifying it. She declares, "Dass sein Zorn sich verzogen, / weiss ich auch" (MD 771). (I know that his anger subsided.) She eagerly asks if Waltraute's visit means that Wotan has forgiven her, hoping of course that he has, and betraying persistent and deep attachment to him. In the next scene, she changes her mind and her story, for now she feels she fully understands his punishment as including the humiliation of being abducted and belonging to any man who comes along. Brünnhilde now feels Wotan is deliberately making a mockery of her. She puts things together to come to the wrong conclusion.

In the second act, when she ascertains that Siegfried has stolen the ring from her (though this fact is also distorted by false assumptions—she doesn't know about the potion), she interprets this, too, as Wotan's doing. She exclaims, "Heil'ge Götter, / himmlische Lenker! / Rauntet ihr dies / in eurem Rat?" (MD 789) (Holy gods, divine rulers! Is this what you counsel me?) The Valhalla-theme makes the allusion explicit. She misinterprets Siegfried's betrayal of her as Wotan's doing— which it is, of course, but only indirectly. She feels, though, that it was planned by him as part of the punishment he has inflicted upon her. She even calls upon Wotan in the Vengeance Trio. The Immolation Scene in the third act is her reckoning not with Siegfried, but with Wotan.

This thesis that I have advanced, though, is much more complex than it may seem. The idea that the *Ring* thematizes interpretation can be made more specific. For one thing, the *Ring* is really about itself. Insofar as the *Ring* loops back on itself when the figures interpret events that have occurred in this fictional world, the *Ring* thematizes its own interpretation. Insofar as the narratives show different versions of events and varying interpretations of the world in which these characters live, the narratives thus explicate the drama in which these figures exist. Furthermore, because the narrations explicate the drama, they are instances of Romantic irony or innertextual reflection of the text upon itself. Abbate's discussion of narrative as performance points out a "play within a play" structure, which is also the essence of Romantic irony. Thus the duality of enactment and narrative retelling in the *Ring* can be explained as an instance of Romantic irony. Through it, I would propose, the *Ring* thematizes itself and its own interpretation, and in doing so explicates itself.

That the *Ring* is itself an explanatory story, a myth in the extended sense, and that it is, furthermore, composed of recycled pieces of genuine mythology, gives my theory a further complexity. The *Ring*, as I discussed in chapter 1, is mythological in several ways. Insofar as it is an explanatory story (and one that happens to be made up of mythological raw material), the *Ring* thematizes itself in thematizing myth, that is, in showing the characters formulating explanatory stories. Furthermore, insofar as it thematizes myth, it conversely comments upon and thus thematizes itself and its own significance.

However, when one considers that these explanatory stories in the tetralogy are meant to explicate the quasi-mythological world in which these characters find themselves, one may conclude that the *Ring* is a musical-dramatic discourse on mythological hermeneutics. The *Ring* is comprised of scraps of mythical raw material pieced together on the stage of reflection. It is a synthetic myth that is made up of shreds of genuine myth. Thus it has different textual levels, and it generates itself by mythological self-reflection, as I will show. Not only do the narratives of the figures, in explicating the drama, establish the *Ring* as self-referential. By depicting the figures struggling to understand the mythical objects or conventionally mythological trappings of the work, the *Ring* shows specifically mythological interpretation such as Wagner presents in *Oper und Drama*. In other words, the *Ring* thematizes its own fragments of mythological or legendary raw material, and in doing so it demonstrates Wagner's aesthetic program of mythological refabrication and reinterpretation from the second part of *Oper und Drama*.

Schnädelbach notes how the tetralogy thematizes its own raw material and thereby generates itself when he mentions that for Wagner, the drama brings forth myth, not vice versa. This process happens before our eyes and ears. The work demonstrates not only its own musical genesis, the evolution of a cosmology from a single chord, as in the prelude to *Rheingold*. In thematizing the formation of myth, the work also thematizes the production of its own raw material. One could say that it thus dramatizes its own contents. In this way, the drama becomes self-referential and reflective. Therefore, one can conclude that the *Ring* is a Romantic drama. It is, in other words, a self-conscious work—a tragedy on the level of reflection—because it is a myth on the level of reflection. The *Ring* loops in on itself both interpretatively and temporally. Thus it shows its own genesis in mythological interpretation. It also depicts various phases of mythological fabrication. It recapitulates the process of myth production and thus the composition of both itself and of its own raw material also.

I am not the first to assert the self-referentiality of the *Ring*. It is generally acknowledged that the tetralogy thematizes some of Wagner's major philosophies. Stefan Kunze, for instance, writes that Wagner's myth does not mean only itself. It is, according to Kunze, a transparent medium for Wagner's conception of drama.[27] Kunze points out that the dramas proceed circularly, in a spiral motion. Kunze writes that the basic plots and conflicts of Wagnerian dramas consist of individual forces, persons, and actions emerging from a condition that is pre-individual, nameless, and timeless, and which ultimately return to this state. The plot consists of the atonement of guilt and alienation, a restitution of the primal state. When his analysis of Wagner's dramas is understood with reference to the function of myth in nineteenth-century aesthetics (which I outlined in chapter 1), then, I would add, Kunze actually proposes that the dramas thematize not only their aesthetic theory and but also, in particular, their raw material.

In Wagner's dramas, according to Kunze, individualization leads to the destruction of the individual and thus to dissolution in a state that transcends individuation and is therefore represented as redemption. Kunze writes that myth, because it suggests a condition that precedes individuation, is thus the raw material that corresponds to the Idealistic conception of art, for the mythological raw material of Wagner's dramas gives them an atemporal quality and thus situates them in an imaginary realm of the general, absolute, and eternally valid. In thus arguing that individuation is the fault that fatally afflicts Wagner's characters, Kunze draws a parallel between the mythological raw material and the plot of the drama, thus outlining how Wagner's dramas thematize not only Wagner's concept of art, but in particular the mythological nature of their own raw material. In this way Kunze draws a parallel between myth as the raw material and as the implicit theme of the dramas. In other words, the myth that has come to define the form (as tragedy, for Wagner) has a content that can be considered as the drama thematizing myth.

Jean-Jacques Nattiez argues that the *Ring* enacts Wagner's theory of the history of music, and it portrays the unity of the arts, the loss of this unity, and its rediscovery.[28] He theorizes that the *Ring* is the artistic metaphor of a theoretical construct elaborated in tandem with it. Kunze implicitly argues that Wagner's dramas are about myth; Nattiez points out that they are metaphorical. I wish to combine these two approaches and take the metaphoricity of Wagner's works further. Wagner's *Ring*, I would suggest, is about myth as metaphor. It reflects the multilayered and dual nature of Wagner's theory in all its paradoxes.

I would like to combine the ideas that I have generated so far and by doing so propose a new approach to how the *Ring* can be understood in conjunction with the theory presented in *Oper und Drama*. I will argue that the *Ring* is a tragedy on the level of reflection because it is a myth on the level of reflection, that is, a myth about myth. Thus it is a complex, double-layered tragedy. It has a myth (or myths) within myth, a kind of textual or ideological "doubling" similar to that which one finds in novels that thematize language or writing. Abbate has pointed out that there are instances of "layered time" in the music of the *Ring*. Because the *Ring* is a modern myth, its "mythical" nature is not simple. The work, I would suggest, has "layers" of myth. When one considers that the *Ring* is an explanatory story that uses mythical material, and that the characters within the tetralogy show the process of myth formation, it becomes evident that the *Ring* has layers of myth. It is self-referential and doubly "mythical."

I would suggest that Wagner's *Ring* is a "mythical palimpsest" in an abstract rather than a concrete sense. It actually thematizes the notion of myth as metaphor. I will explain how the *Ring* is not so much a transparent medium for specific mythical stories presented in Greek works that can be considered analogues of the *Ring*, but instead uses myth in a general and self-referential or reflective way. It thematizes its own raw material, mythology, at the level that I will call "myth as form." Furthermore, as the ideal can only be portrayed indirectly in the sensual world, so can myth only refer indirectly to political reality. Myth can be political only by referring to itself.

In the *Ring*, mythology is a dual phenomenon. Wagner, one must recall, regards form (tragedy) with regard to content (myth). Form is content, and vice versa. In the *Ring*, I would suggest, myth—the content or raw material that has come to define the form (tragedy)—has also become the content of this content (or form), for the work thematizes myth. In other words, form and content mirror each other, and under this first content (which has come to define form) there is yet another layer of content. This, I would empha-size, is appropriate for a synthetic and modern myth, a myth on the level of reflection. Bernhard Heimrich, as I discussed in chapter 1, argues that in the case of Romantic irony, form has become the content of a form. Some-thing similar happens in the *Ring*.

In *Oper und Drama*, Wagner distinguishes a kind of natural art (percep-tion) and "artistic" art (myth, the communication of the perceived image), with Greek tragedy as the artistic realization of Greek myth thus raising this whole process to a higher level. Similarly, the *Ring* has real mythological objects and explanatory stories in a second-hand myth based on conventional myth. This duality of myth creates a tension within the work of art similar to the ancient/modern dichotomy of fate that I pointed out earlier in discussing *Oper und Drama*. The *Ring* is full of doublings. Things exist on two levels, events are overdetermined (externally and internally), the real is mirrored in the ideal, myth has a metaphorical significance, and the work as a whole is mirrored in various miniature ways within the work itself.

The *Ring*, I would argue, enacts the complexity of Wagner's theory of myth from *Oper und Drama*. Furthermore, because the work as a whole, this entire synthetic myth, is a metaphor for history, telling as it does of the beginning and destruction of the world, it also has within itself not only a self-referentiality as regards myth, but it contains within itself an interrelation of history and myth. It has mythological objects within a quasi-mythical myth, stories within stories, and perspectival fictions within a larger fiction. That myth is, to Wagner, metaphorical, and the *Ring* is mythical in several senses, creates metaphors upon metaphors, and myths about myth.

Furthermore, mythical objects in the tetralogy have metaphorical significance, and I will subsequently demonstrate the problems that this state of affairs causes for the critic trying, like the characters, to interpret this strange kind of quasi-mythical world. In this manner, the *Ring* thematizes itself in a seemingly endless hall of mirrors. It contains metaphorical myth and historical reflections of the figures upon myth that explicate the mythical raw material, just as *Oper und Drama* does. I would suggest that the *Ring* thematizes its own metaphoricity as a modern myth that explains and is supposed to change history. Similarly, the *Ring* portrays the beginning and end of history as well as portraying its own creation and reception.

A discussion of the central symbol of the work, the ring named in the title, reveals these various facets of the work and shows how form has somehow become content. The ring is both objective and subjective. Dahlhaus notes how, in the absence of unity of action in the *Ring*, the plot that revolves around this ring unifies the tetralogy and thus holds this huge work together.[29] The *Ring* tetralogy is a curious mixture of the literal and the figurative or symbolic, the magic and the metaphorical, the real and the ideal, if you will, the concrete and the psychological. It has a "dual" structure, like a tale by E.T.A. Hoffmann. The ring and its curses, I will suggest, form the rip in the textual fabric of the *Ring* tetralogy.

It is generally recognized that the gold and the ring forged from it stand for the evil of capitalism, the greed for wealth, the desire to amass material possessions. The ring, though, works on two levels, the material and the symbolic. The stipulation that one must renounce love to gain power over all the world by means of the ring establishes the central duality of the cycle,

the dichotomy of love versus power. The ring, then, has a symbolic significance. This may seem like a trite assertion, but it is important for my
discussion to remember that the ring stands for something on the level of
ideas, on what I will therefore call the "ideal" level. The "ideal" level thus
explicates the "real" level. The work interprets itself, as is appropriate for
a self-conscious, modern myth. The ring stands for the abstract notion of
the renunciation of love for power. It has abstract significance. The metaphorical level allows one to establish the link to world-history. Wagner's
Ring can be understood as a metaphor for world-history only when this
equation is mediated by ideal, abstract concepts.

The scene between the Rhinemaidens and Alberich is, in fact, full of irony.
The Rhinemaidens' flattery of Alberich can only be described as ironic.
Furthermore, it seems odd that they even tell him about the significance of
the gold.[30] This is, of course, necessary for the textual structure of the work
of art, and it does get the plot moving. After Woglinde sings the exposition
of the renunciation-motive, telling Alberich about the special properties of
the gold, Wellgunde takes her turn, boasting, "Wohl sicher sind wir / und
sorgenfrei, / denn was nur lebt will lieben, / meiden will keiner die
Minne." (We are certainly safe and free from care, for whatever lives wants
to love, nobody wants to shun love.) Woglinde then chimes in, singing, "Am
wenigsten er, / der lüsterne Alp; / vor Liebesgier / möcht er vergehn"
(MD 533). (Least of all this lustful dwarf; he is perishing of love.) Saying or
singing something can have profound consequences. Articulation can be
deadly.

With reference to this scene, one can even say that enunciation leads to
renunciation. In telling Alberich about the special properties of the gold,
they prompt his fulfillment of these conditions that they feel are impossible.
It is, of course, ironic that the Rhinemaidens think there is so little danger,
especially from Alberich, that they can blab all about the power of the gold.
The scene seems oddly contrived or "staged." Harry Kupfer's Brechtian
staging of *Rheingold* with the gods demythologized—in which instead of
the traditional eye patch Wotan sports a pair of sunglasses—seems appropriate to the work, for the world of the drama does not seem properly
mythological.

Deryck Cooke points out that, though Alberich is obviously drawn from
the Andvari of the Scandinavian sources, nowhere in any of the sources
does a creature go to a river and meet three water-nixies, try to woo them,
discover gold that can be stolen and made into a ring conferring absolute
world-dominion by renouncing love or by any other means, and then
perform that feat. In fact, Cooke discusses the various elements of this scene
and in doing so shows how it is Wagner's own invention, despite its
profoundly mythical character. The ring itself, then, the object upon which
I am centering my analysis, has no actual prototype in the sources. The ring
may seem mythological, but upon close analysis, it is really not. In that

respect, it is a microcosm of the work as a whole. It represents the tetralogy in a very real way. It is, paradoxically enough, both mythical and modern.[31]

What functions beautifully on the "ideal" level does not, however, work quite consistently on the mythological or fairy-tale, or at any rate *fictional*, level. This is the plane of the simple story-line, the one on which magic is allowed. By definition, the magic of the ring is only useful to Alberich, who cursed love when he stole the gold. And with the ring he does, of course, enslave the Nibelungs, as shown in the third scene of *Rheingold*. But this is the extent of the magical powers of the ring. Alberich evidently cannot use it against Wotan and Mime when they confront and capture him in Nibelheim. In this way problems arise when one tries to analyze the *Ring* as some kind of mythological world in the traditional sense. The *Ring* echoes, rather, Wagner's schema of shifting mythological interpretation and perspectival redefinition from *Oper und Drama*.

The ring, though, serves to instigate a power struggle. The ring is a symbol of power or wealth not only to the spectator or listener, but to Wotan and the other characters, this is how it functions. The fact that Wotan is forced to either temporarily ransom or permanently surrender Freia to the giants in payment for his fortress further reinforces the power versus love symbolism. Alberich's power is (or would be) a threat to Wotan's. The rest of the tetralogy is linked to the building of Valhalla and the story of the ring by the notion of the "free hero" (presumably Siegmund, but the idea catapults into Siegfried as well) whom Wotan begets to do what he cannot. The importance of the ring is primarily in the eye of the beholder. Wagner comments, in his letter to Röckel from which I cited earlier, on how Brünnhilde sees the cursed ring as a token of Siegfried's love. Dagmar Ingenschay-Goch notes how the ring means something different to Waltraute than to Brünnhilde.[32]

The ring is a strange mixture of the subjective and the objective, the metaphorical and the literal. It is not even consistently a power symbol, for different characters see it differently. It also works inconsistently. Its significance and power seem to be perspectival. It works according to how one interprets it. The magic of the ring is curious indeed. The ring apparently depends on its wearer for its function. Wagner explains, in the letter to Röckel of 25/26 January 1854 from which I cited earlier, that Brünnhilde follows Siegfried/Gunther so readily in the first act of *Götterdämmerung* "eben weil dieser ihr den *Ring* entrissen, in welchem sie einzig auch noch ihre Kraft bewahrte"[33] (because he snatched the ring away from her, and it alone preserved her power). In writing this, Wagner makes the perspectival, subjective, psychological nature of the ring as a power symbol especially evident. The ring is a symbol of love, not power, to Brünnhilde. Furthermore, it gives her strength by being such a symbol. Is this because she thinks it will? The ring paradoxically collapses the love/power dichotomy in this way, just as it brings the whole world of the *Ring* to ruin. It should, by definition, properly be an instrument of power only to Alberich, who cursed love. By being a symbol of love to Brünnhilde, it also seems a symbol (subjectively, of course) of power. Ironically, the ring does not establish dichotomies as much as it undermines them. It is a paradoxical thing indeed. It defies those dichotomies that define it. It evades any strict determination of what it signifies.

Similarly, the scene in which Alberich curses the ring accentuates the parallel between Alberich and Wotan. The transfer of the ring from the former to the latter seals the fatality of the *Ring* cosmos in an interesting way. In the confrontation between Wotan and Alberich, the two are mirror-images of each other, as Cooke points out in his analysis of the scene.[34] The scene is for this reason a particularly powerful one. Wotan denies that the ring rightfully belongs to Alberich, thus showing his own blindness, as it belongs to him perhaps even less. Wotan accuses Alberich of stealing the ring, but he is, moreover, about to steal it from Alberich. That Loge watches and listens in triumph and amusement further complicates the textual structure of the *Ring*.

Alberich, who ironically seems to have more insight than Wotan does, makes the parallel between him and Wotan explicit. He asks, "Wirfst du Schächer / die Schuld mir vor, / die du so wonnig erwünscht? / Wie gern raubtest / du selbst dem Rheine das Gold, / war nur so leicht / die Kunst, es zu schmieden, erlangt?" (MD 565). (Do you reproach me with having done the deed you wish you had done yourself? How gladly you would have stolen the gold from the Rhine for yourself, if you had known how to forge a ring from it.) After being robbed, Alberich feels he is "der Traurigen traurigster Knecht" (the saddest of all sad slaves). Wotan mutters, "Nun halt ich, was mich erhebt, / Der Mächtigen mächtigsten Herrn" (MD 566). (Now I hold what makes me the most powerful of the powerful lords.) The parallel is obvious. The relationship will, though, via the curse, be ironically reversed.

Alberich warns Wotan not to steal the ring from him, with the words,

Hüte dich, / herrischer Gott!—/ Frevelte ich, / so frevelt ich frei an mir:—/ doch an Allem, was war, / ist und wird, / frevelst, Ewiger du, / entreissest du frech mir den Ring! (MD 565–66)

Watch out, you dictatorial god! The only one I harmed was myself, but you will commit a crime against all that was, is, and will be, if you shamelessly steal the ring from me!

Alberich knows, as he warns Wotan right before being robbed of his treasure, that if Wotan stole the ring from him, Wotan would bring the whole universe to ruin with his own moral demise. The prediction comes true in an unexpected way. Alberich passively makes it come true. He works on Wotan's mind and thus, via the redundant curse which is not really magical, indirectly causes him to fulfill it. The prophecy comes true in a literary-critical way, as I will show in the next chapter.

The curse that Alberich places upon the ring is even more interesting than the curse through which it belongs to him. This simple gold ring works in an exceedingly complex and nonmythological way. One traditionally thinks of a curse as something metaphysical, especially in a mythological work that also features a Tarnhelm, a dragon, giants, potions and the like, but upon closer inspection, this curse seems to lack any kind of (conventionally) magical properties. Alberich, with his curse, condemns the owner of the ring to care ("Sorge") and fear ("Furcht"), and any who do not own it shall, Alberich pronounces, be eaten away by envy ("Neid"). All will desire it, Alberich states, but nobody will enjoy it. The lord of the ring shall, Alberich predicts, be the slave of the ring. But this is nothing supernatural. Rather, it is merely a commentary on the symbolic significance and the function of the ring within the tetralogy.

The curse is not really a magical requisite, nor is it the raving of a maligned subhuman creature worthy of neither attention nor close analysis. It is rather a very intricate structure of Romantic irony. When he pronounces the curse in *Rheingold*, Alberich does say that the ring will bring misfortune and death to all who wear or possess it. But this, too, can be explained simply, on the symbolic level, that is, to mean that the characters will destroy each other because of their avarice. As Deryck Cooke writes, "Alberich does not really need to put the curse on the ring, we might say, since it is already there in the nature of things."[35] Alberich's curse seems merely rhetorical, a verbal (and musical) gesture.

The curse can be interpreted, like the power/love significance of the ring itself, as real or ideal, literal or figural. One can expect the work to function the way a traditional myth does, or one can know that these objects often have only metaphorical significance and thus an almost allegorical function. One could say the ring was cursed from the beginning. Furthermore, Erda tells Wotan to flee the curse. Wotan gives the ring to the giants, but he does not flee the curse, thus indicating that this curse works in an odd way. The curse, in fact, states that all who wear the ring shall die, but Wotan was told by Erda that he would die anyway, and so would everything else. It thus seems pointless for Wotan to be overly concerned about the power of the ring (which, unlike the Tarnhelm, Alberich could not demonstrate for him in Nibelheim) or its curse. If he had been another type, he might have forgotten all about it, but he lets it get to him.

Alberich even notes how his second curse somehow mirrors or "potentiates" his first. The curses seem to form mirrors in mirrors, a kind of telescopic structure, as the text progressively unfolds itself. Despite his wrath, Alberich eloquently comments on the correspondence, and with regard to the textual structure of the *Ring*. The redundancy of this curse is not meaningless, but very significant. "Wie durch Fluch er mir geriet, /

verflucht sei dieser Ring!" (MD 566). (As it came to me through a curse, may this ring be accursed!) The second curse actually forms a commentary on the symbolic significance of the ring. Thus the text further explicates itself in layers. It progressively folds and unfolds, getting (as does Wotan) worn and torn as it goes along. It seems to have boxes in boxes, or mirrors in mirrors.

Alberich comments upon and summarizes his curse, ironically calling it a "blessing," and pronounces, concluding his solo, "So segnet / in höchster Not / der Nibelung seinen Ring:— / behalt ihn nun, / hüte ihn wohl! / Meinem Fluch fliehest du nicht!" (MD 567). (Thus the Nibelung blesses his ring, keep it, guard it well! You will not flee my curse!) Then he scurries away to watch the performance. Alberich is clever in his own powerlessness. He turns the tables on Wotan and runs the show himself. It takes only a few choice words. Wotan is nominal head of the gods, but Alberich, ironically enough, has psychological counter-control. He knows how to get to Wotan and thus passively influence the course of the drama.

The curse of the ring is actually, it seems, a kind of psychological dependence. The words of the characters make this obvious. Alberich says to Hagen in *Götterdämmerung* that the curse is useless against Siegfried, for besides being fearless, he does not understand what the ring stands for. Wotan also mentions to Erda in the third act of *Siegfried* that Siegfried is immune to Alberich's curse. The ring, with its curses, works on a conceptual level, that is, an internal and psychological level, but not, it seems, on the story level. It stands for something (in somebody's perception), such as power or love, but is not magical in a literal, objective, and conventional way. The redundancy of the curse is, however, anything but useless. Words can sometimes kill more effectively than magic. Alberich's verbalization of the curse is, rather, vital to the progress of the drama, as I will show. The ring, one could say, is (figuratively) cursed for anyone who knows of its symbolic significance.

Knowing that the ring is cursed, however, creates special problems for Wotan. In a modern myth, this is catastrophic. It entails reflection, self-consciousness, and eating from the Tree of Knowledge a second time. Furthermore, to Wotan the curse that Alberich pronounces has special nonmagical properties that make it doubly deadly and thus bring the whole fictional world to ruin. Critics have noted that in the legends on which the *Ring* is based, the curse of the dwarf does not bring the gods to ruin.[36] This happens, I will show, in a specifically modern way. Because Alberich has made the curse explicit to Wotan, who believes in it, the curse works beautifully. If one thinks the ring is cursed, one makes it an object of the most lethal sort. The curse works best and most tragically when one is aware of it. The curse needs to be internalized in order to be fully effective. Paradoxically, only then can it be conquered. Self-consciousness can, after all, be redemptive.

Loge clearly establishes the parallel between the *Ring* and *Oper und Drama*, showing the similarity of Alberich's curse with the "love-curse" of Antigone when he asks Wotan, "Lauschtest du / seinem Liebesgruss?" (MD 567). (Did you hear his love-greeting?) The term "love-greeting" is, of course, meant ironically. Alberich's "love-greeting" is a sinister one indeed, and Wotan, though he heard it, attached no importance to it, because he was too preoccupied with admiring the ring. The crucial thing is not what one has (objectively) done or will do, but rather whether one wants to (subjectively) listen to others. Listening is not always a simple matter. Then, one must interpret what one hears. Really, anybody can say what he or she wants to, without it necessarily proving true. Alberich has no special talents or supernatural powers.[37] He is, after all, only an ugly dwarf.

Erda, in contrast, deserves more credibility than Alberich. However, she speaks truisms, things Wotan ought to know already. Nobody can deny that Erda appears when she does because she is needed at this point in the drama. Wotan's predicament, both the outer one and the inner one, demand it. She even admits it, thus aiding the critic who is interpreting the drama: "Doch höchste Gefahr / führt mich heut / selbst zu dir her" (MD 572). (The most dire danger leads me to you now.) Her words, though, are strangely uninformative. Just as the Greek oracles spoke truths in very cryptic ways, Erda's pronouncements are dependent on interpretation, and when one considers how carefully Wagner thought about this warning, one must conclude that he meant it that way.

She reinforces what Alberich says about the ring, that it will bring ruin to whoever possesses it. She also pronounces the truism that everything will one day end (that is, regardless of what happens to the ring). Erda is much less subtle than Alberich was with his moralistic character parallels. She is stern where Alberich was eloquent. They both know something, though, that Wotan, head of the gods, strangely enough does not know. The critic could derive various interpretations for Erda's lines. Does Erda's warning mean that Wotan is mortal, or does she just foretell the end of the work of art via Wotan's self-destruction and Brünnhilde's redemptive act?

Erda blatantly tells Wotan to give up the ring. She states, succinctly enough, "Ein düst'rer Tag / dämmert den Göttern:— / dir rat ich, meide den Ring!" (MD 572). (A dark day will dawn for the gods. I advise you to shun the ring!) Erda tells Wotan, almost tauntingly, to ponder her words in care and fear, which are, Cooke notes, the same mental and emotional states to which Alberich's curse condemned him. It seems as though she, too, knows they are in a contrived, symbolic work of art, and her dramatic function is to foreshadow the future not to the audience so much as to Wotan.

Erda has actually foretold the end of the tetralogy, and now Wotan listens. Erda seems to have mythological authority, and Wotan obviously believes in myth. Erda's prophecy disturbs him; he begs her to stay, going into a panic as she starts to vanish. The words echo in Wotan's mind. He replies, "Geheimnis-hehr / hallt mir dein Wort" (MD 572). (Your words echo mysteriously in my mind.) The echoing of these words can be an aural or a musical-dramatic form of the mirrorings of Romantic irony. Through it, the *Ring* will, via Wotan, interpret itself. Erda's disappearance is just as necessary for Wotan's mental state as was her appearance. She explicates her warning, as does Alberich his curse. "Ich warnte dich; / du weisst genug: / sinn in Sorg und Furcht!" (MD 572). (I have warned you; you know enough: think about it in care and fear!) Wotan's reflection is the crucial element of the drama. He follows her advice and shuns the ring, but to no avail. He must learn to die.

Erda has a profound effect on Wotan, who was previously oblivious to Alberich's ravings. He now begins to think there may be something to this curse. The world was, of course, inevitably going to end, as Erda states. But in a very real way, Wotan also *makes* the prophecies come true. Wotan eventually wills the end, as Waltraute reports in the *Götterdämmerung*, and he refuses to eat Freia's apples any more. The two senses of the ring exist primarily in Wotan's consciousness, and also in the audience interpretation of the drama. This is how they motivate the plot. If the *Ring* is an "analytic drama," it is Wotan who does the innertextual analysis.

Wagner, in the letter to Röckel of 25/26 January 1854, wrote that Alberich and his ring could not harm the gods if the latter were not ready for it, and in saying this, Wagner indicates that the curse is not a strictly and traditionally magical one. Rather, the ring interacts with the individual involved, and Wotan, I will show in chapter 4, is impressionable in a very complex way. Deryck Cooke interprets Erda as embodying a sense of destiny, which reveals itself to certain people at moments of crisis, and thus Cooke argues for an internalization of the dramatic conflict.[38] The other characters seem important only as they relate to Wotan.

Erda's prophecy and Alberich's curse are, it seems, merely props, talismans that work only because Wotan believes they will. That Wotan, as Alberich predicted, cannot flee the curse has more to do with the modern character weakness of this recycled Germanic god than any supernatural properties inherent in this allegedly magical ring. The real progress is an inner one, added to a textual one. Just as in *Oper und Drama* Wagner unworks and interprets traditional notions of tragedy, so, accordingly, does the *Ring*, and in agreement with the treatise. The curse is relative and psychologized. The concept of fate, in the *Ring*, resembles the curse on the ring in being ambiguous and double-layered. "Fate" in the *Ring* is, as in *Oper und Drama*, not magical or metaphysical. Its redundancy indicates the structure of Romantic irony in the *Ring*.

At the end of *Rheingold*, Wotan is beginning to change. Deryck Cooke notes how Wotan's unreflecting optimism and lordly arrogance give way to a sense of guilt.[39] He is unnerved when Fafner clobbers Fasolt to death, an event that Loge ironically congratulates Wotan upon, as it shows the good fortune of one whose enemies are killing each other off. He comments on his misdeeds, "Mit bösem Zoll / zahlt ich den Bau!" (MD 574). (I have paid for this building with an evil deed!) He now starts turning inward. Wotan interprets Fafner's murder of Fasolt as an effect of the curse. He comments, "Furchtbar nun / erfind ich des Fluches Kraft!" (MD 574). (Now I see the terrible power of the curse!) The drama progresses and thus rushes to its end, as I will show in chapter 4, through Wotan's innertextual interpretation of it.

When Fafner kills Fasolt, Wotan echoes the formula taught to him by Erda, thus internalizing the prophecy. "Sorg und Furcht / fesseln den Sinn— / wie sie zu enden, / lehre mich Erda:— / zu ihr muss ich hinab!" (MD 574). (Care and fear possess me, may Erda teach me to end them, I must descend to her!) Donner cannot possibly clear the air effectively. The actual tragedy, the inner drama, the exercise in mythological-tragic hermeneutics, has begun. Everything centers on Wotan's perception of events and his growing inwardness. He is to attain a suicidal kind of self-consciousness. The end cannot be averted, and Wotan begins to reflect upon this, for the future as well as the past, as Erda has taught him. The gods perish, even though they have regained Freia. The cure, it seems, was merely cosmetic.

When Fricka asks Wotan what the name "Valhalla" signifies, he tells her that the ensuing drama will explicate this for her, thereby giving a prospective textual interpretation of the drama to come. In doing so, he designates the castle as an ironic structure, for it is built on a contradiction.

Fricka: Was deutet der Name? / Nie, dünkt mich, hört ich ihn nennen.

Wotan: Was mächtig der Furcht / mein Mut mir erfand, / wenn siegend es lebt, / leg es den Sinn dir dar. (MD 576)

Fricka: What does the name mean? I never recall having heard it before.

Wotan: What my courage devised to combat fear will live triumphantly and show you its meaning.

The fortress is no longer even a godly castle that has been paid for with stolen gold. Rather, it has become a monument to Wotan's fear of the end. His attempts to avert the end backfire miserably. The rest of the tetralogy retroactively demonstrates his ironic reflections on and reactions to the events of *Rheingold*. And when Wotan watches his own drama from the outside, the world it depicts, as I will explain in chapter 4, must end.

❧

The ring, I would suggest, is the epitome of metaphor. This, one could say, is its curse. The metaphoricity of Wagner's myth, which derives from its modernity, brings the world of the *Ring* to ruin, and in that sense it actually constitutes the curse on the ring. Accordingly, the ring pulls all who come in contact with it into its syntactical web of mythological metaphoricity. The work explicates itself with reference to the ring. The statement of Woglinde concerning the potential symbolic significance of the gold, and the curse that Alberich places on the ring, explain the function of the ring within the work of art.

The ring is explicitly metaphorical, and the world of the *Ring* is not consistently and conventionally mythical. The ring establishes what I will call a metaphorical structure of signification. It is metaphorically cursed. One could say that the curse that somehow works the doom of the gods establishes a dual or an ironic structure. The ring hovers between the real and the ideal levels. The curse refers to the objective reality, the reality of the work of art as a work of art, as a modern quasi-mythological music-drama. The *Ring* progressively unfolds as the abstract, metaphorical significance of traditionally mythological elements is presented.

In this way the *Ring* progresses on its own momentum. It enacts its own production and by extension that of its raw material. Thus I would argue that the *Ring* stages its aesthetic presuppositions. The action of the *Ring* is inherent in its aesthetic program of mythological refabrication, and also somehow latent in its raw material. The dramatic conflict unfolds naturally and consistently from its very nature. One could say that the plot of the *Ring* is determined by the self-consciousness of a modern mythical world. Furthermore, because the *Ring* progressively unfolds, it is a supreme example of what Friedrich Schlegel termed "progressive Universalpoesie."

Insofar as the *Ring* shows the vacillation between the real and ideal levels of understanding that Kunze has discussed and that I have pointed out, I would suggest that the tetralogy dramatizes Romantic aesthetics. It shows the process of making things that are real and material, such as the ring, into things that are symbolic. It depicts an interrelationship of history and myth, objective and subjective. The narratives constitute internal self-reflection of the work, and thus the work contains a dialectic of consciousness and self-consciousness that would also qualify it as an example of Schlegel's "progressive Universalpoesie." Thus the *Ring* is no doubt a transcendental drama.

As a modern myth made of mythical raw material, the *Ring* creates, however, a hermeneutic dilemma. The ring, and the drama(s) by that name, exist(s) on two levels, the real and the symbolic, the literal and the metaphorical. Furthermore, these levels sometimes diverge in a disorderly way. At times, one level will be at work, and then another. This destroys the work of art. The structure of signification gets messy as the work nears its conclusion and the fictional cosmos rushes to its inevitable end. The ring—the title object and the prime impetus of the action—by having both a traditionally mythological and a metaphorical significance, mirrors (as a microcosm) the work as a whole as a modern reworking of mythology, an interpretation of mythology (the Oedipus myth in particular, as theoretically dictated and outlined in *Oper und Drama*), as a metaphor for history.

The metaphysical trappings (such as fate and the ring) are unworked and demythologized. These mythological requisites have only metaphorical significance at times. Thus Wagner's *Ring* has what I consider a double vision. Myths are usually not abstract and explicitly allegorical, curses are traditionally metaphysical and magical, and fate is normally considered insurmountable, objective, and numinous. The work simply does not function like a traditional, conventional myth. The figures do not act in a way that fulfills their mythological functions. The supposedly magical objects are dematerialized and given symbolic significance in a modern way. The gods, moreover, have modern psychological depth. The work has a Romantic irony that appropriately enough brings the disjointed world it portrays to ruin. In this way, Wagner's historical consciousness is evident in the *Ring*, and it causes the modernity and self-consciousness of this myth.

The Rhinemaidens, for instance, can make prophecies, and they see through the falsity of the gods' grandeur, for instance, as they comment accordingly upon the Entrance of the Gods into Valhalla at the end of *Rheingold*. They are, however, anything but numinous and mythical. In fact, they are silly little creatures who do not know, and ironically perhaps know all too well, not to keep quiet about the magical (but not too magical) properties of the Rhinegold. Ironically, these earth- or water-spirits such as Erda and the Rhinemaidens, and even Loge, the fire-god, while blatantly mythological in appearance or costume, name, and heritage, seem to exist more for foreshadowing, as some kind of modern omniscient narrator in a work with Romantic irony, or a Brechtian "epic theater" device. They are apparently mythological, but they fulfill a definitely nonmythological, modern function in the work of art as a whole.

Similarly, the gods that Wagner puts onstage are not divine. Dahlhaus points out that mythical figures are one-sided, whereas Wagner's are split, contradictory, and differentiated. He cites Wotan as an example.[40] Dahlhaus also notes that in myth there is no place for reflection such as can be expressed by dialogue and rhetoric.[41] Thus the *Ring*, I would argue, is not properly mythical. It has reflection, in fact self-reflection, and this is appropriate to its very nature, for it is a myth on the level of reflection. In the *Ring*, I will demonstrate, reflection and self-reflection actually work against mythology or the properly mythological quality of the raw material to revolutionary purposes and thus aim to influence history. Wagner's characters are known for their wordiness, and their long (unmythological) narratives in which they reflect on their dramatic situations. Wotan's monologue, which I analyze in chapter 4, exemplifies this trait to the utmost. The mythological nature of the raw material, I propose, decisively influences the course of the drama. The weakness of the gods is due to their existence in a modern mythology. The inconsistencies of the *Ring* demonstrate the basic paradox of the *Ring* as a nineteenth-century mythological work of art.

The *Ring* has a forced unity of history and myth, a phenomenon that stems from its being a modern myth to explain a historical progression and a cycle of music-dramas based on mythological raw material but assembled on a modern stage of consciousness. The gods have, within outwardly mythical raw material, a historical existence. Erda makes it clear that they are temporal, that is, historical. Stefan Kunze writes that one tends to overlook the discrepancy between the world of Germanic gods and heroes, on the one hand, and the modern industrial society that is mirrored therein. Furthermore, Wagner's gods and heroes are broken just because of the rift between art and life, which is only exaggerated by the desire to bridge this gap.[42] In this manner, I would suggest, the *Ring* mirrors the theory presented in *Oper und Drama*. Creating a modern myth that is a metaphor about history produces not a strictly mythical work, but a conglomeration of myth and history, modern self-reflective gods, and textual chaos.

Furthermore, the characters in the dramas, in telling stories to try to understand and explain the world in which they find themselves, are making a strange nonmythological, interpretive or critical commentary on a drama cycle that gives a modern synthetic refabrication of mythology. They struggle to come to grips in their modern minds with the mythological requisites that they find around them and thus to reconcile themselves with the world in which they live. The work has different levels of meaning. Objects such as the ring are at times only psychologically important. Their significance is perspectival. This confuses the characters and causes the discord of the world depicted in the tetralogy. The figures onstage apparently do not know where they are or what roles they should be singing. They often seem confused, or as though they had forgotten their lines. By using myth as metaphor, Wagner places his characters into considerable textual confusion and hermeneutic indecision, and primarily Wotan, though in the guise of a Germanic god, must come to terms with his own mortality.

The internalization of the dramatic action (which is thus paradoxically not dramatic in the usual sense) shows myth to be, under the surface, really a mode of being or a state of mind. In *Oper und Drama*, Wagner reduced it to as much. Thus, within the *Ring* as an entire text, there is an interplay between history and myth comparable to that which Wagner theoretically outlines in *Oper und Drama*. Myth has a subjective aspect. The mythical raw material has an additional, extended layer of myth. It contains a subtle interplay of history and myth within mythical material and under the outwardly and apparently mythical surface. Reflection of a historical psyche on a mythological object can, oddly enough, demythologize it, as Wagner does with the traditional tragic curse and the concept of "fate" in his exegesis of Greek mythology in *Oper und Drama*. The *Ring* itself is a mythical work that is a metaphor both for history and also for Wagner's theory of art.

Within the drama, for instance, the ring is a mythological object that is supposedly magical, but it apparently has merely metaphorical significance. Mythical objects in the tetralogy that have metaphorical significance are in this way demythologized, dematerialized, and thus the *Ring* is a strangely paradoxical work. They don't work as real objects, but only as metaphors. Thus the *Ring*, at times, dematerializes its own mythological content. The tetralogy contains a tension between the literal and the figural, the magical and the metaphorical, the concrete and the abstract, and the real and the ideal. Furthermore, when myth is reduced to a state of mind within an apparently mythological drama, the work of art falls apart and is destroyed from the inside. As the mythical objects are strangely dematerialized, ultimately myth has a dangerous psychological relativism. In Wotan's mind, myth is eventually reduced to metaphor. This causes a catastrophe for the world of the *Ring*. The modernity of the work unmasks its metaphoricity. Within the story, the mythological objects are in the last resort reduced to mere metaphor.

Udo Bermbach comments that not only the ring, but all the symbols in the *Ring* are ambivalent and dysfunctional. The ring makes no character ruler of the world. The spear does not guarantee law and order; in fact, Hagen's spear is a murder weapon. Nothung the sword is shattered and reforged, and thus alienated from its original function. It is used as highly controversial evidence against Siegfried in *Götterdämmerung*. Furthermore, the Tarnhelm neither protects Alberich from being captured, nor does it veil Siegfried effectively when he appears as Gunther to abduct Brünnhilde. The dysfunctionality of the symbols, rather than showing, as Bermbach argues, the self-destruction of bourgeois society and its institutions,[43] stems, I would say, from the basic contradiction of a modern myth, the paradox of using traditionally mythological objects on a level of self-consciousness and reflection. The psychological, subjective significance overshadows the objective, material function of these objects.

In this way, the *Ring* shows that it is a modern rebirth of tragedy, and not the genuine article. The mythological nature of the *Ring* is second-hand, recycled. It is reused, unclean, and ungenuine. The beginning of *Rheingold* may seem to represent a state of nature, a condition of mythical timelessness, but (as directors such as Patrice Chéreau, who portray the Rhinemaidens as prostitutes, point out) the state of nature was already defiled before the prelude because (as the Norns later narrate) Wotan has already broken a branch from the World Ash Tree. Nature and culture, one could say myth and history are, in the *Ring*, strangely simultaneous. The metaphoricity of the work, the modernity of Wagner's myth, the ambiguity of its mythological nature, is what has polluted the Rhine.

It is as though Wagner had pasted mythological elements together within his "Kunstmythos," as in a collage, that is, he uses them to form a new myth. Figures with modern psyches or a modern consciousness seem to be running around a mythical landscape, basically unsure of where they are, and they run into mythical beings and props or plot-elements. When Erda appears at the end of *Rheingold*, Wotan doesn't even know who she is. He asks, "Wer bist du, mahnendes Weib?" (MD 571). (Who are you, woman who warns me?) Ironically, Wotan, who is ostensibly the ruler of the world, seems to be the newcomer into his own world. It is as though he had been cast into a role that he did not really know. Erda, the primeval goddess, just happens to appear at the right time at the end of *Rheingold*, when the situation, Wotan's predicament, demands it (on cue, so it seems). She is, however, strangely uninformative. Later she even withholds information, as though angry at Wotan for waking her up and having banished their daughter Brünnhilde.

Wagner's historical consciousness is mirrored by the fictional self-consciousness of some of his figures. Not only do they speak eloquently where genuinely mythical figures are less wordy, and reflect where their prototypes would simply do deeds. At times they seem keenly aware that they are onstage in costume and participating in a performance. Erda introduces herself to Wotan and explains her own mythological function, with what seems Romantic irony because it is a self-consciousness of her own textuality similar to that of the characters in Friedrich Huch's *Holländer* parody, or the title character of Heinrich Heine's Tannhäuser poem. Furthermore, it is highly debatable whether or not she really fulfills her mythological function. In *Rheingold* she speaks trite assertions, and later she is very uninformative, almost as though she had forgotten her lines.

At times, the *Ring* even seems almost comical in the unexpected turns that the action takes, the uncertainty of the figures, and their reflection upon their strangely unserviceable mythological surroundings. *Rheingold*, for instance, though a totally serious drama, has the quality of a modern mythological farce or a parody. The music to which Froh gallantly rushes in to rescue Freia in the second scene definitely has an ironic or even a comical effect. Wotan, whom one usually considers most powerful of the gods, engages in ungodly machinations to placate his wife. He is unsure of his own authority, and he shows a nonmythological and very human insecurity, as he desperately tries to get out of the quandary he is in.

The first evening of the tetralogy basically shows the problems of a dysfunctional family. These are definitely not typically mythical figures. The audience of *Rheingold* witnesses the domestic plight of Wotan and Fricka, and hears the marital discord of the gods.[44] This is punctuated by Freia's melodramatic cries to her brothers for help, and her teary laments that Wotan is abandoning her. Comedy arises from the incongruity between the mythical raw material or subject matter and the plot that is happening onstage. Fricka's despair at the promiscuity of the Rhinemaidens, for in-stance, has an almost comical effect. In the last evening of the cycle, watching Siegfried, the traditional Germanic hero, getting teased by the Rhinemaidens provides comic relief in what is usually considered an unmitigated tragedy and a totally serious drama.

Thomas Koebner points out that whenever myth dictates that a figure in the *Ring* do something, the character does the opposite of what the tradition would have him or her do.[45] If in mythical narrations a schema is visible to which the figures conform, Koebner explains, that is, if their actions repeat a model or a subtext, then the *Ring* seems to break these traditions and contradict any kind of ritual repetition or adaptation. In other words, it is mythical in isolated elements, but not in overall quality. For example, Alberich steals the Rhinegold, an event that was unexpected and unheard of. The Rhinemaidens certainly didn't expect it. In doing so, he revolts against the rule. Wotan builds Valhalla out of anxiety about the end, a deed unworthy of a genuinely mythological god. Siegmund unexpectedly and rebelliously refuses to go to Valhalla. In the third act of *Siegfried*, Wotan goes to Erda at the quintessential mythical location, the center of the world, but she can't answer his questions. Ironically, in this scene Wotan tells Erda more than she tells him. He informs her about Brünnhilde's past and future, which Erda, strangely enough, seems not to know. In this scene, Erda even admits that she is confused by the turn of events that has taken place since she was last awakened, that is, she does not even understand what is going on any more.

Wagner's myth, when compared with its subtexts, is thus out of joint. The characters make decisions that seem to contradict their mythical nature. They do not do what they as mythical figures are supposed to do. I would add that perhaps this is because they are modern mythical figures, and the world of the *Ring* is thus not really mythical. It is as if the Nibelung legend (or a conglomerate of Nordic legends) inevitably got distorted, bent out of shape or knocked out of whack, by being transported into the nineteenth century, and it just didn't work right any more. The *Ring* is full of ironic reversals, such as Brünnhilde's disobedience of Wotan.

The places where the *Ring* unfolds itself by explicating the ideal or metaphorical significance of its real or mythological pieces of raw material can be considered Wagnerian or mythological-hermeneutical variations on what Bernhard Heimrich calls "reductions." These are instances where the characters seem to comment upon and interpret the quasi-mythological modern music-dramas in which they find themselves, that is, their stage surroundings, and try to figure out just what this all may mean. It is almost as though some of them know they are onstage, but others do not. The curse that Alberich places on the ring, which I discussed earlier, is an example of this. The title object is not necessarily cursed at all in the sense of it being really a magical item, such as would be the case in a traditional, genuine myth. The *Ring* is made up of outwardly mythological pieces of raw material and contrived, phony scenes.

The plot of the *Ring* consists not only of reductions, but also of what seem to be a number of improvisations. With reference to the theory of Bernhard Heimrich, these reductions and improvisations establish the Romantic irony of the *Ring*. In addition, the improvisations also place the *Ring* and in turn the aesthetic theory represented by tetralogy into the context of the Romantic notion of art as improvisation. Thus the tetralogy thematizes itself and its own implicit aesthetic theory. The characters seem to be making up the story as they go along, as nobody seems to know what is going on or what will happen. It is as though the characters were playing the children's game of telephone with the ring of the title, just as the Norns take turns telling (or retelling) the story in succession, throwing the thread of destiny from one to the other. The dialogue of Fricka and Wotan in the second act of *Walküre* decides not only Siegmund's fate but the course of the drama as well.

Eckart Kröplin places Wagner within the context of his "theatrical" century. Wagner, he explains, was a performer; he had a histrionic personality. Kröplin discusses how he "staged" the revolution and "directed" in Haus Wahnfried.[46] Abbate's work also suggests the "theatricality" of the *Ring*. Abbate suggests that the transcendent narrative of the Rhinemaidens can only occur offstage. With this distinction between onstage and offstage, she proposes the notion of the *Ring* as somehow portraying a musical-dramatic "stage-world."[47] I feel that these ideas can be extended to the mythological nature of the work. I would suggest that the various levels on which things work, and the inconsistencies, ironic reversals, and self-consciousness of the characters create an atmosphere of the "stage-world" type.

In this manner the *Ring* actually stages its own performance. Insofar as the *Ring* depicts the characters reflecting on the course of the previous dramatic action (in its quasi-mythological nature) it loops back onto itself and then schemes in a foresightful effort to determine the future course of the action, and look forward to what will come, with the answer to the Norns' question significantly vague. That even Erda and the Norns do not know what will happen next is due to the improvisational nature of the work. It therefore thematizes its own performance and demonstrates a specifically Wagnerian kind of Romantic irony. The *Ring* depicts a "stage-world." It is a nineteenth-century, phony, synthetic, stagey, and "staged" myth. I would suggest that the *Ring* depicts its own performance. Like a comedy by Ludwig Tieck, the *Ring* is a staging of a staging. It actually seems to rehearse its own staging.

The *Ring* seems theatrical because the mythological nature of the world depicted is obviously not genuine. The work unmasks itself as a modern music-drama that has been pieced together out of elements of traditional myth, which are then used in a modern way. For instance, Alberich and Erda both seem strangely to know more about the course of the drama than Wotan does, as though only they had read the score before the performance. Everybody except Wotan seems "in on" the story or the ploy, and they have apparently conspired against him backstage. Wotan, however, thinks the drama is real-life. He later learns of his own fictionality. It is amazing how fast news travels in the world of the *Ring*. Certain characters seem automatically to know of past events without even having heard the lengthy narratives of other characters. Loge and Hagen, for instance, know of previous dramatic events. Given the insufficiency of Eternal Wisdom in the guise of Erda and the Norns, this is curious indeed. In *Götterdämmerung*, Hagen seems to know everything that has happened beforehand. He even informs Siegfried about what the Tarnhelm is.

It is as though Alberich were a producer, saying backstage, "Let's pretend this ring is cursed," or, "Let's act as though the ring were cursed." Accordingly, Loge seems to be the stage director, at least in *Rheingold*, executing the concept of the production on the stage by manipulating and directing the action. Alberich's exhortation to the sleeping Hagen in the second act of *Götterdämmerung* would be, according to this interpretation, not so much to regain the ring as to keep playing the game, stage more pranks, continue the deception, and thus keep the show on the road. The ironic reversals show the characters unsure of what to do. They seem to be making the script up as they go along and as the performance progresses. In this way, too, the work recounts or recapitulates its own genesis, not just musically in the evolution of the cosmology from a single chord. This thematization of its own conditionality and formal performance, like its historical consciousness, stems from its modernity and clearly establishes the Romantic irony of the work.

Furthermore, this stage-world has an implicit "play within a play" structure. This exists beyond the consideration of narrative as performance. The *Ring* contains various instances of this. That modern directors are fond of having figures onstage at times when the work does not actually demand their presence, shows that they have noted that the *Ring* often uses an implicit "play within a play" device. The *Ring* has "repeated mirrorings" of a stage-world, levels of play-acting, within it just as it has levels of music. Drawing a parallel with Tieck's *Der gestiefelte Kater* might seem to some to be totally out of place. However, when one considers that both are modern-day resuscitations of folk-literature that have various textual levels and that the *Ring* has Romantic irony, the comparison is suddenly and unexpectedly justified. The ironic reversals of the action of the *Ring* make the characters seem as though they are in costume and unsure of their lines, uncertain of what to do next.

The tetralogy, in fact, is full of characters that are "staging" things, that is, manipulating others. In *Rheingold*, Loge mentions "with warmth" ("mit Wärme") (MD 546) that Wotan might steal the ring from Alberich in order to restore the gold to the Rhinemaidens, seeming to delight in his fore-knowledge that Wotan wants nothing less than to give up the ring. At the crucial moment in the last scene, when the giants demand the ring, Loge says ironically that Wotan is going to give it back to the Rhinemaidens. Loge manipulates Wotan and Alberich, tricking the latter into transforming himself via the Tarnhelm. Wotan manipulates the Volsungs, in raising Siegmund and hardening him to misfortune so as to better equip him to return the Rhinegold, and Hagen "stages" the whole mess that culminates and explodes in the second act of *Götterdämmerung*. Before he kills Siegfried, Hagen "stages" a case of perjury as an alleged justification of the murder, inducing it chemically (and involving two different substances, in the first and third acts). This implicit "play within a play" structure participates in the essential irony that I have discussed. Eventually it encompasses the whole drama and in the final cataclysm wrecks the sets, props, and costumes.

ᡖᴥ

I do not intend any close or extended musical analysis of the *Ring*. However, no discussion of the *Ring* would be complete without some treatment of the music, and thus I do wish to present some general ways in which the music can be considered suitable to the dramatic theory I have previously summarized and the interpretation of the dramas that I have outlined. In various ways which I will briefly sketch, the music is appropriate to the derivative mythological nature of the *Ring*. I will leave it to musicologists to expand upon these notions for further research and analysis.

Music is the only adequate expression of, or medium for, myth because both appeal to feeling and pre- or nonrational faculties. Lévi-Strauss likens music, that is, a score, to myth in that both have a synchronic as well as a diachronic aspect. The issue, though, is much more complex, as the mythological nature of the *Ring* is synthetic, modern, and second-hand. The reflexivity or self-referentiality of the work as regards myth is reflected in, or echoed by, the music. The music is, in various combinations of these terms, mythical, metaphorical, and interpretatively relative. Ultimately, it echoes the subjectivity of the characters in this self-reflective myth.

Not only can one draw an analogy between myth and music, as Lévi-Strauss does. The fact that the drama is doubly mythical and that the music can be considered in some ways mythical creates a multilayered structure. The various levels interact, comment upon each other, and feed into each other. Not only does the musical texture, as Abbate has shown, have several layers, participating in the Romantic irony of the work and creating extra layers of significance. The myth of the *Ring*, as with those myths retold in *Oper und Drama*, is metaphor, and thus the music reveals the metaphoricity of myth and also shows a subtle interplay between history and myth. In this way, the music is suitable to the dramatic and ambiguously historical-mythological content of the work.

The musical structure mirrors or echoes the basic metaphoricity of the work as a whole, adding to the multileveled textual structure of myths and metaphors that forms the essence of Romantic irony. The work is in various ways a mass of mirrorings and/or echoings. These Romantically ironic structures both create and undermine meaning. Just as the *Ring* is a metaphor for history, with the ring of the title acquiring metaphorical significance, so does the *Ring* have, through its "Leitmotiv" system, what one could call "metaphorical" music. Insofar as the motives "stand for" things—by "things" meaning not only objects, but also characters, or even intangible states of mind—they are metaphors. Dahlhaus refers to the music as "tönenden Metaphern"[48] (resounding metaphors) and calls it "musikalische Metaphorik"[49] (metaphorical music). In this way, the music is mythical, as myth is a metaphor that explains something and thus gives it meaning. The music echoes the internal hermeneutical process of the drama.

Furthermore, music, as Carl Dahlhaus points out, has in itself no object; it is not conceptual.[50] This is the state of the Rhinegold, I would add, before it is stolen and cursed. Similarly, Hans Mayer writes about Wotan's spear, "Er *ist* vor allem, dann erst *bedeutet* er."[51] (First it *is*, then it *signifies*.) Mayer then continues to parallel Wotan's acquisition of his spear with Alberich's theft of the Rhinegold.[52] The *Ring* is about giving meaning, interpreting, and insofar as this is the origin of myth, the tetralogy is about itself as myth. Just as the *Ring* is, on the story level, about metaphor, interpretation, and giving meaning, and the ring is redefined by the characters, the "Leitmotive" acquire meaning, though often only approximate and tentative, through association with the drama. The ambiguity of Wagner's music consists of the shifting meanings that the musical phrases, key relationships, or other devices acquire through the course of the drama.

Thus, bringing the music into an ideological analysis of Wagner's *Ring* does not necessarily yield the meaning of the work that is absolutely true. Using the music to interpret the drama also creates an interpretative dilemma. The music itself is still a matter of interpretation. One must interpret what a musical repetition may mean. Even the meaning of a "Leitmotiv" itself can be a matter of interpretation. As music is semantically unspecific, the meaning of the "Leitmotive" is established by association. Their repetition can sometimes only add to the interpretative dilemmas. Assigning a label to a "Leitmotiv" and then arguing from this specification of its meaning to interpret a repetition of this motive seems somehow unsatisfying, circular, based on a fallacy. In this manner Wagner's motives seem to defy semantic specification, their systematic labelling being associated more with Hans von Wolzogen than with Wagner himself.

Furthermore, the significance of the motives or their repetition is not always self-evident. Deryck Cooke, for instance, has discussed how the meaning of motives can be debated.[53] Critics acknowledge that in the musical-dramatic world of the *Ring*, meaning can be problematic. One could, for instance, extend Abbate's ideas about the perspectival nature of epistemology in the *Ring* and argue, with a hermeneutic twist on the "voices" in the score, that when Siegfried hears Mime's offer of refreshment as an attempt to murder him, perhaps Wagner is letting the audience hear Siegfried's interpretation of Mime's seemingly kind offer of refreshment. Similarly, at the end of *Rheingold*, when the same motive to which Alberich placed the curse on the ring sounds right after Fafner kills Fasolt, perhaps the music is giving the audience Wotan's interpretation of the murder as an effect of Alberich's curse.

Perhaps the distrust of narrative to which Abbate points reflects Wagner's theory of language and his language skepticism from the second part of *Oper und Drama*, and his view that verbal communication, and in the *Ring* thus music too, has "fallen" and is somehow, in the modern world, impure, decadent, and thus unreliable. Abbate has demonstrated this, and it is also intrinsic to the "Leitmotiv." The entire text that constitutes the *Ring* is out of joint and remarkably modern. Its implicit Romantic irony lends itself very well to a post-structuralist analysis. The work repeatedly loops in upon itself, and in interpreting itself shows the relativity of meaning and subjectivity of myth. The fact that it is a modern work seemingly masquerading as a traditional myth makes it a strange drama indeed. Not only does the music interpret the drama. The musical phrases themselves are open to interpretation. Often the significance of a musical phrase is not definite at all.

Thus the music participates in this process of making myth, that is, interpretation. In this way, the musical form is appropriate to the drama. The music also sends out an invitation to the viewer or listener to interpret the drama. Furthermore, by not only interpreting the drama but by also being itself open to interpretation and thus inviting the viewer or listener to actively participate in the hermeneutic process, the music creates one more layer of meaning. It helps express that the story itself is about interpretation and understanding, and thus about the process of creating myth, and therefore about itself and its own artistic program. Analyzing the music of the *Ring* involves interpretation. For instance, a motive can sound ironically, linking several contrasting scenes, as I pointed out in my first chapter. Thus the music, by means of the system of motives, participates in this process of progressively creating meaning, of the "repeated reflections" of which Schlegel (if I may be allowed to mix visual and auditory imagery) writes. The music participates in the process of interpretation and "potentiation."

Furthermore, these musical metaphors can themselves work on several levels, and thus they raise things from the individual to the symbolic level in their process of interpreting the drama, and in this way show the mythicization of history. In raising the individual to the general, one is, temporally speaking, raising history to the level of myth. In this way even the music of Wagner's *Ring* strides the dual levels of the real and the ideal. In this way, too, the musical form is tantamount and appropriate to the mythological form (and content). Giving definite names to the motives seems to violate the work of art by doing an injustice to the complexity of the work of art, which resides in the shifting meanings and usages of these musical phrases. The *Ring* is a structure of shifting significance with regard to the music as well as the dramatic action. As the music comments upon and interprets the drama, therefore the critic is called upon to interpret an interpretation, as I have analyzed Wagner's interpretation of the Oedipus myth, or the drama itself is to embody an interpretation of the Oedipus myth. The drama is thus mythical at one remove.

Werner Breig discusses the complex way in which Wagner uses his system of motives in the *Ring*.[54] Breig points out that even when it is possible to label a motive verbally, the motive often functions less to simply characterize something specific than to associate different things and differentiate a specific thing. Persons, objects, and abstractions merge together. Some motives designate objects and abstractions; for example, the same music is used for the spear and for treaties. Some music characterizes persons and objects (Loge is seen in his sapient form and as fire) or persons and abstractions (the same music is used for Freia and for youth). Similarly, I would add, the ring can be considered a literal object or a symbolic entity, as the real thing that it is or the ideal, metaphorical significance it acquires in the drama.

Secondary figures such as Erda and Gutrune have only one motive. Main figures, however, are seen under several aspects, and therefore they have various motives. Wotan has the music of Valhalla or of the spear. Brünnhilde is seen as a Valkyrie or a loving woman. Siegfried is heralded by his horn call, but he is also designated by his heroic Siegfried-theme. In the case of motives that do not designate characters, but rather objects, abstract concepts (which these objects may be interpreted as representing), or even states of mind, the issue is much more complex. Music, via the motives, can be varied and thus it can show complex, fluid interrelationships within myth.[55] Breig points out that the music must be grasped as process, rather than as stasis. Similarly, there is a historical relativity in the mythological interpretation that Wagner presents in *Oper und Drama*. He is, it seems, implicitly aware of this. The meaning of the music shifts. Meaning is relative; interpretation is both textimmanent and somehow unreliable.

Dahlhaus, too, points out that the motives of the spear and the sword designate the objects themselves, even resembling the object in their notation (the spear-motive resembling someone striding with a spear pointing downward, and the sword-motive resembling someone brandishing a raised sword), but they are also symbolic for the realm of contracts and the realm of freedom.[56] Thus it is difficult to give precise meaning to the motives. Their meaning changes, like the significance of the ring. Furthermore, it vacillates between the real and the ideal, the concrete and the symbolic, the literal and the figural, the mythological and the metaphorical. This is the problem with any interpretation of the music of the *Ring*. The music is appropriate to the mythological form, for it lets things merge into one another, raising the individual to the level of the general when it links things via symbolism. The music, one could say, creates myth. History is the individual and specific; myth is the general and timeless, the basic abstract schema to which all existence conforms.

Furthermore, the music both establishes and undermines meaning, just as Romantic irony both builds and destroys a fictional world, and mythology is a hermeneutical schema the historical relativity of which Wagner was conscious. Dahlhaus comments upon how, when the motive of the ring is transformed into the Valhalla-motive in the scenic transformation between the first two scenes of *Rheingold*, Wagner is showing that Wotan is possessed with the same greed for power as Alberich.[57] The "Light-Elves" and the "Dark-Elves" reflect each other, like a positive and a negative. Moreover, when set against the chromaticism and dissonance of the ring-motive, which in reality speaks the truth about the Valhalla-motive which is derived from it, the solidity that the diatonicism and consonance of the Valhalla-motive seems to express is somehow undermined and shown to be deceptive. The Valhalla-motive is thus as innerly broken as the triumphal music of the Entrance of the Gods into Valhalla at the conclusion of *Rheingold*, which Loge comments upon with the pronouncement that the gods are rushing to their end. In thus interpreting the drama, the music, which itself shifts in significance, echoes the schema of mythological interpretation and hermeneutic relativity that Wagner presents in *Oper und Drama*.

Not only is music appropriate to myth in that it lets things merge fluidly into each other and raises the individual to the level of the general, symbolic, and thus mythicizes history, thereby formally reflecting the nature of the *Ring* as an artistic explanation of history. Motivic recurrence in itself designates the music as somehow mythical. Basic to the idea of myth is the notion of repetition. Kurt Hübner draws an analogy between the "Leitmotive" and the "Archái" of mythology.[58] "Leitmotive," according to Hübner, are the means with which to clearly express the "Archái" of myth. Just as the "Archái," as elements of myth, stand in complex relationships, so do the motives. Motivic recurrence, according to Hübner, expresses the mythical world-view of the *Ring*.

Hübner explains that the drama contains or is based on primal events— for example, Alberich cursed love, or Wotan carved a spear from the World Ash Tree. These are mythical events, Hübner explains, in the sense that they cannot be temporally dated. They are numinous primal events, that is, "Archái." They are also mythical insofar as they are mirrored in temporal happenings, and they recur there when similar things happen. Wotan's crime continues to have an effect when society is founded and myth, because of greed for power, is misused. Alberich's curse is working wherever nature is destroyed. Thus a correspondence can be established between the musical form and the dramatic content. Both are not only retrospective, referring all earthly reality to primal events; they also raise history to the level of myth.

Furthermore, the music can even raise something to mythical stature by associating it with a more numinous reality, a basic pattern or, in this case, the plot of divine entities who are somehow "running the show" and determining the course of the dramatic action. Dahlhaus points out that the tragedy of Wotan, the outwardly more mythical action, the tragedy of the gods, gives higher significance to the drama of the Volsungs, the (half-) mortal progeny of Wotan.[59] The metaphorical structure of the music communicates this additional level, this mythical significance. Within outwardly mythical raw material, the music raises history to the level of myth.

But this has an important subjective aspect. The retrospective orientation of the music expresses the reflection of the dramatic characters. Being an explanatory system imposed by mankind onto objective reality, myth is actually a state of mind, a psychological reflection of or upon external reality. As an interpretative schema that enables one to make sense of reality, it exists in one's perception and subjectivity. Thus problems arise when it has become, in the case of Wotan, corporeal reality in a fictional universe. The ambiguity of the music derives from the subjectivity and solipsism of myth in the *Ring*.

Wagner explained the two functions of "Leitmotive" as anticipation ("Ahnung") and remembrance ("Erinnerung"), but Carl Dahlhaus notes that the "Leitmotive" almost always express a remembrance, and seldom an anticipation. The motives, "tönende Erinnerung" (resounding memory), connect the present with the past. He explains that the weight of the past entails reflection, the medium of which the "Leitmotiv" is.[60] Thus retrospection entails subjectivity. The "Leitmotive" form a network of musical reflections, creating what Dahlhaus calls "ein musikalisches Reflexionsdrama."[61] They reflect each other, thus reinforcing the mythical nature of the drama, the sense of repetition and timelessness that the work creates. The music expresses that the drama is somehow generated through the reflection and interpretation of the characters.

Furthermore, the music shows an interplay between history and myth that is going on within the characters, as is appropriate for a drama in which the most important "action" is an internal kind of process. The motives are the adequate means of musical expression for a drama that is constituted to a large extent by the reflection and interpretation of the characters onstage. The psyches of the characters are primarily what are reflecting. Myth is a reflection of the individual psyche upon the outside world, a metaphor, an explanatory system. Dahlhaus points out that the retrospective orientation of the music, the fact that the majority of the motives are those of remembrance, is appropriate for a drama in which the events of the past cast a huge shadow over the present action of the drama.[62] The motives express the eternal psychological recurrence of what is past. Dahlhaus notes that the "Leitmotiv" technique expresses the continual presence of what is past.[63] Thus, the mythical and the metaphorical music expresses or echoes the self-reflection of the characters within this doubly mythical music-drama.

Others, too, have noted the mythological-psychological significance of Wagner's system of "Leitmotive." Nattiez quotes Lévi-Strauss as saying that myth is timeless; it explains the past, present, and future. In likening this to the Norns' Scene that opens *Götterdämmerung*, Nattiez shows that the *Ring* thematizes myth. Freud's rejection of historical contingencies also proclaimed the death of the subject; it is the unconscious that is speaking.[64] Catherine Clément draws an analogy between music and the unconscious.[65] Both express, or raise events to, a mythical timelessness. They defy temporality. The music reflects or echoes the timeless nature of myth.

Therefore, the music echoes the mythical nature of the drama and the relative, subjective nature of myth. The analogy between myth and psychology that these critics have drawn is no coincidence. The music of the *Ring*, I propose, represents the remembrance of a past that has become regulatory for one's present situation and thus mythical. When the subjectivity of myth and of the significance of musical phrases is coupled with the relativity of interpretation and the instability of meaning, one sets the mythical-historical musical-dramatic stage for the solipsism into which Wotan lapses.

The essential irony as regards myth, I would argue, comes from supposedly representing a *second* state of naiveté or unconsciousness. The gods must end because the work is a synthetic, modern myth that uses mythological raw material, and the basic paradox of a modern, self-conscious restitution of myth is what brings the fictional world of the *Ring* to an end. Roland Barthes calls mythology a "second order system of signification." That which is a sign, that is, the concept and the image, the signified and the signifier, in the first semiological system, becomes a mere signifier in the second. What is in the first system "meaning," that is, the final term, is in the second system "form."[66]

This semiological distinction is applicable to the multilayered textual structure that forms the *Ring*. Mythology, which for Wagner defines the form, has been doubled in a similar way in this work. Because of the indeterminacy and overdetermination of meaning in Wagner's tetralogy, the *Ring* is what I would call, building on the definition of mythology by Roland Barthes, a "second order mythology." The mythological objects that

I consider signs in this system of signification have extended, abstract significance as well as their original meaning. Romantic irony can be very dangerous. The modernity of the work is what destroys the fictional world portrayed therein. Furthermore, the "Götterdämmerung," the end of the gods, happens because the work has, via Wotan, unravelled or "deconstructed" its own metaphorical structure of signification.

NOTES

1. George Bernard Shaw, *The Perfect Wagnerite: A Commentary on the Niblung's Ring*, 4th ed. (New York: Dover Publications, Inc., 1967). The work was originally published 1898; the 4th ed., 1923.

2. For his critique of Shaw's interpretation, see Deryck Cooke, *I Saw the World End: A Study of Wagner's "Ring"* (London: Oxford University Press, 1979), pp. 15–25.

3. Hans Mayer, "Wagners 'Ring' als bürgerliches Parabelspiel," in *Anmerkungen zu Richard Wagner* (Frankfurt am Main: Suhrkamp, 1966; 2d ed., 1977), pp. 100–111; Udo Bermbach, "Die Destruktion der Institutionen. Zum politischen Gehalt des 'Ring'," in *In den Trümmern der eignen Welt: Richard Wagners "Der Ring des Nibelungen"*, ed. Udo Bermbach, Hamburger Beiträge zur öffentlichen Wissenschaft, vol. 7 (Berlin: Dietrich Reimer, 1989), pp. 111–44.

4. Robert Donington, *Wagner's "Ring" and its Symbols. The Music and the Myth* (London and Boston: Faber and Faber, 1963). For his critique, see Cooke, pp. 25–36.

5. See Jean-Jacques Nattiez, *Wagner Androgyne*, trans. Stewart Spencer (Princeton, NJ: Princeton University Press, 1993), pp. 226–33.

6. Richard Wagner, *Sämtliche Briefe*, vol. 4, *Briefe der Jahre 1851–1852*, ed. Gertrud Strobel and Werner Wolf (Leipzig: VEB Deutscher Verlag für Musik, 1979), pp. 173–76 (here cited from p. 175, capitalization added).

7. Cosima Wagner, *Die Tagebücher*, 4 vols., 2d ed., ed. Martin Gregor-Dellin and Dietrich Mack (Munich: Piper, 1976, 1982), vol. 3, p. 223 (entry of 10 November 1878). I have used the translation by Geoffrey Skelton, *Diaries*, 2 vols. (New York: Harcourt Brace Jovanovich, 1978/80), vol. 2, pp. 194–95. Citations will hereafter be given in my text by volume and page numbers, with the German reference preceded by the abbreviation "CT," and that of the translation by the abbreviation "D."

8. Wolfgang Schadewaldt, "Richard Wagner und die Griechen," in *Richard Wagner und das neue Bayreuth*, ed. Wieland Wagner (Munich: Paul List, 1962), pp. 149–74 (here I am citing especially pp. 166–74).

9. Michael Ewans, *Wagner and Aeschylus: The "Ring" and the "Oresteia"* (New York: Cambridge University Press, 1982).

10. See: Ulrich Müller, "Richard Wagner und die Antike," in *Richard-Wagner-Handbuch*, ed. Ulrich Müller and Peter Wapnewski (Stuttgart: Alfred Kröner, 1986), pp. 7–18 (here cited from pp. 14–15); Dieter Bremer, "Vom Mythos zum Musikdrama. Wagner, Nietzsche und die griechische Tragödie," in *Wege des Mythos in der Moderne. Richard Wagner, "Der Ring des Nibelungen"*, ed. Dieter Borchmeyer (Munich: Deutscher Taschenbuch Verlag, 1987), pp. 41–63 (here cited from pp. 55–58).

11. See: Werner Breig, "Das Schicksalskunde-Motiv im *Ring des Nibelungen*. Versuch einer harmonischen Analyse," in *Das Drama Richard Wagners als musikali-*

sches Kunstwerk, Studien zur Musikgeschichte des 19. Jahrhunderts, vol. 23 (Regensburg: Gustav Bosse, 1970), pp. 223–34.

12. Hans Mayer, "Der 'Ring' und die Zweideutigkeit des Wissens," in *Richard Wagner: Mitwelt und Nachwelt* (Stuttgart: Belser, 1978), pp. 230–35.

13. See the chapter, "Ödipus und 'Der Ring des Nibelungen'," in Dieter Borchmeyer, *Das Theater Richard Wagners: Idee, Dichtung, Wirkung* (Stuttgart: Reclam, 1982), pp. 230–53 (here cited from p. 238).

14. Rainer Franke, *Richard Wagners Zürcher Kunstschriften: Politische und ästhetische Entwürfe auf seinem Weg zum "Ring des Nibelungen"*, Hamburger Beiträge zur Musikwissenschaft, vol. 26 (Hamburg: Verlag der Musikalienhandlung Karl Dieter Wagner, 1983). Some of the terms and phrases he uses are: "Wotans Staat" (p. 281), "Wotans Gesetzesstaat" (p. 295), "die Staatsweisheit Wotans" (p. 277).

15. Franke writes, "Wotan ist also personifizierter Staatspolitiker und Träger der Idee von der Notwendigkeit eines Staates" (p. 284).

16. Peter Wapnewski, *Der traurige Gott. Richard Wagner in seinen Helden* (Munich: C.H. Beck, 1978; Deutscher Taschenbuch Verlag, 1982), pp. 26–27.

17. See note 3 above.

18. Herbert Schnädelbach, " 'Ring' und Mythos," in *In den Trümmern der eignen Welt: Richard Wagners "Der Ring des Nibelungen"*, ed. Udo Bermbach, Hamburger Beiträge zur öffentlichen Wissenschaft, vol. 7 (Berlin: Dietrich Reimer, 1989), pp. 145–61 (here I am referring to pp. 154–58).

19. Richard Wagner, *Sämtliche Briefe*, vol. 5, *September 1852–Januar 1854*, ed. Gertrud Strobel and Werner Wolf (Leipzig: Deutscher Verlag für Musik, 1993), pp. 185–90.

20. Franke, p. 310.

21. Borchmeyer, *Das Theater Richard Wagners*, pp. 237–38.

22. On Wagner's revolutionary activities, see: Rüdiger Krohn, "Richard Wagner und die Revolution von 1848/49," in *Richard-Wagner-Handbuch*, ed. Ulrich Müller and Peter Wapnewski (Stuttgart: Alfred Kröner, 1986), pp. 86–100; Gregor-Dellin, "Beziehungen zum Sozialismus," in *Richard Wagner—die Revolution als Oper*, Reihe Hanser, 129 (Munich: Carl Hanser, 1973), pp. 20–41; Gregor-Dellin, *Richard Wagner: Sein Leben, Sein Werk, Sein Jahrhundert* (Munich: Piper, 1980), pp. 242–76.

23. Richard Wagner, letter to August Röckel of 25/26 January 1854. Richard Wagner, *Sämtliche Briefe*, vol. 6, *Januar 1854–Februar 1855*, ed. Hans-Joachim Bauer and Johannes Forner (Leipzig: VEB Deutscher Verlag für Musik, 1986), pp. 59–76 (here cited from p. 67).

24. *Sämtliche Briefe*, vol. 6, p. 68.

25. Gregor-Dellin, *Richard Wagner: Sein Leben, Sein Werk, Sein Jahrhundert*, p. 288; "Beziehungen zum Sozialismus," in *Richard Wagner—die Revolution als Oper*, p. 34.

26. Carl Dahlhaus, *Richard Wagners Musikdramen* (Velber: Friedrich, 1971), pp. 133–34.

27. The following is summarized from: Stefan Kunze, *Der Kunstbegriff Richard Wagners: Voraussetzungen und Folgerungen* (Regensburg: Gustav Bosse, 1983), pp. 182–85.

28. Nattiez, pp. 53–90.

29. Carl Dahlhaus, *Wagners Konzeption des musikalischen Dramas* (Regensburg: Gustav Bosse, 1971), p. 31.

30. Donington (pp. 55–59) discusses this "slip."

31. Cooke, pp. 134–42.

32. Dagmar Ingenschay-Goch, *Richard Wagners neu erfundener Mythos: Zur Rezeption und Reproduktion des germanischen Mythos in seinen Operntexten*, Abhandlungen zur Kunst-, Musik- und Literaturwissenschaft, vol. 311 (Bonn: Bouvier Verlag Herbert Grundmann, 1982), p. 53. See also Peter Wapnewski, "Der Ring und sein Kreislauf. Überlegungen zum Textverständnis der 'Götterdämmerung'," "*Götterdämmerung*": *Programmhefte der Bayreuther Festspiele* (1984), pp. 25–50.

33. *Sämtliche Briefe*, vol. 6, p. 71.

34. See: Cooke, pp. 148–49, 158–60, 268–73, et passim.

35. Cooke, p. 224.

36. Gregor-Dellin, *Richard Wagner: Sein Leben, Sein Werk, Sein Jahrhundert*, p. 364.

37. Donington (p. 107) asks where Alberich gets the power to curse the ring after all.

38. Subsequent mentions of Cooke, which cite specifically his discussion of Erda, will be, unless otherwise noted, to *I Saw the World End*, pp. 226–33.

39. Cooke, p. 232.

40. Dahlhaus, *Wagners Konzeption des musikalischen Dramas*, p. 31.

41. Dahlhaus, *Wagners Konzeption des musikalischen Dramas*, p. 37.

42. Kunze, p. 187.

43. Bermbach, p. 134.

44. Cooke points out that Wotan has "in-law trouble." P. 153, n. 5.

45. Thomas Koebner, "Minne Macht. Zu Richard Wagners Bühnenwerk *Der Ring des Nibelungen*," in *Die Nibelungen. Ein deutscher Wahn, ein deutscher Alptraum*, ed. Joachim Heinzle and Anneliese Waldschmidt, Suhrkamp Taschenbuch 2110 (Frankfurt am Main: Suhrkamp, 1991), pp. 309–32 (here cited from pp. 324–25).

46. Eckart Kröplin, *Richard Wagner: Theatralisches Leben und lebendiges Theater* (Leipzig: VEB Deutscher Verlag für Musik, 1989).

47. Carolyn Abbate, *Unsung Voices: Opera and Musical Narrative in the Nineteenth Century* (Princeton, NJ: Princeton University Press, 1991), pp. 203, 238–40.

48. Dahlhaus, *Wagners Konzeption des musikalischen Dramas*, p. 105.

49. Dahlhaus, *Wagners Konzeption des musikalischen Dramas*, p. 22.

50. Dahlhaus, *Richard Wagners Musikdramen*, p. 88.

51. Mayer, "Wagners 'Ring' als bürgerliches Parabelspiel," p. 101.

52. Mayer, "Wagners 'Ring' als bürgerliches Parabelspiel," p. 102.

53. Cooke, pp. 37–73.

54. Werner Breig, "Wagners kompositorisches Werk," in *Richard-Wagner-Handbuch*, ed. Ulrich Müller and Peter Wapnewski (Stuttgart: Alfred Kröner, 1986), pp. 353–470 (on the "Leitmotiv" in the *Ring*, see pp. 421–26).

55. See also Borchmeyer, *Das Theater Richard Wagners*, p. 135.

56. Dahlhaus, *Richard Wagners Musikdramen*, p. 113; *Wagners Konzeption des musikalischen Dramas*, p. 42.

57. Dahlhaus, "Die Musik," in *Richard-Wagner-Handbuch*, ed. Ulrich Müller and Peter Wapnewski (Stuttgart: Alfred Kröner, 1986), pp. 197–221 (here cited from p. 208); "Musik als strukturale Analyse des Mythos. Claude Lévi-Strauss und 'Der Ring des Nibelungen'," in *Wege des Mythos in der Moderne. Richard Wagner, "Der Ring des Nibelungen"*, ed. Dieter Borchmeyer (Munich: Deutscher Taschenbuch Verlag, 1987), pp. 64–74 (here cited from p. 69).

58. Kurt Hübner, *Die Wahrheit des Mythos* (Munich: C.H. Beck, 1985), pp. 399–401.

59. Dahlhaus, *Wagners Konzeption des musikalischen Dramas*, p. 105.

60. Dahlhaus, "Die Musik," p. 212; *Wagners Konzeption des musikalischen Dramas*, pp. 42–43.

61. Dahlhaus, *Wagners Konzeption des musikalischen Dramas*, p. 21.

62. Dahlhaus, "Wagners Stellung in der Musikgeschichte," in *Richard-Wagner-Handbuch*, ed. Ulrich Müller and Peter Wapnewski (Stuttgart: Alfred Kröner, 1986), pp. 60–85 (here cited from p. 70).

63. Dahlhaus, *Wagners Konzeption des musikalischen Dramas*, p. 17.

64. Nattiez, pp. 248–53. I have for a long time felt that motivic repetition in Wagner's *Ring*, especially in Siegfried's wood-bird narration in *Götterdämmerung*, could be effectively analyzed with reference to Freud's essay "Über das Unheimliche," in which he psychoanalytically explicates Hoffmann's story *Der Sandmann* by discussing the repetition compulsion in the unconscious.

65. Catherine Clément, *Opera, or the Undoing of Women*, trans. Betsy Wing (Minneapolis: University of Minnesota Press, 1988), pp. 164–70.

66. Roland Barthes, *Mythologies*, trans. Annette Lavers (New York: Hill and Wang, 1972), pp. 111–17.

Chapter 4 ❧

Wotan's Monologue: Mythological Deconstruction

A quote from Cosima's diaries seems to make the link between what happens in the *Ring* and the aesthetic program of *Oper und Drama* clear, thus establishing that the *Ring* exemplifies Wagner's theory of tragedy. Cosima writes, on 4 July 1873,

Nach Tisch Gespräch über Siegfried und Brünnhilde, dass ersterer nicht tragisch sei, weil er nicht zum Bewusstsein seiner Lage kommt, ein Schleier ist über ihm, seitdem er Brünnhilde für Gunther geworben, aber alles unbewusst, der Zuschauer erkennt es. Wotan und Brünnhilde sind tragisch. (CT II, 703)

After lunch conversation about Siegfried and Brünnhilde, the former not a tragic figure, since he does not become conscious of his position, there is a veil over him since winning Brünnhilde for Gunther, he is quite unaware, though the audience knows. Wotan and Brünnhilde are tragic figures. (D I, 653)

In both *Oper und Drama* and this quotation from Cosima's diaries, Wagner is concerned with the process of becoming conscious. Tragedy, he felt, could not exist without a figure being aware, conscious, of it. In the *Ring*, accordingly, the real tragedy is the drama of Wotan and Brünnhilde. They are tragic figures, for in the course of the tetralogy they come to consciousness, to a full realization of what has happened and why it has happened. The process of coming to consciousness that the characters undergo within the drama parallels the course of the drama with the reception of the drama (that is, the audience should come to a revolutionary consciousness by experiencing the drama).

I have argued that the *Ring* is a Romantic tragedy, with, of course, Young German political implications. It is more precisely an unworking of tragedy that metaphorically and self-reflectively demonstrates its revolutionary purposes. Wagner uses layered aesthetics to the end of politics. Accordingly, the *Ring* exemplifies Wagner's theory of tragedy and myth, that is, mythological drama as a modern rebirth of Greek tragedy, through a clear and ultimately catastrophic depoliticization of the drama and by demonstrating a dialectic of consciousness and self-consciousness such as is represented by the reflections upon and interpretations of Greek mythology in *Oper und Drama*.

In this chapter, I wish to investigate more closely just how the ring works the doom of the gods, which is, I would argue, revealed by an analysis of Wotan's monologue. This is where the *Ring* begins to deconstruct itself. In this chapter, I will first of all show how the relationship of Wotan and Brünnhilde is another aspect of the dual nature of the *Ring*, and then how Wotan, himself a historical-mythological composite, is thus the Wagnerian tragic hero, that is, the tragic hero of which Wagner writes in *Oper und Drama*. I will delve, via an analysis of his monologue, into the intricacy of this figure. In his monologue, Wotan reflects upon the previous course of the drama. Because he exemplifies the theory of *Oper und Drama*, and he is a god besides, Wotan's mythological nature is highly suspect. Thus the self-consciousness that he achieves through innertextual reflection is self-destructive.

This monologue, being the peak of the pyramid that the drama theory of *Oper und Drama* forms (the schema that the *Ring*, I am arguing, conforms to), is the pivotal point of the *Ring*. Furthermore, this monologue embodies and exemplifies the paradoxical nature of Wagner's drama theory and thus of the *Ring*. It therefore lends itself quite readily to an analysis that uses the tools of post-structuralism. I would suggest that Wagner's Romantic transcendence of tragedy in the *Ring* may very well consist of Wotan's rising above his dramatic situation, in fact, above the very form of the drama as art itself. When he does so, Wotan puts the *Ring*, as Derrida would say, "under erasure." Reflection of Wotan upon the ring and its curses brings him to self-consciousness, and thus his monologue is an instance of Romantic irony. In the process, the mythological nature of the *Ring* falls apart, as does the fictional cosmos that the work depicts. The theater set of the *Ring* eventually and inevitably collapses. The *Ring* cosmos ends at the finale of *Götterdämmerung* because the work has deconstructed itself.

≥∌

Due to the heroic nature of the Siegfried legend, one would think, upon first reception of Wagner's *Ring*, that Siegfried is the tragic hero. He is certainly a mixed figure, neither totally good nor blatantly evil. He is also exceptional. The bright-eyed lad who does not know fear was certainly intended by Wagner as a positive figure, as he represents some kind of naive, childlike existence. Upon closer examination, though, this hypothesis of Siegfried as the tragic hero proves, upon almost all counts, false. Exploring this conjecture about Siegfried qualifying as the traditional tragic hero blatantly refutes it and confirms my argument that the *Ring* is not a traditional tragedy.

Unlike the traditional tragic hero, Siegfried does not suffer. Wapnewski has explained, and very beautifully, that unlike most other Wagnerian characters, Siegfried does not suffer, for he does not know fear.[1] Furthermore, Siegfried does not come to consciousness of his transgressions. Michael Ewans calls it an "anagnorisis," thus deeming it a tragic recognition, when Siegfried praises Brünnhilde with his dying breath,[2] but I would say that the delirious man does not really acknowledge his guilt. His awakening of Brünnhilde, but not his transgression against her, comes to consciousness when Hagen restores his memory. He dies as "der überfrohe Held" (MD 804) (the much too happy hero). Moreover, Siegfried has no inner conflict. He does not question his position in the world or vis-à-vis the gods. He is, ironically, oblivious to them—he encounters Wotan the Wanderer directly, but he has no idea who the old stranger is.

Nor does Siegfried even qualify as the Wagnerian tragic hero. He does, of course, fulfill Wagner's demand that the hero become innocently, unconsciously guilty. But Wagner felt that the conflict of the individual with society should take place within the hero. Siegfried lacks this complexity, this added dimension. Siegfried's virtue, his appeal, is his simplicity. Concerning the political interpretations of the *Ring* that associate it with the founding of the German "Reich," Gregor-Dellin writes, "Aber Siegfried ist ein reziproker Held und der Ring eine Kosmologie eigener Art."[3] (Siegfried is a reciprocal hero and the *Ring* is a unique cosmology.) The *Ring*, I have been arguing, similarly, does not refer to political reality. In writing that Siegfried is a "reciprocal hero," Gregor-Dellin might very well mean that he is an anti-hero. I will examine, furthermore, the unusual and idiosyncratic nature of the cosmology that the *Ring* presents.

Wagner's designation of Brünnhilde and Wotan as the tragic characters of the *Ring* reflects his aesthetics of untragic tragedy. Brünnhilde has traits of both the traditional and the Wagnerian tragic hero(ine). Furthermore, the *Ring* contains a complex constellation of interrelated figures. Critics have pointed out that Brünnhilde displays the basic features of Antigone according to Wagner's analysis of the Oedipus legend.[4] This idea, though, falls short of encompassing the full scope of the matter and the complex way in which the characters in the *Ring* exemplify Wagner's reworking of tragedy as presented theoretically in *Oper und Drama*. Brünnhilde seems to, significantly enough, mirror a part of Wotan.

In *Götterdämmerung*, of course, Brünnhilde seems to have the distinguishing characteristics of the tragic hero(ine). The drama demonstrates the relation of a woman to the gods, and it shows a woman in a metaphysical dilemma. Brünnhilde constantly tries to come to terms with Wotan. Abbate has shown how the music of *Götterdämmerung* establishes Brünnhilde's tragic-heroic persona (as opposed to the "romantic victim," what Abbate refers to as "voice-Brünnhilde").[5] Perhaps the fact that Brünnhilde's role fulfills more traditional requirements of tragedy in *Götterdämmerung* can be correlated with Wagner's reversion to forms of "grand opera" such as duets and other ensemble pieces in this work. In the duet in the third act of *Siegfried*, too, the music is more traditional in this regard. Now that Brünnhilde is mortal, she and Siegfried sing as in a more traditional "grand opera" duet, with simultaneous and imitative vocalizing.

Furthermore, Brünnhilde comes to full consciousness of her dramatic dilemma, just as Wagner designated tragedy as a process of psychological realization. Wagner wrote that Siegfried must die so that Brünnhilde can gain wisdom (entry of 6 September 1871; CT I,435; D I,410). In the Immolation Scene, when she says, "Alles, Alles, / Alles weiss ich" (MD 813) (Now I know all), she isn't so much referring to what the Rhinemaidens told her, that is, the cause of Siegfried's death, but the whole larger picture, focussed on Wotan, of the whole lousy system that she sees through. The entire scene is actually an accusation of Wotan. One usually thinks of the gods of tragedy sitting in judgement over mankind. Ironically, Brünnhilde, who is now a mortal, pronounces a harsh indictment of the god whose reign is ending. The tetralogy clearly glorifies the principles she champions over those that brought Wotan to ruin. When analyzed with regard to traditional theoretical notions, the tragedy of the *Ring* seems oddly inverted. Similarly, the Rhinemaidens, the meek and silly creatures of the deep, saw through the empty grandeur of the gods at the end of *Rheingold*.

The interaction of Wotan and Brünnhilde is, however, a complex one. A consideration of Brünnhilde as a traditional tragic heroine clearly does an injustice to the work, for it fails to account for the tetralogy with reference to Wagner's redefinition of tragedy in *Oper und Drama*. In the treatise, as I have shown, Wagner overturns and undermines traditional tragedy theory. If *Götterdämmerung* is Brünnhilde's tragedy, then *Walküre* is Wotan's tragedy. The rest of the *Ring* is a tragedy about the tragedy of *Walküre*. The *Ring*, one could say, contains a tragedy within a (larger) tragedy, like boxes within boxes, just as *Oper und Drama* contains interlocking interpretations of myths, traditional elements of tragedy and their reinterpretation. Thus the entire plot structure of the *Ring* tetralogy is one of the potentiated "repeated mirrorings" of Romantic irony. Significantly enough, the drama of the mortals is embedded in that of the gods, which seems only appropriate. Wagner defined tragedy with regard to myth, and thus one can suspect that the *Ring* somehow undoes its own mythological raw material, which, I will demonstrate, is precisely what happens.

Wotan and Brünnhilde clearly have complementary roles in the *Ring*. Wotan makes a change of heart, a figural change; the god becomes a father in the third act of *Walküre*. Brünnhilde, who is literally stripped of her immortality, metamorphoses from being a Valkyrie to being a mortal when she is awakened in the third act of *Siegfried*. She even, in her "role" as Valkyrie, guards her father's back in battle. The two characters seem almost like mirror-images of each other. Wotan says to her, before his monologue, that he speaks to himself when he talks to her. With regard to these two figures, one could even say that the outer is really the inner, with Brünnhilde representing or mirroring a part of Wotan. She does say that she is his will. The reciprocity of these two characters causes the *Ring* to progress to its conclusion. Brünnhilde's tragedy undoes Wotan's. When the action is internalized, one character can, paradoxically, be a part of another.

In this sense, I would call the *Ring* a "double tragedy." Furthermore, Brünnhilde's tragedy clearly interlocks with Wotan's. That the music of *Götterdämmerung*, according to Dahlhaus, embeds the events of this last drama into the "Göttertragödie,"[6] as I noted in chapter 3, further emphasizes the reciprocity of these two characters and the fact that Brünnhilde's tragedy is like a smaller box within Wotan's tragedy, with the two dynamically interacting. The musical allusions are the auditory expression of this interpretative reciprocity, which can be considered a distinctively Wagnerian instance of Romantic irony. As the action of the *Ring* depends upon how each character perceives, that is, understands and interprets, his or her respective environment and thus dramatic situation, one could further argue that the two tragedies explicate each other in the *Ring*, interacting in a hermeneutic way and thus propelling the drama forward (and back).

Accordingly, Brünnhilde interprets the events of the present tragedy with reference to Wotan's tragedy, at the same time misinterpreting them. Brünnhilde constantly betrays her attachment to Wotan and her mythological origins within this fictional cosmos. Cooke comments upon the dramatic irony that Wotan asks, while confiding in Brünnhilde in his monologue, where he can find a free hero, and Brünnhilde subsequently reveals herself as just such a free agent when she defies his command and shields Siegmund in battle.[7] Brünnhilde, however, is also in some way a part of Wotan. She is, after all, his will, as she says in the second act of *Walküre*, thereby prompting the decisive monologue of Wotan.

Critics like to discuss another duality of the *Ring*, what I would explain as a mythological-tragic inversion, by referring to its compositional history. The genesis of the *Ring* has been well documented by, among others, Carl Dahlhaus.[8] Roughly speaking, the *Ring* was the result of an extensive backward expansion. Wagner originally planned a drama on the Siegfried myth, that is, *Siegfrieds Tod*, which he terms in *Mein Leben* a tragedy (as opposed to *Der junge Siegfried*, which he appended to it and called a "heroisches Lustspiel") (heroic comedy).[9] Wagner then expanded the

drama he originally planned backwards, visualizing, so to speak, or dramatizing the prehistory of it and embedding the story of Siegfried into that of
Wotan.

Critics discuss the various conclusions that Wagner wrote for the cycle,
and they debate to what extent his reading of Schopenhauer in 1854
influenced the *Ring*, and in what way the *Ring* shows a turn from Feuerbach
to Schopenhauer, from revolution to resignation. Discussing the compositional history of the *Ring* thus raises the issue of how one is to weigh the
external and the internal motivations that the characters in the *Ring* experience, the outer and the inner dramas, the two extremes of Shaw and
Donington. Some attribute what they consider to be the change in conception that the *Ring* underwent to Wagner's disillusionment at the failure of
the revolutions of mid-century and his subsequent abandonment of political action.[10]

At any rate, Wagner shifted from portraying the final catastrophe itself
to also showing the causes of this catastrophe. Instead of merely showing
Siegfried's death, Wagner wished to explore *why* Siegfried has to die. One
can of course debate, as Gregor-Dellin does, the validity of attributing this
change of emphasis to political events. Gregor-Dellin argues that the contradiction was within Wagner himself.[11] This fails, however, to explain how
this dual structure works artistically in the finished product. It is question-
able if one is even justified in using it as an explanation, and whether it
really explains anything at all. I wish to discuss the matter in literary-critical
terms instead. Whatever the cause of it, the *Ring* has a double-tiered
structure that is, I would suggest, just one manifestation of the fundamental
duality that I have been investigating.

Carl Dahlhaus, however, has proposed that Wotan is the tragic hero.[12]
One could build on this idea and conjecture that in expanding the *Ring*
backwards and embedding the story of Siegfried into that of Wotan, Wagner
moved the tragedy, so to speak, entirely upstairs. This option warrants
expansion. Wagner, I propose, has thus, via Wotan, internalized the structure of tragedy. In doing so, he has unworked the metaphysical aspect of
tragedy, as would be consistent with the influence of Feuerbach at this time
of his life, turning the traditional structure of tragedy not only upside-
down, but also inside-out. I would also suggest that perhaps this is why the
drama is, one could say, a mythologically hermeneutic one.

When analyzed with regard to traditional tragedy theory, one must
conclude that through this backward expansion the tragedy of the *Ring*
became reflexive, and that the *Ring* is a self-referential tragedy. One could
even theorize that the drama explicates itself, and that it thematizes the
main principles of the traditional tragedy. In keeping with its theoretical
framework as presented in *Oper und Drama*, the *Ring* is the rebirth of tragedy
on the stage of reflection. In other words, the *Ring* is a tragedy about tragedy.
In thematizing the main principles of the traditional tragedy, it reflects upon

them and redefines tragedy, thus demonstrating the theory presented in *Oper und Drama*.

Although, as Borchmeyer notes, it is a frequent theme of myth that the gods need mankind,[13] tragedy traditionally deals with the relation of mankind to the gods. Insofar as Wotan's dilemma is how to beget a free hero, the *Ring* explores the position of the gods vis-à-vis mankind. In "directing" his progeny and trying to overcome his fate, Wotan eventually watches and explicates his own drama. The conflict, the dichotomy, of free will and destiny, central to the traditional structure of tragedy, is a theme of the cycle. The decisive dialogue of Wotan and Fricka in the second act of *Walküre* centers on this issue. Thus the *Ring* is a self-referential tragedy; it explicates itself. It thematizes the basic premises of tragedy. Furthermore, in doing so, it reflects the reflexive structure of *Oper und Drama*. Wotan and Fricka discourse and debate on free will and custom (or, in artistic terms, innovation and convention) as though they had read the treatise.

In doing so, they argue about the future course of the work of art in which they are participating, and how the "inner" drama (of the mortals, that is) and thus their own "divine" drama, shall end. Furthermore, in his monologue, Wotan applies this theoretical apparatus and fatally reflects upon his own dramatic dilemma. A consideration of Brünnhilde and Wotan as the Antigone and Creon from Wagner's interpretation of Greek tragedy in *Oper und Drama*, such as Rainer Franke proposes,[14] ignores the internalization of the dramatic conflict in Wotan. It simply does not go far enough. Furthermore, the inner is usually more important to Wagner than the outer. Accordingly, his works need to be analyzed, so to speak, from within.

Various critics have argued for the centrality of Wotan in the *Ring*, and the internalization of the drama in him. Dahlhaus notes that the Wotan-plot is a monodrama or psychodrama, with Fricka and Brünnhilde almost like allegories for Wotan's inner processes.[15] Others have argued similarly. Deryck Cooke calls the two opposite sides of Wotan's character that are represented by Fricka and Brünnhilde the "old" Wotan and the "new" Wotan respectively. Fricka, Cooke explains, embodies all of Wotan's old ideas, such as power, law, and stability; Brünnhilde represents his new plans, which go against his laws.[16]

Carolyn Abbate takes a musical slant on this same basic idea of the internalization of the drama in Wotan.[17] Abbate points out that Wotan's narration is cyclic. Wotan's monologue, Abbate explains, consists of variations of a myth that is at the center of the *Ring*, the renunciation of love to acquire power. The monologue, according to Abbate, presents history as a repetition. The semantic repetition of a recurring sequence has forced Wotan into foreseeing the future repetition. His moment of revelation is brought about, Abbate shows, by the formal structure that his narrating has engendered. The cyclic repetition of the narrative has compelled him to a future action. The music of the monologue, Abbate explains, expresses

Wotan's despairing view of history. Abbate argues that in his monologue Wotan hears the music he is singing to, and hears the form that his story has taken, which thus compels him to repeat the story of the renunciation of love for power and abandon Siegmund.

Gregor-Dellin, too, has noted that the *Ring* is really the story of Wotan, adding that the other figures represent or embody principles that are at war within Wotan himself. (In other words, I would add, the outer is really the inner.) The Wotan-scenes are, Gregor-Dellin points out, the ones in which the meaning of the work is best revealed. The processes taking place within Wotan, the forces that are at conflict within him, are at the same time presiding over the development of the figures whom he has begotten. Ultimately he is guilty for their fate, for he is, in his greed for power, the root of all evil. All the other figures are, according to Gregor-Dellin, in some way part of Wotan. Thus Gregor-Dellin argues for the internalization of the dramatic conflict or tragedy in Wotan.

His tragic contradiction, Gregor-Dellin explains, that of originally having created the laws and then having transgressed them himself, brings his end inevitably and also the end of those beings whom he brought to life for the purpose of saving him from the end. The events of the tetralogy, Gregor-Dellin observes, seem almost predetermined. The figures act under a fate that has been imposed on them by Wotan, and which seems to arise from the mysterious curse of the ring. This interpretation, though, creates many problems. As it outlines only one side of a duality, it raises more questions than it answers. Wotan, Gregor-Dellin suggests, creates the fate of others. But what about his own? How does he transcend tragedy, then? Who rules over the god and creates the fate of the ostensible ruler of the fictional mythological universe?

In the present chapter, I will further explore and apply this idea of the drama, tragedy, or dramatic conflict being internalized in Wotan. I would argue that Wotan is the nontraditional "tragic hero" whom Wagner describes as the protagonist of his reworking or deconstruction of tragedy. Wotan, by exemplifying the self-referentiality of the tragic nature of the *Ring*, clearly qualifies as the Wagnerian tragic hero. Wagner termed Wotan "die Summe der Intelligenz der Gegenwart"[18] (the sum of the intelligence of the present), indicating that he united all sorts of things within himself, as Wagner, in *Oper und Drama*, wrote that the main character of the art-work of the future should. The tragedy of the *Ring* actually takes place within Wotan himself.

I would argue that not only the dramatic conflict is internalized in Wotan. That the other figures are embodiments of forces or processes within Wotan is not the only way in which the drama is internalized in Wotan. Not only, furthermore, does the *music* come from within Wotan, as Abbate has suggested. In *Oper und Drama*, Wagner defines tragedy with regard to its mythological raw material. Thus I would argue that if the tragedy of the

Ring takes place within Wotan himself, then the mythological nature of the drama may very well come from Wotan, too. In a letter to Liszt of 3 October 1855, Wagner designated the scene of Wotan and Brünnhilde in the second act of *Walküre* as the most important scene of the whole tetralogy. Scholarship has not yet exhaustively explicated this monologue with regard to the theme of mythological refabrication in the *Ring*. Despite the wealth of material that has been written about it, this monologue, I feel, warrants more analysis. I wish to explore the complex processes that take place in Wotan and how, via Wotan, this mysterious curse really works the doom of the gods.

Furthermore, if tragedy for Wagner has to do with coming to consciousness, then the fact that Wotan, according to Wagner, rises to the tragic dignity of willing his own destruction would imply that Wotan comes to consciousness in his monologue. Just how and why Wotan rises to the tragic dignity of willing his own destruction, and just what the nature of his tragic insight is, warrant further investigation. The consciousness that Wotan attains is, I will argue, the one that Wagner's typical tragic hero according to the theory of *Oper und Drama* should achieve in the art-work of the future. Furthermore, this is the episode in which the revolutionary mythical music-drama stages its own reception. Accordingly, I will argue that Wotan, in his monologue, experiences his own drama.

Carl Dahlhaus notes that in the narratives (the prime example of which is, of course, Wotan's monologue) the characters become conscious of the present. In such instances memory of the past and anticipation of the future meet with each other.[19] That the drama is internalized in Wotan proves catastrophic for the falsely mythological stage-world of the *Ring*. Myth, the content that has become form and the form that has then in turn become the content of this form/content, has become subjective. Wotan's monologue gives a psychogram of tragedy. When myth has become a state of mind, then the doubling of the inner (the psychological) with the outer (the external props and sets that make the drama seem genuinely mythological) sets the stage for a Wagnerian catastrophe. Just how and why Alberich's curse works the doom of the gods, if it does this at all, awaits adequate explanation. I will argue that it seals the end of the fictional universe in a post-structuralist way. It deconstructs the outward drama by dematerializing it.

Brünnhilde, in *Siegfried* and *Götterdämmerung* (the two dramas of the *Ring* in which she is mortal) demonstrates the self-referentiality of the *Ring* by showing the relation of a woman to the previous events of the tetralogy. As she comes to grips with the other characters onstage, she also reflects upon her former (mythological) self. As a mortal, though, Brünnhilde looks at tragedy from below. Wotan, however, looks at tragedy from above. He surveys his dramatic situation, examines his own character, and in doing so takes the work apart. As opposed to Brünnhilde in *Götterdämmerung*,

Wotan is, in *Walküre*, a god. I would argue that in his monologue, Wotan fatally reflects upon myth and his own mythical nature. This leads him to, I will argue, will the end of the gods. I will thus propose a new explanation of how the curse on the ring works the end of the gods.

Siegmund's death, the immediate cause of Wotan's despair in the scene that I will discuss, forms a turning-point of the action only with reference to Wotan's fear that Alberich may regain the ring. This death does not, then, necessarily lead to the end. Although Siegmund's death is an apparent turning-point of the drama, it does not, however, necessarily entail Wotan willing his own destruction. The answer to why, at the end of Wotan's monologue, he wills the end of the gods must be sought in his idiosyncratic relationship to the mythical world in which he exists. Exploring what Siegmund's death really has to do with Alberich's ring will yield an answer to what makes Wotan function. Fricka gets her way at first; it seems that the conservative order will triumph. After she leaves, however, Wotan gets more radical than ever. Siegmund's death may seem to have little to do with Alberich's ring. Wotan, however, thinks it does. In other words, this, too, is his interpretation.

Abbate's discussion of Wotan's narrative as a performance that contains the tetralogy in microcosm points out the Romantic irony of the monologue, designating it as a "play within a play" that mirrors in miniature the work as a whole. By containing the tetralogy in microcosm, I would add, Wotan's monologue reflects the Romantic irony of the work as a whole. Everything converges on that one object I have discussed as the main impetus and unifying element of the tetralogy, the (supposedly) accursed ring. The fact that *Walküre*, or the *Ring* in general, is a Wagnerian tragedy means that it transcends tragedy. In rising to the tragic dignity of willing his own destruction, Wotan rises above the drama and in doing so transcends his dramatic situation and the mythological raw material of the drama also.

Critics write that Wagner restored myth only to destroy it.[20] The *Ring* destroys myth, one could say it deconstructs itself, in a way that is firmly rooted in its theoretical presuppositions and its aesthetic program of mythological reinterpretation and social revolution of history through mythological reconstruction. Thus the *Ring* is the appropriate musical-dramatic counterpart of Wagner's conflation of aesthetics and politics in *Oper und Drama*. It demonstrates Wagner's theory of revolution through aesthetic mythological reinterpretation. Wotan dissects and interprets from within the mythicized version of history that Wagner has theoretically built in *Oper und Drama*.

Furthermore, Wotan's monologue shows how the inner can affect the outer, and thus how one's perception of the past can determine, in a way, the future. The *Ring* is both regressive and progressive, like the myth of Oedipus that Wagner explicates in *Oper und Drama*. In this way, the *Ring* somehow stands for the processes by which myth can change history, and art can revolutionize reality. Wotan's fate (to die, that is) has been decided since before *Rheingold*. The *Ring*, however, also presents the idea that in a dialectical way, through interaction with the external world and upon the prompting of others, one decides one's own fate. That is, whether or not one thinks one is in a myth seems to determine one's real musical-dramatic location. The *Ring* is full of the phenomenon of characters writing the script for others. By destroying itself, I would suggest, the *Ring* shows how music-drama can change society.

Analyses of the *Ring* with reference to *Oper und Drama* have already highlighted the fact that Wagner uses myth as raw material for his tetralogy. They have expanded the parallels between this mythical story with the myth of Oedipus, the most obvious parallel being the similarities between Brünnhilde and Antigone; and they have drawn comparisons between the incest of the Volsung twins, which Wotan tries (unsuccessfully) to vindicate in his dialogue with Fricka, and that of Oedipus and Jocasta, which Wagner sees in a positive light. However, the links between *Oper und Drama* and *Walküre*, especially with reference to Wotan's monologue, warrant further investigation. The interconnections go far beyond those just mentioned. The complex psychological and (as he is a fictional character) literary-critical, textual processes that take place in Wotan are rooted in Wagner's aesthetics.

In *Oper und Drama*, Wagner interprets and relativizes myth, arguing that the art-work of the future should interpret myth. The *Ring*, like the second part of *Oper und Drama*, is about interpretation, specifically mythological interpretation. In addition, the *Ring* is a modern reworking or interpretation of mythological elements. The different levels in *Oper und Drama* represent facets of, and confusion in, Wotan himself. I would like to discuss the *Ring*, in particular Wotan's monologue, by understanding Alberich's curse with reference to Wagner's analysis of the traditional tragic curse in *Oper und Drama*. That Wotan's declaration of the end in his *Walküre* monologue seals the doom of the gods of the *Ring* is, of course, self-explanatory. But in ways that go far beyond the obvious, during the course of the tetralogy and in a process that culminates in his monologue, the course of action exemplifies Wagner's theory of tragedy from *Oper und Drama*.

It seems a commonplace of Wagner scholarship that the doom of the gods is caused by the curse that Alberich has placed on the ring. However, the world was going to end inevitably, that is, regardless of what happens to the ring. Erda made that clear three evenings before the end actually takes place. Wotan's monologue seals the doom of this cosmos in another way entirely. Wotan's thought processes actually enact Wagner's revolutionary deconstruction of Greek tragedy when he reflects on the ring and the curse that Alberich has pronounced upon it. Romantic irony proves, in Wotan's monologue, catastrophic. Concepts from post-structuralism will prove instrumental in my analysis, for, I will be arguing, Wotan's monologue seals the fate of the fictional universe by unravelling the structure of signification of the work of art.

Deconstruction is not simply a matter of locating a moment of ambiguity or irony ultimately incorporated into the text's system of unified meaning, but rather a moment that genuinely threatens to collapse that system. To deconstruct a text one finds the vulnerable textual passage, just as Hagen aims his spear at that spot in Siegfried's back. Wotan's proclamation, in his monologue, of the end of the *Ring* cosmos, I propose, is the paradoxical moment that collapses the system of signification and literally the fictional cosmos portrayed in the *Ring*. In the light of more recent literary-critical trends, Lévi-Strauss' designation of Wagner as the originator of the structural analysis of myth clearly falls short of explaining Wotan. In this monologue, Wotan performs a process I would call "mythological deconstruction."

In the second act of *Walküre*, known primarily for its lengthy stasis, Wotan does make a pivotal decree. He mirrors his previous command to Brünnhilde to shield Siegmund in the coming battle with Hunding by pronouncing at the end of his monologue that Siegmund should lose the battle. But Fricka badgers him into this. Wotan's monologue is, furthermore, an apparent turning-point of the action, insofar as Siegmund's death is a direct reversal of the course that he has been planning the action to take. Siegmund's death, though, has relatively little effect on the external action except insofar as Wotan is thereby encouraged or actually coerced to relinquish control over it. However, when the *Ring* is analyzed with regard to the theory of mythological refabrication presented in *Oper und Drama*, it becomes clear that Wotan's monologue is, I would argue, a crucial point of the *Ring* in quite another sense. Wotan's decree of Siegmund's death may not be the result of Wotan's inner progress. Retelling the story, however, proves cathartic.

In willing his own destruction and that of the mythological world in which he lives, Wotan is destroying the outwardly mythological raw material of the *Ring* tetralogy. One could say he is deconstructing the work of art via its mythological nature. Moreover, he specifically dismantles or deconstructs the drama at the nodal point of its mythological nature, the title object. In Wotan's monologue, I propose, the work of art actually undermines the structure of signification that is created by its modern reworking and reinterpretation of mythological raw material. The structure of signification established by the ring and the ambiguous dual-layered curses associated with it subsequently unravels. Disaster ensues when it comes apart, for it drags the whole dramatic structure of the text down to ruin with it. The structure of signification represented by the ring is, it proves, certainly one of difference.

Furthermore, this mythological deconstruction is a direct result of the basic paradox of modern mythological reconstruction on a stage of self-consciousness, which is, as I have shown, outlined in Wagner's theory of *Oper und Drama* and which forms the aesthetic program of the *Ring*. The basic contradiction of music-drama as a nineteenth-century, modern metaphorical reinterpretation of mythology with the aim of commenting upon and thus revolutionizing society through art brings the world of the *Ring* to ruin. The joy of never being finished consists, with the repeated performance of the *Ring* cycle, of experiencing the repeated mirrorings of Romantic irony repeatedly falling apart. The dual metaphoricity of the *Ring* proves self-destructive. The two kinds of metaphoricity, that is, of the work as a metaphor for history and the ring as a metaphor within the modern myth, cancel each other out and seal its fatality.

Wagner wrote that whereas Greek tragedy was conservative, modern tragedy should be revolutionary. In Greek tragedy, according to Wagner, "fate" is really a fiction of society. The tension between Wagner's interpretation and what he sees as an interpretation, that is, the dichotomy of the metaphorical and the mythical, the duality of the figural and literal meanings of the tragic curse, is in the *Ring* internalized in Wotan to a revolutionary conclusion. The *Ring*, after all, portrays not only the beginning, but also the end of history. Wotan's monologue, I will argue, is where the art-work of the future stages its own reception. In his monologue, Wotan is both within the drama and outside of it; the creator and spectator of the work of art; the author and the audience simultaneously. In Wotan's monologue, dichotomies merge, collapse into each other, and are obliterated. Wotan's monologue, as the pivotal point at which the work turns from portraying its creation to somehow portraying its reception, functions as the mythical-historical mirror, the hinge at which articulation and difference converge.

It might seem incongruous to some to liken Wotan to a figure from a fictional work by E.T.A. Hoffmann, whose stories resemble, rather, comic opera, while Wotan's monologue is deep, ponderous, and totally serious. The decisive "event" that occurs during the narration of this monologue is, however, internal and, one could say, hermeneutic. A similar process to that which Strohschneider-Kohrs outlines in *Prinzessin Brambilla* takes place, I would argue, in the *Ring*, as it thematizes, via Wotan, its own aesthetic program in the form of endless reflections. Here Wotan rises above the drama, just as Celionati rises above the work of literature in which he exists. Like Celionati, Wotan analyzes the story from the outside while still being a part of the plot and participating in some way in the course of the action, even if this entails, paradoxically, not participating in it.

Building on the work of Strohschneider-Kohrs that I summarized in chapter 1, I would suggest that Wotan's monologue constitutes an instance in which the fictionality of the work is questioned or broken by a fictional character. As Celionati mirrors E.T.A. Hoffmann, Wotan mirrors Wagner. In his monologue Wotan, a character in the drama, observes and comments upon the action from above. In doing so, Wotan, another charlatan, another

Celionati, negates the fictionality of the work of art in another way from
that in which Celionati, according to Strohschneider-Kohrs' analysis, does.
As Wagner, in *Oper und Drama*, unworks myth, so does Wotan, and his
consciousness is revolutionary to the aesthetically utmost. He takes the
eraser to the score of the *Ring*.

In his monologue, as he retells the story of the previous events, Wotan
psychologically and in an idiosyncratic way enacts Wagner's interpretation
of Greek tragedy from *Oper und Drama*. Wagner theorized that the traditional tragic curse was merely a figural one, a fiction of society, and not a
literal, magical one. It portrayed how a conservative society saw a free
thinker or nonconformist. Wagner interprets Greek tragedy as an interpretation. Wotan actually enacts the undoing of this interpretation in self-recognition. He reverses it, and thus mythological music-drama portrays its
own reception as well as production and demonstrates its own aesthetic
program. In this way, Wotan's reflection upon myth mirrors Wagner's
mythological reflection in *Oper und Drama*. The two processes can also be
seen as reversals, for Wotan dismantles the work of art that *Oper und Drama*
theoretically builds.

I would argue that in the course of this monologue, by telling of his past
transgressions, Wotan grows in self-knowledge, and as a result he comes to
see the curse that Alberich has placed on the ring as a figural one, an abstract
one, and not a literal one. It is metaphor, not myth. Furthermore, in gaining
an insight into the metaphorical nature of the curse on the ring, Wotan
learns of the metaphoricity and thus the fictionality of the entire synthetic
mythological work of art in which he finds himself. In addition, he gains
an insight into the textual nature of his own existence. In this manner,
Wotan's monologue demonstrates the revolutionary potential of Wagner's
aesthetics of mythological self-reflection. It is the aesthetic counterpart, the
artistic mirror, of the revolutionary overthrow that the aesthetic program
of the work dictates that the *Ring* should indirectly cause.

Much has transpired between the previous drama and *Walküre*. Deryck
Cooke explains that Loge has abandoned Wotan; Fafner has turned himself
into a dragon and he guards the ring and the Tarnhelm in a cave; Alberich
has begotten a son on a mortal woman to be his agent in his attempt to
regain the ring; Wotan has ordered that the bravest heroes shall go to
Valhalla after their deaths in battle to defend it against any possible attack;
Wotan has fathered nine Valkyries to incite men to heroism and choose the
bravest among the slain; and the Volsung twins were begotten on a mortal
woman with the intent that Siegmund shall be Wotan's own agent in his
attempt to regain the ring. Wotan has done all this in his own interest. He
is afraid that Alberich may regain the ring, which is the reason for the army
of heroes to defend Valhalla. Wotan himself cannot act, due to the contracts

that he has made and that he is morally bound to uphold. Siegmund, his agent, is there to prevent Alberich from regaining the ring. The magic of the ring, after all, is only useful to Alberich, whose power would then undermine Wotan's.[21]

I would add that a major change, however, has taken place in Wotan himself between these two dramas. The night with Erda has not only brought Wotan's drama its lead soprano role, Brünnhilde. Wotan has evidently learned hermeneutics, which he practices in his monologue. Because he has descended to Erda, he has learned how to rise above the drama. He has also learned to play the game. It is no coincidence that Loge is absent; Wotan does not need him any more. Wotan is no longer the one being manipulated. He has assumed the role of theater director himself. Furthermore, Deryck Cooke points out that Wagner uses three of the periphrases for Wotan from the *Poetic Edda* in *Walküre*: "Walvater," "Heervater," and "Siegvater," derived respectively from the Old Norse names of Odin as battle-god: "Valfadir," "Herfadir," and "Sigfödr."[22] Peter Wapnewski explicitly states Wotan's function as director of this "theater within a theater" when he writes that in Act I, Wotan, as father of the Volsung twins, is invisibly present as "Regisseur des Schicksalsdramas"[23] (the director of the drama of fate). Wapnewski further comments, concerning the events of the first act, that not the free will of free individuals acted, but, rather, predetermined roles were mechanically performed.[24] Furthermore, Wotan has a new role within the mythological substance of the tetralogy. In *Walküre*, Wotan appears in the persona of Odin, the Old Norse battle-god.

Wotan's dilemma, though, is that the hero he creates will inevitably remain unfree. He cannot "program" a hero to be free; this is a paradox. Thus the conflict between freedom and custom is somehow intrinsic to Wotan's dramatic situation. Fricka, though, is very concerned with the mythological substance of the drama. She is more conservative than Wotan. The gods, she thinks, need to survive this performance. Fricka feels the gods will perish as such when they transgress the laws that they should be upholding. She asks, "So ist es denn aus / mit den ewigen Göttern, / seit du die wilden / Wälsungen zeugtest? / Heraus sagt ich's; / traf ich den Sinn?" (MD 606). (So are the eternal gods finished, since you fathered the wild Volsungs? The gods are finished, I said; is this what you mean?) Not only does the sword get smashed in the second act. Wotan shatters the very substance of the mythological music-dramas in which he exists. Ironically, the gods end anyway, even though (and in a way, because) Fricka wins the argument.

Deryck Cooke explains that the second and third acts of *Walküre* are based on four short passages of source material.[25] For instance, the dialogue of Wotan and Fricka actually has no basis in the mythology that Wagner used as his raw material. Other parts of the drama under discussion are radical expansions or synthetic recombinations of scant fragments in the sources. The majority of Wagner's scenes in these acts have no exact equivalents in the mythology, then, but are based on general ideas contained in the mythology, such as Odin the battle-god telling a Valkyrie which side to take in a battle, or the battle-god being defeated in an argument with his wife. Cooke notes that the only basis in the mythology for the scene that follows Fricka's exit is that Odin ordered Brynhild to give victory to Hjalmgunnar, which she was unwilling to do.[26] In other words, this scene in *Walküre* that I will now discuss is synthetic, refabricated, counterfeit modern mythology. Furthermore, I would argue, it unmasks itself as such.

I wish to analyze Wotan's fictional thought processes more thoroughly. I will investigate, in doing so, just what the nature of his tragic (or therefore untragic) realization really is. This monologue gives valuable information concerning Wotan's state of mind and his dramatic dilemma. From this monologue, one can speculate about his perception of the curse that Alberich has placed upon the ring, note the effect that the other characters have had on him, and observe just how the action of the drama and the musical-dramatic conflict of the *Ring* are internalized in Wotan. It will then become apparent that the chief god is, indeed, in a deep and seemingly insurmountable dilemma much more complex than regaining a simple (objective) magical ring.

Wotan's monologue lays bare the psychic and multilayered textual artistic depth of this fictional character, this modern-minded and nineteenth-century ancient mythological Germanic god in costume. Wotan, I propose, shows the textual confusion that Wagner inflicts on his characters by placing them in a myth that is reflective, that is, self-referential, and that has metaphorical significance. In his monologue, of course, Wotan shows characteristic nonmythological introspection as he reflects and discourses upon his nondivine powerlessness. Furthermore, when one considers how the *Ring* thematizes its own raw material, then it becomes clear that Wotan's despair is indeed warranted.

In his monologue, Wotan analyzes the previous course of the action, and in doing so, he performs innertextual hermeneutics. His stance, though, turns out to be an implicitly post-structuralist one. Wotan deconstructs myth when, in an instance of Romantic irony, he interprets the drama in which he exists and reflects upon the curse that Alberich has placed on the ring. In doing so, he reflects upon the entire quasi-mythological story of the tetralogy of music-dramas in which he exists. As a result, the ambiguity of the term "myth" inevitably brings him to ruin. The two meanings of it, as mythical raw material and reflective interpretation of one's surroundings, work against each other and destroy the fictional world of the *Ring*. In his monologue, Wotan becomes conscious of the metaphoricity of myth and of his own intertextuality. As a myth about myth, and a modern synthetic work that uses traditional mythological motives and objects in a metaphorical way, the *Ring* must rush inexorably to its inevitable end.

Wotan is the epitome of modern mythological self-reflection. This monologue is much more than the redundant narration that it may seem to be. Wotan is sorting through the previous events of the tetralogy and thus the various textual layers that I have discerned in it. In the *Ring*, I have been arguing, narrating really means reflecting upon the story, and that in turn means performing mythological hermeneutics. Wotan interprets the drama in which he finds himself. For this reason, Wotan's thought processes have grave results for the work of art in which he finds himself. In retelling the story, Wotan undoes it. His threat to Brünnhilde, when she dares to defy his command, that he can throw the entire cosmos into ruin, resembles Friedrich Schlegel's theory of Romantic irony, which stated that the task of the artist was alternately creation and destruction. This is basically what Wotan does in his monologue.

That the ring is cursed for one who knows (or rather thinks) that it is cursed seems to indicate that the *Ring* portrays the tragedy of self-consciousness. In Wagner's unworking of traditional tragedy theory, this implies, in turn, that such a drama transcends tragedy. In Wotan's monologue, I would argue, he becomes fully conscious of his dilemma. Furthermore, that Wotan comes to consciousness in his monologue means that he attains self-consciousness of his false mythological nature. In this monologue, moreover, Wotan achieves the consciousness of myth that excludes mythological consciousness. When one analyzes Wotan's monologue with regard to Wagner's theoretical unworking and redefinition of tragedy in *Oper und Drama*, then one has to agree with the composer that *Walküre* is, indeed, as Wagner wrote, the most tragic of his works.

Wotan's monologue is really an exercise in hermeneutics, and mythological hermeneutics at that. During the course of his monologue, Wotan either explicitly or implicitly interprets the words of the Wala and Alberich. The monologue is not a simple narration of past events for the sake of recapitulating them for the audience; rather, it is a subtle exercise in textual exegesis from within a work of art. Erda and Alberich have left traces in Wotan's psyche. The important thing is how Wotan combines and perceives them. In his *Walküre* monologue, Wotan reacts to Alberich's pronouncement(s), he puts things together in his mind, he retells the story, he associates Alberich's curse and Erda's prophecy, and he has a "delayed reaction."

The notion of the palimpsest, the distinction between an original text and a reinscribed text, is an important one to deconstruction, which finds texts under texts and subtexts within texts. In retelling the story as he does in his monologue, Wotan simultaneously reinscribes and erases the text. In doing so, he demonstrates Wagner's method of mythological narration and historically conditioned textual exegesis from *Oper und Drama*. Thus the *Ring* rehearses its own grammatological structure. Erda has simply made Wotan

aware of his own mortality. The interpretative relativity and psychologically internalized subjectivity of myth brings Wotan to ruin when he reflects
on it too much. Whether or not the ring can really work the doom of the
gods is irrelevant—Wotan *believes* it can. The curse on the ring is more
Wotan's thing than Alberich's.

The focus of Wotan's attention as he delivers the monologue is, of course,
the accursed ring. In his monologue, I would argue, to be specific, Wotan is
subtly dismantling the quasi-mythological universe in which he exists via
a dematerialization of the ring, the curse that Alberich has placed upon it,
and thus by extension the very mythological substance of the *Ring*. One
could say that he is demythologizing the work of art in which he exists by
reducing myth to metaphor. This happens according to the interpretative
schema of *Oper und Drama*. Siegmund's death may seem tragic, but the real
drama of the *Ring* is Wotan's inner one.

The immediate cause of Wotan's despair when he sings his monologue
is his imminent decree of Siegmund's death. The monologue, though, goes
much deeper than this, as Wotan's problem also goes much deeper than
this. In retelling the story, Wotan touches upon the various inner and outer
causes of his dramatic dilemma, his perception of the interplay between the
subjective and the objective that has led to his present predicament. His
situation is a paradoxical one, and he has mostly made his problems for
himself. He is guardian of the laws, but he has broken (and wants to
continue breaking) them. His predicament seems truly hopeless and irre-
solvable. He wants it both ways; he wants both love and power. Furthermore, in a very real way, he has driven himself to despair. Ironically, Wotan
has made his own predicament and has even indirectly helped work the
real end of the gods, in large part through his conscious effort to avert the
end. He has gotten himself tangled up in his double-dealings.

The dilemma that Wotan laments in this monologue, though, is actually
caused by his dual and paradoxical existence as a nineteenth-century phony
recycled god. His dramatic plight is rooted in the theoretical aesthetic
program of *Oper und Drama*, insofar as it dictates a modern-day revival of
mythological drama. His "role" in the performance, one could say, is not
clearly defined. In many ways, Wotan is a contradictory, paradoxical figure.
He exists onstage, but the essence of the problem he is lamenting is that he
cannot participate in the action surrounding the supposedly cursed ring.
He is a god, but he must come to grips with his own mortality, which Erda
has informed him of. The work is full of paradoxes and contradictions, a
fundamental one being the simultaneity of history and myth, the paradox
of which Stefan Kunze and Tibor Kneif have written.

In this way, Wotan is caught in the dichotomies of myth and modernity,
magic and morality, that form the basic conflict of the *Ring*. Wotan's immediate situation is a strange and unique one indeed. He is musing about an
odd magic ring, though he has evidently failed to notice that it has demon-

strated only psychological properties; the ring is supposedly cursed, or at least Wotan thinks it is. Moreover, his dilemma is a problematic moral one, for his treaties keep him from preventing Alberich from regaining it. One could say that Wotan embodies the dual nature of the *Ring*. He is both human and divine, historical and mythological, modern man and Germanic god. Thus Wotan's problems go far beyond his own particular dramatic situation. Not only is Wotan the central figure of the tetralogy. He embodies in particular the paradox of its mythological nature.

Thus Wotan's dilemma is symptomatic of the problematic mythological nature of the work of art as a whole. Not only has he created his own dramatic dilemma for himself. When one looks deeper, it thus seems that his main problem is congenital. Wotan's dilemma, I would argue, is essentially the paradox of his own fictional or textual existence as a nineteenth-century synthetic reconstitution of Germanic mythology. He is straddling the two textual levels that I have distinguished in the *Ring* tetralogy. He is supposedly a Germanic god; this is his role in *Walküre*, but he is bound by modern morality. As an extension of this idea, and an application of it in literary-critical terms, one could say that the ring is apparently cursed, and supposedly can accord Alberich power over Wotan, but the god is bound by modern morality from acting directly on his own behalf. Thus the *Ring* works on two levels, the real and the ideal, in a lopsided way, and to Wotan's detriment. Deryck Cooke comments on the irony of the brief meeting of Fricka and Brünnhilde at the entrance of the latter and the exit of the former, as Fricka refers to Wotan with one of the grandiose titles of the battle-god ("Heervater," MD 610).[27]

Furthermore, the very fact that Wotan has helped cause his own dramatic dilemma also seems strangely to indicate that he was created to fit this mythical cosmos. That the drama is internalized in Wotan means that his self-reflection is fatal. It effectively undoes everything he has previously attempted. In recapitulating the story, he destroys the work of art, exploding it from the inside out. In this monologue, reconstruction pivots into deconstruction. The monologue is the innermost limit of the hall of mirrors, or the smallest of the boxes within boxes. When Wotan deals with his own past, he deconstructs his own alleged identity and the entire *Ring* cycle, that is, his persona and the work in which he exists. The *Ring* presents an artistic myth, a phony cosmology, a false origin.

His outburst about having touched Alberich's ring, which he voices right before his lament over having to decree Siegmund's death, seems to indicate that he interprets the necessity of Siegmund's death as an effect of Alberich's curse. It is, of course, necessary because of the contradiction that he has created for himself, the paradoxical situation of willing a hero to be free to accomplish what Wotan wants him to, and of being guardian of the laws while breaking them all to keep his power. One could, for the sake of analysis, devise a scale for Wotan's transgressions and his acknowledgement of guilt. There is the belief that the ring will work his end (through Alberich and Hagen, with the ring being magic); that he touched the ring, and therefore the (magical) curse will not flee him; or, that it's his own fault for touching the ring and trying to keep his power through wrongdoings. This last possibility would imply a recognition that Wotan himself has done wrong, and that the curse on the ring is only a figural one.

Wotan's lament is phrased ambiguously enough, too. He exclaims, "Ich berührte Alberichs Ring,— / gierig hielt ich das Gold! / Der Fluch, den ich floh, / nicht flieht er nun mich" (MD 616). (I touched Alberich's ring—I greedily held the gold! The curse that I fled will not flee from me!) The monologue is thus ambiguous as regards what Wotan considers the curse to be—the real, magical curse, or the figural, symbolic, psychological one. The ambiguity of the monologue reflects the dual layers on which the *Ring* and its title object function. Wotan is confused, and understandably so. In discussing Hans Blumenberg's *Arbeit am Mythos*, Norbert Bolz calls narration "die Zauberkraft der sogenannten Geisteswissenschaften"[28] (the magical power of the humanities). Through introspection and narration, Wotan performs mythological suicide and transcends the doubly mythological work of art in which he exists.

I would extend and build upon Abbate's theory about the music of the monologue coming from Wotan. Not only does the music seem to be coming from Wotan, as Abbate has shown. It is as though Wotan had conjured up the outwardly mythological nature of the cosmos in which he exists. Myth is a kind of cyclical and fatalistic world-view. It implies forcing something that happened in the past into a world-view that is cyclical, recurrent. One sees reality or the present in relation to preconceived patterns. The mythological nature of the material somehow reflects Wotan's world-view, as does the musical repetition echo his state of mind. Wotan has, accordingly, made the ring and its curses regulatory for his life and therefore the course of the previous dramas.

Thus, not only has Wotan created the dramatic situation in which he finds himself. The entire drama is his story. He has, in other words, produced the tetralogy himself. Wotan, I would argue, has evidently conjured up the apparently mythical raw material. The conflict of the drama is, after all, internalized in him. The inner has become the outer. Thus it is his drama. It shows his perspective; it is written from his viewpoint. I have been arguing that he is the only one who doesn't know that it is only a performance. This is the nature of his decisive and nontragic recognition. The monologue shows how he has, indeed, caught himself in his own textual snares.

The mythological raw material also seems appropriate to his self-image. It represents a kind of wish-fulfillment. Wotan desperately wants to be immortal. His previous efforts to fend off the end of the gods show that this is what he has been striving for. He fathered the Valkyries to fortify Valhalla and thus to help him keep his power, in denial of the truth proclaimed to him by Erda. Wotan wishes he were a mythological figure, that is, a timeless and eternal being, but he is not; Wagner's *Ring* shows the gods suspended in a precarious way in some odd realm between history and myth. His psyche is evidently a historical, modern one. The mythological material is, in ways, at odds with the content. Wotan initially refuses to accept that his power, that in fact the world at large, is not eternal. Wotan evidently, and incorrectly, believes he is in a real myth, a work of genuine or one could say first-order mythology. Wotan, however, is merely a trace of what he is supposed to be and what he wants to be. When discussing Wotan's mono-logue, Carl Dahlhaus points out that the musical motives which express Wotan's inner state are appropriate to a situation in which a god is no god.[29]

Wotan's psychological and mythological defense mechanisms have evi-dently been working full strength until the second act of *Walküre*. Then they weaken, as he experiences self-doubt and anguish, and the Valkyrie must fail to carry Siegmund to Valhalla. However, through introspection, Wotan evades the curse entirely. The consciousness that Wotan achieves when he rises to the tragic dignity of willing his own destruction is an insight into his own fictionality. As in the reception of drama as Wagner describes it in *Oper und Drama*, the inner affects the outer decisively. With Wotan's change in self-image, the viability of the mythological universe of the *Ring* takes a turn for the worse and it starts to disassemble. When his historical psyche reflects on his mythological persona, the character split from which he is suffering becomes catastrophic to the world he has conjured up. Wotan's monologue is a mythological musical-dramatic "talking cure" of sorts. It frees him from his inner conflict in the most profound way.

In the last analysis, myth is really a state of mind, and when Wotan penetrates the falsity of the theater set around him, it virtually crumbles. Wagner apparently felt that myth was a state of mind. He reduces it to psychology in *Oper und Drama*, feeling that it can be used as a metaphor for history. In the *Ring*, though, the subjective has become objective. Wotan exists, though on a stage, in a fictional work. Myth, furthermore, is perspec-tival. The persona of Wotan in this work therefore greatly affects his world-outlook. As Wotan grows to a deeper understanding of the work of art in which he exists, he unworks his mythological world-view. As Wotan turns inward and the mythological cosmos nears its end, the work of art unravels. Wotan undoes and unworks the mythological music-drama in which he exists with reference to, according to, Wagner's own schema. Wotan's deconstruction, the destruction of the state, is an act of free self-de-termination, as he gradually frees himself from his own shackles.

In this monologue, Wotan shows a strange mixture of self-knowledge and deception, or introspection and self-delusion. He is a god, but he is confronted with a problem that is not typical for a divine and almighty being. Thus the confusion that Wotan shows, I would say, stems from the dual and modern nature of the mythological work in which he exists. It seems as though the contradiction between the mythological objects and the modern interpretation of them that he is starting to formulate in his more sophisticated reflection drives him to despair. He sees a mythical world around him. It is at least apparently mythical. He is trying to deal with it and accomplish what he sets out to, but somehow he is still at odds with his environment. The raw material surrounding him, though outwardly mythological, is nineteenth-century synthetic musical-dramatic myth.

Wotan is apparently suffering from ontological uncertainty. He seems uncertain just where he is, what kind of a being he is, or what he should do next. He is less a crafty politician or an almighty genuine Germanic god than the confused renegade whom John Tomlinson portrayed in the Harry Kupfer Bayreuth production, madly racing around the Bayreuth stage and whacking it with his Lucite spear in utter frustration, like a child throwing a temper tantrum. Wotan is perplexed, furious, and dejected, unsure of how to solve his dramatic dilemma, and uncertain what to do next. He is trying to be something or someone he is not. Psychologists would probably diagnose Wotan as suffering from the imposter syndrome. He is playing a role that he is not entirely suited for.

Because Wotan ascribes to a mythological world-view, he feels, and fears, that the curse on the ring can and will magically work the doom of the gods. This is why he has been trying to prevent Alberich from regaining it. The magical curse fits his mythological world-view. He lets the ring work the end of the gods, however, in another way than he expects; he wills the end because he thinks the ring will work the end of the gods. The model, Abbate says, is enactment followed by narration. I would reverse this—Wotan's narrative, I would argue, is also followed by enactment. He makes what I would consider to a large extent a self-fulfilling prophecy. Doing so, however, necessitates a hermeneutic sleight-of-hand that actually erases the curse completely. Erda and Alberich write the script; Wotan reinscribes it and in doing so learns how to follow it.

The work within which Wotan exists is, it is true, supposedly mythological. That is, it seems mythological, and it looks mythological. It is made out of raw material that was originally mythological. But this apparently, outwardly mythological nature of the *Ring* cosmos is deceptive. Wotan's existence is actually temporal; Erda has made this clear. Wotan's existence is really mortal, as much as he would like to deny this mortality and defy the end. Real gods are immortal. His wrath indicates how Wotan's own mortality infuriates him. Tibor Kneif remarks that the words of Erda that state that all will have an end some day are, paradoxically, proclaiming not a historical consciousness so much as a liberation from history.[30]

A work that is both a metaphor of history and a metaphor of itself as a metaphor for history will eventually and inevitably wring itself out of shape entirely, come apart at the seams, and split completely. Wotan's modern psychic reflection and thus his ensuing self-reflection, which this mono- logue under discussion represents, necessarily relativizes the mythological universe portrayed onstage and dematerializes, or, in literary-critical terms, deconstructs it. Similarly, Wagner's *Oper und Drama* implicitly demon- strates how myth, in the nineteenth century, is constantly relativized by history, and thus it becomes ungenuine and ironic. In post-structuralist terms, one could say that it represents an absence, rather than a presence.

The mythological cosmos of the *Ring* exists, in actuality, only "under erasure." It is necessary, but neither genuine nor present. Only in his absence is Wotan, as Dahlhaus points out, a god. His invisible presence is more powerful than his visible one.[31] Dahlhaus notes that the retrospectively oriented music in the tetralogy, the motives of reminiscence, are associated primarily with Wotan and his tragedy.[32] Dahlhaus comments on the para- dox that Wotan, who is a god but certainly not very divine in *Rheingold*, attains, through means of the music, mythic grandeur in *Götterdämmerung*, the drama in the tetralogy from which he is ostensibly absent.[33]

This duality of the *Ring* cosmos is exemplified by the ring and its curses. The ring, as a microcosm of the work as a whole—the central title object that holds the tetralogy together—exists accordingly on two levels: it is apparently a real magical mythological requisite, and it has metaphorical significance. The seemingly mythological requisite, then, can be seen as a real magical token, an objective entity, a literal mythological object, or a metaphorical thing, a subjective, figural token, just as language can be either literal or figural. As the ring is redefined, Wotan grows to an understanding of its symbolic significance and discards his mythical world-view. In doing so, he wills and works his own end. The two strands that I have distin- guished eventually converge. Dualities begin to cave into each other. Wotan follows Wagner by his method of mythological interpretation—but in- nertextual analysis proves dangerous. This reflexivity destroys the dra- matic form that Wagner has created. The work, by folding in upon itself, starts collapsing entirely.

By extension, then, the curse on the ring can be literal or figural, magical or metaphorical, depending on one's world-view. The curse on the ring, too—Alberich's "love-greeting"—can be interpreted as figural, like the "love-curse" of Antigone or the "love-sword" of Creon's son. When Wotan wills the end, this distinction between the literal and the figural is erased. Wotan not only creates a myth, he also unworks it. Wotan's desire for and fear of the ring clearly indicates that he sees this object as a mythical object. Furthermore, Wotan has felt, and still feels, that the ring is really, literally, cursed. But the curse on the ring is figural, a metaphor. It is as though, as if, it were cursed. In pronouncing the curse, one could say, Alberich tropes the ring. Wotan gradually comes to understand what metaphor is.

The struggle that forms the conflict of the *Ring* occurs between Wotan and Alberich. These two warring parties, however, are reflections of each other. Wotan, in his monologue, says that Alberich is working toward the end of the gods. But this is merely the opposition of the Light-Elves and the Dark-Elves, and thus not a strict dichotomy at all. Wotan, however, still apparently fears Alberich. To Wotan, the opposition is literal, whereas to the outside critic, it is merely metaphorical, for the parallel between the Light-Elves and the Dark-Elves shows that they are basically made of the same stuff.

Whether things in the drama, though, are real and/or metaphorical depends on the characters' perceptions of them. It is, in other words, perspectival, just as myth can exist on a superficial plane of significance or on the deepest metaphorical level. Wotan obviously sees his situation in opposition to Alberich. Wotan fortifies Valhalla via the Valkyries to defend it against a possible attack. Siegmund is there to prevent Alberich from regaining the ring. The magic of the ring is only useful to Alberich, who cursed love, and thus it would not work for Wotan anyway. The outwardly mythological appearance of the *Ring* cosmos is, however, a facade, a theater set. Wotan has been projecting, fighting his own shadow. Now he gives up and deconstructs his own dramatic significance and with it the surrounding drama also.

I would expand Abbate's theory that in his monologue Wotan hears the music he is singing to, and argue that hearing the music he is singing to and hearing the form his story has taken implies perceiving the formal structure of the work. This in turn means learning or knowing that one is in a fictional work, that is, achieving fictional self-consciousness. One could argue that consequently Wotan becomes aware of his own textuality. This is an experience that penetrates the two levels that I have discerned, and the spanning of which constitutes Romantic irony, that is, the fiction of or within the work, and the objective reality of the work of art as a work of art.

Furthermore, Wotan's understanding of the curse on the ring, I would propose, substantiates this idea, for in the course of the monologue this, I would point out, changes radically. In retelling the story and performing textual interpretation by summarizing the previous events of the tetralogy, Wotan rises above the drama and takes it apart from his vantage point of being both within the drama and somehow outside of it. In doing so, he reduces the ring to its symbolic significance, and he learns of the abstract, extended nature of Alberich's curse, thus gaining an insight into his own fictionality or intertextuality.

Wotan follows Wagner's lead as outlined in *Oper und Drama* by retelling a story. The layers of Wagner's theoretical text, however, converge in Wotan's mind. The story that the hypothetical Greek society has imposed upon the tragic hero merges with Wagner's anti-metaphysical unworking of this story. The curse that was portrayed as literal is merely figural; the mythical is actually metaphorical. The two interpretations clash in Wotan's mind to disastrous effect, just as the *Ring* depicts its own genesis and reception. The textual layers work against each other to have a general collision effect. After he has dematerialized the ring and by extension the work named after that object, he rejects the outward trappings of myth. Therefore, when Wotan performs the mythological reflection of *Oper und Drama* in the *Ring*, in demonstrating the reception of the work of art by rising above it and becoming the spectator, he somehow reverses the compositional processes that Wagner is justifying in the treatise.

As *Oper und Drama* reflects upon the process of creating myth and theorizes that music-drama should by its reception progress mankind forward to utopia by in some way reversing the course that history has previously taken, so does Wotan try to explain the world in which he exists, that is, the work of art, and in doing so destroys it by attaining fictional self-consciousness. Wotan thereby demonstrates the paradox of a work of art that portrays both history and itself as myth. The reflexivity of the work counteracts its fictionality. In his Romantically ironic scheme of mythological interpretation and revolutionary aesthetics of audience reception that Wagner outlines in *Oper und Drama*, he metaphorically draws a parallel between ontogeny and phylogeny. This mirroring, too, of the individual and the rest of the species is present in Wotan's monologue.

In willing his own destruction, Wotan brings the entire fictional world to ruin with him. Alberich had correctly warned him of the danger Wotan would incur if he stole the ring to pay for his castle. Wotan, however, interprets and thereby destroys the work of art as art, fulfilling in a very different way Alberich's prophecy that Wotan's theft of the ring will destroy the entire fictional cosmos. Alberich sized up Wotan well when he predicted that Wotan could not flee the curse. In *Rheingold*, the pronouncement seemed a magical curse that was totally in place in a mythological universe, but it all depends on how one interprets it. The prophecy comes true in a complex and nonmythological way. Its enunciation only has made it true; it is, though, really no more magical than the curse of the ring. Through innertextual hermeneutics, Wotan deconstructs the structure of significance that the *Ring* has evolved.

Wotan's monologue contains the essential paradox that Wotan fears the ring will allow Alberich to conquer the world and in that way work the end of the gods; and Wotan, furthermore, feels that this ring is not only magical in a conventional way, but that it is also cursed in such a way besides. Wotan expresses in his monologue that Alberich is working toward the end, that Alberich gained power with the ring, and that if he regains the ring Valhalla has lost the battle. Wotan, however, gives up and *wills* the end. For this reason, I feel that it is deconstructive. This monologue thus warrants more attention than it has been previously given. The self-recognition that Wotan apparently achieves in this monologue is that if he is bound by modern morality, tormented by modern psychology, and haunted by a ring that is symbolic of the evil of capitalism, he is not an almighty god presiding over a genuine mythological cosmos. Almost in revenge, it seems, he therefore destroys it.

Wotan tells Brünnhilde, in narrating his past to her, what happened between *Rheingold* and *Walküre*. He recalls,

Von dem Ende wollt ich / mehr noch wissen; / doch schweigend entschwand mir das Weib.— / Da verlor ich den leichten Mut, / zu wissen begehrt es den Gott: / in den Schoss der Welt / schwang ich mich hinab, / mit Liebeszauber / zwang ich die Wala, / stört ihres Wissens Stolz, / dass sie Rede nun mir stand. (MD 612–13)

I wanted to know more about the end of the gods, but the woman silently vanished. Then I lost my carefree courage, the god desired knowledge; into the depths of the earth I descended, conquered the Wala with the magic of love, and disturbed her pride, so that she would tell me more.

He wanted to know how the tetralogy will end. This is ironic. He eventually decides this himself.

In a sense, the ring does work the doom of the gods, but in another way, Wotan's proclamation of the end of the gods somehow negates the ring as an instrument of doom. The ring that works the doom of the gods is actually a stage prop and nothing else, and Wotan reveals it as such. Wotan actually wills the end of the gods, which he has envisioned as being worked by the ring in the sense that the ring will directly cause it by having some supernatural magical properties. He proves himself wrong, however, and causes the end himself. Wotan's declaration of the end of the gods is therefore truly a paradoxical moment. By willing the end himself, Wotan obviates the interpretative distinction between the literal and the figural curse, for he essentially negates the ring as an instrument of doom, transcends his dilemma completely, and takes fate into his own hands, as he now assumes control of his dramatic situation.

The end of the gods, which was inevitable from the start, is actually a self-fulfilling prophecy insofar as Wotan wills it. Thus he creates his fate himself. He even helps make it happen by refusing to eat Freia's apples and having the World Ash Tree hewn and placed around Valhalla, which (indirectly) causes Brünnhilde and Loge to ignite the castle along with Siegfried's funeral pyre. In different ways, the curse is, one could say, both fulfilled and negated by the end. A further paradox resides in the fact that by renouncing his power he affirms the laws that reinforce his rule, the system that he should be upholding.

One may debate whether at this point in the drama Wotan feels the ring is literally cursed, or if he has an insight into the metaphoricity of the curse. But this is, due to his declaration of willing the end of the gods, irrelevant. It no longer matters. If he submits to what he sees as the literal curse, he erases it in doing so. Willing the end negates the mythological nature of the fictional world. It reduces the ring to its purely metaphorical significance. Because Wotan wills the end, the curse of the ring is thus not mythological;—it has a merely metaphorical curse. In other words, no magical curse works the end of the gods.

If Wotan ever once felt that the ring was literally cursed, he effectively nullifies the curse by willing the end. The curse is thereby reduced to a recognition of its metaphorical significance, the vice of avarice, the curse of greed for gold. The literal is thus reduced to the figural. Furthermore, in submitting to what he feels is the literal curse on the ring (in a Schillerian way), Wotan would be in some way saying that it is only a figurative curse, for he wills his own end, and thus the (real) curse does not really work the end of the gods. The end is inevitable, and it has been from the beginning. Paradoxically, the curse destroys the gods when it no longer exists.

Moreover, this would further imply that Wotan has gained an insight into the metaphorical curse, which would also mean that in renouncing his power, he negates the curse. He atones and reforms by willing the end. Paradoxically, in taking the curse upon himself and willing his own destruction, he negates the curse, conquering it internally (psychologically) and externally (via Brünnhilde, who mirrors and is a part of himself). The ring, one could say, is now no longer cursed at all. The curse has been eliminated, in post-structuralist terminology erased, by Wotan's act of self-destruction. Because he wills the end, that is, he recognizes that he has done wrong and the end of the gods is a necessity, he is reducing the ring to its metaphorical significance. This further implies that he has gained an insight into the false modern fictionality of this quasi-mythological cosmos. In other words, he now indicates that he realizes that he himself has been at fault. This implies that he finally understands the figural level of the *Ring* tetralogy.

In willing his own (physical) end, I would therefore argue, instead of fighting a literal curse, Wotan assumes the metaphorical curse. Therefore in an indirect way, Wotan is expressing that he understands the metaphoricity of the entire quasi-mythological work in which he exists. He has become fully conscious of his own textuality. In relinquishing the world to the unborn son of Alberich and willing the end, Wotan is showing a tacit recognition that in a very different way he himself has cursed the ring all along, and that the literal curse never really existed as such. Thus in Wotan's monologue, the textual levels of the ring and the *Ring* collapse into each other, which means, in turn, the total collapse of the system of signification that is held together by this ring. He is delving down in some way to the figural level of the work. This entails, however, a recognition and a rejection of the falsity of the literal level of the *Ring*.

The *Ring* thus, because in it Wagner has reconstituted myth, also inevitably destroys myth. The textual layers converge in and on Wotan. As Wotan comes undone, so, too, does the modern mythological structure of signification of the text in which he exists. In coming to understand Alberich's curse, and making stories (metaphors, myths), Wotan, I will argue, "deconstructs" or undoes myth, going from myth to history, like reading Novalis' *Heinrich von Ofterdingen* backwards. Ensuing events move the work to the human plane of action. Brünnhilde is robbed of her immortality in the third act of *Walküre*. The Gibichungs represent the human world in *Götterdämmerung*. Myth self-destructs with Wotan.

One can see Wagner's *Ring* as an inverted myth, an anti-myth, a "myth" in some kind of negative or paradoxical sense. It is almost as though Roland Barthes were commenting on the *Ring* when he writes in *Mythologies*, "Truth to tell, the best weapon against myth is perhaps to mythify it in its turn, and to produce an *artificial myth*: and this reconstituted myth will in fact be a mythology."[34] Hermeneutics engenders cosmic crises when meaning violates the raw material that is used to convey it and the drama turns itself inside out. The mythological content that defines the form of tragedy for Wagner is in Wotan's monologue undermined by the content that it must portray. The literal and the figural converge. The work subsequently falls apart. Wotan's dilemma is truly unsolvable in any viable way. At the end of the tetralogy, the work has dismantled its rhetorical structure. Ironically, the figural curse is the real one, and the literal one is just a figment of Wotan's imagination.

One might even suspect that it is to keep up his divine pose, and smoothly fit his deconstruction into the *Ring* as a whole, that Wotan interpretatively echoes the words of Erda and assures Brünnhilde, "Jetzt versteh ich / den stummen Sinn / des wilden Wortes der Wala" (MD 616) (Now I understand the mute sense of the strange words of the Wala), and then repeats Erda's prophecy that when the foe of love begets a son, the end of the gods is near. Wotan evidently still fears Alberich and Hagen. He fulfills this forecast, too. It is, however, ambiguous. It later proves true, but not in the way in which Wotan expects. Hagen's murder of Siegfried gives Brünnhilde a redemptive insight, and causes her to burn Valhalla and thus "redeem" Wotan. Perhaps, though, Wotan previously interpreted Erda's words about Hagen literally, and now he understands the "mute" (that is, hidden or extended) sense.

When he sings, "Das Ende" (the end), as Abbate notes, the music stops and Wotan puts an end to the cycle of repetition. In arguing that the form of his narrative, the cyclic musical substance that mirrors the successive repetitions of a basic myth, the renunciation of love for power, has compelled Wotan to abandon Siegmund, that is, to perform this same renunciation again, Abbate overlooks the fact that the love/power dichotomy is here collapsed. This paradox is inherent in the fact that he must perform a last repetition to put an end to the cycle of repetitions. Wotan can't win. His existence as the Wanderer is a kind of living death. After Wotan sings "Das Ende," the music stops, as Abbate observes—but then, I would add, it continues. Wotan's mythological essence is basically an absence, and not a presence. When Wotan refers to himself as a god in the third act of *Siegfried*, Erda reminds him that he is not what he likes to call himself.

In renouncing his power, as he does in this monologue, Wotan, like Derrida, deconstructs metaphysics. He becomes the Wanderer in the next drama, thus having lost some of his divinity, and except in modern productions he is not in the stage action of *Götterdämmerung*. In fact, during *Götterdämmerung* he has even withdrawn from the offstage action as well, as Waltraute reports to Brünnhilde. As Wotan gradually withdraws from the external action of the tetralogy, he turns inward and undergoes internal self-recognition. Wotan bores the "love-sword" into his own heart through his tragic self-recognition, for in his various roles, these various sides of his character, he is a composite of Wagner's interpretations or versions of Antigone, Creon, and Oedipus.

In his monologue, Wotan experiences the self-recognition that the protagonist and audience of the art-work of the future should. Insight into the metaphorical nature of the work of art, which Wotan has gained by reflecting upon the curse on the ring and the previous course of the drama, implies a recognition of his own false, derivative, synthetic and modern nature. In the course of Wotan's monologue, consciousness gradually becomes self-consciousness, just as Wagner, in *Oper und Drama*, wrote that the spectator of a work of art should experience self-recognition. Wotan experiences his own drama, as though from the outside.

The incestuous mirroring of the Volsungs which has brought Wotan to despair is fatally repeated, mirrored to catastrophic results, in Wotan's self-mirroring. When the chief god sees his own image, disaster follows. Wotan laments, "Zum Ekel find ich / ewig nur mich / in Allem, was ich erwirke" (MD 615). (To my disgust I find only myself in everything that I do.) He incessantly sees himself as though in a mirror. The fact that he uses a mirror-image to describe his experience is no accident. Furthermore, this decisive instance of mirroring, this crucial instance of Romantic irony, collapses the mythological nature of the work and thus of the world portrayed therein.

When Wotan experiences self-recognition, he acquires fictional self-consciousness, an awareness of his own false mythological essence. Now he knows the truth about himself. Thus self-recognition for Wotan is a Romantically ironic realization that he has a nineteenth-century psyche in mythological costume. For this reason, I would argue that in his monologue, in realizing that he must give up on the ring, he gains an insight into his own modern textuality. Wotan realizes he is, according to the theory presented in *Oper und Drama*, a Feuerbachian projection of himself. His "mythological" nature must be qualified, put, so to speak, under erasure. Thus self-knowledge entails, for Wotan, self-destruction.

Wotan despairs of his own textuality, and in particular his specific textuality, that is, his modern mythological intertextuality. In *Walküre*, Wotan appears in the persona of Odin, the battle-god. Insight into the metaphorical nature of the curse on the ring and thus the fictional work of art in which he finds himself undermines basic presuppositions for his viable corporeal existence in this false quasi-mythological work of art, this modern and phony mythical universe. Wotan is, in *Walküre*, by definition a god, that is, mythological. That is why, as a result of this self-recognition, he must will his own destruction.

Renouncing his power not only declares the end of the world. It also seals the end of the work of art. Wotan's declaration of the end is thus a reduction, as it refers to both the world depicted within the fiction and the fictional work of art itself. It still fits the fictional persona and blends into the surrounding story, but it also spans the two levels that qualify it as an instance of Romantic irony. Calling for the end of the gods not only ends the cosmos portrayed in the *Ring*. It also destroys the fictional mythological stage-world of the *Ring*. In this manner, when he declares the end of the world, Wotan actually destroys the mythological sets, for he has effectively rejected and negated the literal mythological setting of the *Ring* tetralogy. The metaphoricity of the ring and Alberich's curse obviates and excludes the legitimacy of the mythological world portrayed. Paradoxically, when Wotan gives up on trying to regain the ring from Alberich, he passively accomplishes the destruction of the fictional universe.

When he sends the world around him to ruins, Wotan actually rejects the theater sets of the *Ring*. When he declares the end, then, he is expressing that he doesn't want to be in the *Ring* any more. He doesn't want to finish the performance or even to participate in this drama any more. He just wants it to end. He has already, after all, dematerialized the ring and the curse. Thus he essentially rips down the surrounding sets and makes a grandiose exit. This is his most graceful and painless way out. The modernity, the Romantic irony, of the work destroys him, and he calls for an end not only to the fictional cosmos, but also to the work of art in which he exists.

In fact, declaring the end of the fictional world and the work of art is a necessary result of Wotan's dematerialization of Alberich's ring and curse. Insight into the metaphoricity of the ring and thus by extension the fictional world precludes a belief in the authenticity of Wotan's mythological surroundings. In willing his own destruction, therefore, Wotan is virtually destroying the outwardly mythological raw material. One could say he is deconstructing the work of art via its mythological nature. In reducing the ring and thus the *Ring* to its figural significance, he veritably destroys the literal level of signification. When he wills the end, he actually pronounces a redundancy.

In a sudden change of mind from agony to despair, as the stage direction notes, Wotan decides to call for the end.[35] He exclaims,

Fahre denn hin, / herrische Pracht, / göttlichen Prunkes / prahlende Schmach! / Zusammen breche, / was ich gebaut ! / Auf geb ich mein Werk: / nur Eines will ich noch: / das Ende— / das Ende!— (MD 616)

Be gone, lordly pomp, the boasting and shameful divine majesty! May all that I have built crumble to pieces! I give up on my creation: I only want one thing more—the end! The end!

This can be understood on two levels; the level of the drama, or the level of the fictionality of the drama. Wotan has created his own drama in various ways. He conquered and tamed the fictional world and he wrote the drama as part of Wagner. The pomp that he refers to in the line I just cited seems to refer to Wotan's godly splendor in this fictional universe (which is not really so divine at all), but it can also be taken to mean the grand theater sets as well. It is therefore a reduction. He won't play this role any more. It's false even in its fictionality. The end that he is referring to is the end of the fictional cosmos as well as the final curtain of the performance in which he is participating.

At the end of the monologue, Wotan literally storms off; the stage direction reads, "Er stürmt fort" (MD 618). The sound effects usually include thunder, and the lighting panel makes lightning strike. He leaves Brünnhilde to improvise and make the anticlimactic comment, "So sah ich Siegvater nie, / erzürnt ihn sonst wohl auch ein Zank" (MD 618). (I never saw Victory Father so upset, even though he is sometimes angered by a quarrel.) He storms off the stage (like a singer who has lost his voice and has decided to leave the stage) in divine fury ranting all kinds of threats and telling Brünnhilde (who is left to improvise in order to save the performance) that his wrath can ruin the world, but this is merely a pose. He has essentially ruined the fictional universe already. Furthermore, and as is appropriate, this final renunciation of love for the sake of law corresponds to the loss of his power.

The facade cracks and Wotan cracks up in the third act, when the god becomes a father, when Wotan "breaks character." When he yields to Brünnhilde's plea to surround the cliff where she shall sleep with fire and sings Wotan's Farewell, Wotan's persona changes from the stern god to the loving father. Similarly, in the announcement of death scene in *Walküre*, Brünnhilde tries to play the role assigned to her by Wotan and say her lines, but she can't. These two events interlock to determine the end of the tetralogy, which transcends tragedy, redeems Wotan, and glorifies Brünnhilde. When Wotan "breaks character," he delegates his lead role to Brünnhilde. This is the (figural) destruction of the state that Wagner writes of in *Oper und Drama*, for in this scene, the god becomes a father. In the treatise, Wagner illustrates it with a metaphor, that is, by interpreting the myth of Oedipus. History will be reversed in and by music-drama. The work of art that Wagner sketches in *Oper und Drama* comes apart. The finale of *Götterdämmerung* might seem to be the destruction of the state, but it really isn't. Rainer Franke, for instance, writes that Brünnhilde destroys the state when she throws the firebrand into Valhalla.[36]

In *Oper und Drama*, however, Wagner illustrates the destruction of the state in a myth, that is, a text within a text, and a nonrealistic one at that. It is a figural destruction of the state (by Antigone's "love-curse" making the ruler become a father). If Wagner's *Ring* is not realistic, and it does not portray a real "state," then the destruction of the "state" doesn't have to be a real debacle. The destruction of the state is the yielding of lovelessness to love. Deryck Cooke comments upon how George Bernard Shaw's political interpretation of the *Ring* is useless to explain the third act of *Walküre*, the action of which has moved onto an entirely different plane from the political one. This scene between Wotan and Brünnhilde portrays not a political allegory, but, rather, a father and a daughter, an emotional confrontation between two individuals.[37] Elsewhere in Wagner's dramas, too, one can find a similar phenomenon of an implicit "play within a play" structure breaking down.[38]

In the *Ring*, the "Charaktertragödie" (tragedy of character) overpowers the "Schicksalstragödie" (tragedy of fate), thus conquering the very form of tragedy itself. As the Wanderer, in the riddle game in *Siegfried*, Wotan shows increased self-consciousness. He even makes explicit the parallel between the "Light-Elves" ("Lichtalben"), the head of which is Wotan or "Light-Alberich" ("Licht-Alberich"), and the "Dark-Elves" ("Schwarzalben"), foremost of whom is "Dark-Alberich" ("Schwarz-Alberich") (MD 675–76). He has experienced self-recognition in his monologue. His existence as the Wanderer in *Siegfried* is the outward depiction of his precarious role as actor and spectator, author and audience, which he lamented in his monologue (that is, not being able to regain the stolen magic ring himself). He says to Alberich, "Zu schauen kam ich, / nicht zu schaffen" (MD 693). (I have come to watch, not to act.) This is actually a description of his role as the Wanderer.

He does not even want the ring any more, as he explains to Alberich before Fafner's lair. He will not play that game any more. Alberich, Mime, and Wotan are all at one time or another audience members in the second act of *Siegfried*, assembling to watch Siegfried slay Fafner. Furthermore, the Wanderer speaks of Wotan in the third person. The self is split; the character has two personas. Wotan realizes he is a reflection of Alberich. They relate to each other as a positive to a negative. Moreover, here Wotan himself explicates the structure of the mythological universe of the work of art in which he exists. He no longer needs Loge to traverse the universe and report back to him on it. He has penetrated the textual structure himself.

Wotan's conversation with Erda in the third act of *Siegfried* also shows him somehow changed. In a last desperate attempt to forestall the end, Wotan asks how to stop a wheel that is rolling downhill. But he also asks,

"Wie besiegt die Sorge der Gott?" (MD 720). (How does a god conquer Care?) Real gods should not have cares like this; Erda knows that. He tells Erda, perhaps without total veracity, "Um der Götter Ende / grämt mich die Angst nicht, / seit mein Wunsch es will" (MD 720). (I do not fret about the end of the gods, since I have willed it.) However, in this scene Wotan does show a new inwardness and is quick to realize the folly of his continued efforts to avert the end. He comments on his *Walküre* monologue, after summarizing the events of the previous drama, now leaving his inheritance not to the Nibelung, but rather to the Volsung. He seems to be consciously connecting the present scene with previous ones. He resigns now because of an inner necessity to yield to "dem ewig Jungen" (MD 721) (the eternally young).

Wotan lapses into his former role when he runs to Erda to ask her how to stop the wheel that is rolling downhill, but this doesn't last long. Now he knows that it is only a game. In a role reversal, Wotan tells Erda the future. He knows that Brünnhilde, after she is awakened by Siegfried, will redeem the world. Wotan says to Erda, speaking of Siegfried, "Liebesfroh, / ledig des Neides / erlahmt an dem Edlen / Alberichs Fluch: / denn fremd bleibt ihm die Furcht" (MD 720). (Joyfully in love, without envy, against the noble Siegfried the curse of Alberich weakens, for he does not know what fear is.) Now Wotan knows all about the subtlety and intricacies of the curse on the ring. The Wanderer's music is serene, as though he were transfigured.

Furthermore, Wotan no longer takes Erda seriously. He knows that Erda's statement that all things will end includes herself, too. He destroys her pose of being the "Urwala" and immortal. When Erda tells him that he is no god, he answers, in similar fashion, "Du bist nicht, / was du dich wähnst! / Urmütter-Weisheit / geht zu Ende: / dein Wissen verweht / vor meinem Willen" (MD 720). (You are not what you think you are! Eternal Wisdom is ending; your Wisdom will scatter before my will.) Wotan is now in control of things; he does not let Erda and Alberich pull his strings and control him any more. In commanding her to go back to her slumber, Wotan banishes Erda to the role of audience: "träumend erschau' mein Ende!" (MD 721) (while you dream, watch my end). Erda will be the spectator of the finale. It is Wotan's drama to the very end.

Blocking Siegfried's way to Brünnhilde is, in a way, suicidal. Wagner wrote in his letter to Röckel that Wotan, wanting to be conquered, stands in Siegfried's path out of jealousy for Brünnhilde. In his letter to Röckel from which I cited earlier, Wagner writes,

In solcher Gestalt—musst Du zugestehen—ist uns Wodan höchst interessant, wogegen er uns unwürdig erscheinen müsste als subtiler Intrigant, denn das wäre er, wenn er Ratschläge gäbe, die *scheinbar* gegen Siegfried, in Wahrheit aber für ihn, und namentlich für sich gelten: das wäre ein Betrug, würdig unsrer politischen Helden, nicht aber meines untergangsbedürftigen jovialen Gottes. Sieh, wie er dem

Siegfried im dritten Acte gegenüber steht! Er ist hier vor seinem Untergange so unwillkürlicher Mensch endlich, dass sich—gegen seine höchste Absicht—noch einmal der alte Stolz rührt, und zwar (wohlgemerkt!) aufgereizt durch—Eifersucht um Brünnhilde; denn diese ist sein empfindlichster Fleck geworden. Er will sich gleichsam nicht nur so bei Seite schieben lassen, sondern fallen—besiegt werden.[39]

Thus is Wotan very interesting to us, whereas he would not be worthy of our attention if he appeared as a subtle deceiver who gave advice that was apparently against Siegfried but really for him and therefore for himself too; that would be a deception worthy of our political heroes, but not my god who is happily nearing his end. See, how Wotan stands in Siegfried's way in the third act! He is here, before his demise, finally an instinctive human being, so that—against his intentions—the old pride acts up, and, significantly enough, kindled by rivalry for Brünnhilde, for this has become his weak spot. He doesn't want to be shoved aside, but rather be conquered and fall.

Wagner obviously would not have approved of interpreting Wotan as a "political god." Furthermore, Wotan is fully human in this scene. He acts spontaneously out of human weaknesses and inner feelings. The god has already become a father. Wotan is totally demythologized. He needs only to go to his dressing room after this scene, take off his costume, change into his street clothes, and leave the theater after his final curtain call.

Deryck Cooke speaks of a supersession of Erda by Wotan.[40] In *Siegfried*, he points out, Erda cannot tell Wotan what the destiny of the world is. Wagner, Cooke argues, from his revolutionary standpoint, did not regard the wisdom bound up with a knowledge of human fate as absolute and insurmountable. Fate is to be overcome, and so Wotan's final knowledge is, Cooke explains, a great and final step forward on Erda's. The Norns weave "im Zwange der Welt" (MD 718) (in thrall to the world). Their weaving ends when the youngest Norn can no longer see the future; the destiny of Wotan and the world is in the process of passing beyond the limits of fate altogether. In the third act of *Siegfried*, Wotan says to Erda,

Urwissend / Stachest du einst / der Sorge Stachel / in Wotans wagendes Herz: / mit Furcht vor schmachvoll / feindlichem Ende / füllt ihn dein Wissen, / dass Bangen band seinen Mut. (MD 719–20)

Primevally wise you once pricked Wotan's heart with the thorn of care: your wisdom filled him with fear of the humiliating and hostile end, so that dread possessed his spirit.

Now he gives up "froh und freudig" (MD 720) (happily). He has accepted his paradigmatic artistic nature.

In *Götterdämmerung* there is no self-interest on the part of Wotan. He speaks not of regaining the ring from Alberich to avert the end of the gods, but of throwing the ring back into the Rhine. Waltraute quotes him, "Des tiefen Rheines Töchtern / gäbe den Ring sie wieder zurück,— / von des Fluches Last / erlöst wär Gott und die Welt!" (MD 773). (If she would give the ring back to the daughters of the Rhine, the gods and the world would be redeemed from the burden of the curse.) Considering his refusal to eat Freia's apples, and the fact that the World Ash Tree is piled up around Valhalla and ready to be ignited, he can only be speaking of the internal workings or meanings of the curse when he uses the term "Fluch" (curse). Perhaps Waltraute misinterprets his musings.

Furthermore, in *Götterdämmerung*, Waltraute reports about Wotan, "So sitzt er, / sagt kein Wort, / auf hehrem Sitze / stumm und ernst, / des Speeres Splitter / fest in der Faust" (MD 773). (There he sits, and he does not say a word, on his lofty throne, mute and solemn, the pieces of his spear clutched in his hand.) Wotan is obviously suffering from a musical-dramatic kind of aphasia, and it seems totally appropriate that, following his herme- neutic breakdown, he would experience a pathological inability to commu- nicate. Evidently he is now totally at odds with the formal structure of the *Ring* tetralogy. Now he not only refuses to exist in it (that is, onstage) any more. He will not allow his thoughts to even be quoted in the *Ring*.

Wagner wrote, in his letter to Röckel from which I cited earlier, that the curse would be lifted when the ring is returned to the Rhine. This too, however, is open to the various interpretations that I have proposed for the curse. Wagner writes, "Auch diess lernt Wodan erst ganz am Schlusse, am letzten Ziele seiner tragischen Laufbahn erkennen."[41] (Wotan learns this only at the end, at the conclusion of his tragic career.) Wagner's use of terminology is again very telling. Wotan's career as a god is, according to Wagner, "tragic." He fully comprehends the necessity of returning the ring to the Rhine in order to negate the curse only at the end; and Wagner points out that Loge and Erda did tell him this earlier.

Similarly, "erlösen" (redeem) has other connotations rather than causing a "happy end." Wagner wrote, in his letter to Röckel, that redemption resides, as Wotan finally learns, in returning the ring to the Rhine. Wotan wants to die reconciled and absolved. In her diaries (19 February 1878), Cosima cites her husband as identifying Titurel with Wotan. He explained,

In der Weltentsagenheit wird ihm die Erlösung zu Teil, ihm wird das höchste Gut anvertraut, und nun hütet er es kriegerisch göttlich. (CT III, 47–48)

After his renunciation of the world he is granted salvation, the greatest of posses- sions is entrusted to his care, and now he is guarding it like a mortal god. (D II, 29)

Wotan is redeemed by renouncing his power and willing his own end. Waltraute's words, "erlöst wär Gott und die Welt" (the gods and the world would be redeemed), are accompanied by the same undulating music as Brünnhilde's words in the Immolation Scene, "Ruhe, ruhe, du Gott!" (MD 813). (Rest, O god.)

Along with the scenery, the various layers—the real and the ideal, the subjective and the objective—collapse at the end of the cycle. Paradoxically, when Wotan feels the ring is really cursed, it works the figural end of the "state" (*Walküre*, Act III), whereas when Wotan feels the ring is figuratively cursed, the literal end of the gods happens. Brünnhilde resists metaphor. She denies, or at least seems oblivious to, the metaphorical significance of the ring previously established by Alberich's curses. Brünnhilde makes the figural into something literal, the abstract into something concrete. She cleanses the ring of its significance.

In the Immolation Scene at the finale of *Götterdämmerung*, the ring is purged of its metaphoricity. Significantly, it is destroyed in the process. It no longer signifies. It becomes pure Rhinegold again. Its curses are erased. As the ring is the microcosm that symbolizes the tetralogy as a whole, the work of art at that point ends. The silence that comes at the end of the tetralogy, after the final notes sound, designates the destruction of musical and sung language, and the meaninglessness of nonarticulation. The destruction of the title object corresponds with the final pages of Wagner's score. The two levels that I have previously distinguished, the real and the ideal, existence and meaning, converge. Metaphor becomes catachresis. The figural becomes literal (within the work of art, that is). Form equals content again. And, paradoxically and appropriately, the content no longer exists, as the work is ending.

The destruction of the state of which Wagner writes in his explication of the Oedipus myth in *Oper und Drama*, which occurs at the end of *Walküre* (because it is figural, psychological, inner), needs to be reflected by the end of *Götterdämmerung* as a foreshadowing of the physical destruction of the state that the experience of the drama and process of coming to consciousness can cause. The end of the tetralogy is, Dieter Borchmeyer argues, a restitution of the "mythical" state of nature represented by the musical "redemption motive" ("Erlösungsmotiv").[42] Paradoxically (and appropriately), this corresponds to the end of the work of art. The work unravels; *Oper und Drama* is undone.

Romantic irony, as both Wagner and modern directors have realized, can have societal and political reverberations. For Wagner, in fact, the inner and the outer necessarily entail each other. The past mythicization of history performed by Wagner in writing the *Ring* is mirrored by the future historicization of myth that the performance of the tetralogy will cause. Art both reflects and foreshadows life. At the end of *Götterdämmerung*, the dramas open from myth onto history (which will, or at least, Wagner felt, should be mythicized), and the anticipated future is rehearsed.

NOTES

1. Peter Wapnewski, "Gedanken zu Richard Wagner hundert Jahre nach seinem Tode," *"Die Meistersinger von Nürnberg": Programmhefte der Bayreuther Festspiele* (1983), pp. 2–17.

2. Michael Ewans, *Wagner and Aeschylus: The "Ring" and the "Oresteia"* (New York: Cambridge University Press, 1982), p. 243.

3. Martin Gregor-Dellin, *Richard Wagner: Sein Leben, Sein Werk, Sein Jahrhundert* (Munich: Piper, 1980), p. 361.

4. See: Rainer Franke, *Richard Wagners Zürcher Kunstschriften: Politische und ästhetische Entwürfe auf seinem Weg zum "Ring des Nibelungen"*, Hamburger Beiträge zur Musikwissenschaft, vol. 26 (Hamburg: Verlag der Musikalienhandlung Karl Dieter Wagner, 1983), pp. 303–12.

5. See: Carolyn Abbate, *Unsung Voices: Opera and Musical Narrative in the Nineteenth Century* (Princeton, NJ: Princeton University Press, 1991), chapter 6, "Brünnhilde Walks by Night," pp. 206–49.

6. Carl Dahlhaus, *Richard Wagners Musikdramen* (Velber: Friedrich, 1971), pp. 133–34.

7. Deryck Cooke, *I Saw the World End: A Study of Wagner's "Ring"* (London: Oxford University Press, 1979), pp. 332–33.

8. Dahlhaus, *Richard Wagners Musikdramen*, pp. 83–107; "Über den Schluss der *Götterdämmerung*," in *Richard Wagner: Werk und Wirkung*, ed. Carl Dahlhaus, Studien zur Musikgeschichte des 19. Jahrhunderts, vol. 26 (Regensburg: Gustav Bosse, 1971), pp. 97–115.

9. Richard Wagner, *Mein Leben*, ed. Martin Gregor-Dellin (Munich: Paul List, 1963; Goldmann, 1983), p. 478.

10. Martin Geck, "Wagners 'Ring'—Summe einer Lebensphilosophie," in *Bayreuther Dramaturgie. "Der Ring des Nibelungen"*, ed. Herbert Barth (Stuttgart: Belser, 1980), pp. 309–26; Hans Mayer, "Zerstörung und Selbstzerstörung im 'Ring des Nibelungen,'" in *Anmerkungen zu Richard Wagner*, Edition Suhrkamp 189 (Frankfurt am Main: Suhrkamp, 1966; 2d ed., 1977), pp. 91–99.

11. Martin Gregor-Dellin, *Richard Wagner: Sein Leben, Sein Werk, Sein Jahrhundert*, pp. 360–69. All subsequent references to Gregor-Dellin in this chapter will be to this discussion of the *Ring*.

12. Dahlhaus, *Richard Wagners Musikdramen*, p. 102; "Über den Schluss der *Götterdämmerung*," p. 110.

13. Dieter Borchmeyer, *Das Theater Richard Wagners: Idee, Dichtung, Wirkung* (Stuttgart: Reclam, 1982), pp. 243–44.

14. Franke, pp. 279–80.

15. Dahlhaus, *Richard Wagners Musikdramen*, p. 118.

16. See: Cooke, *I Saw the World End*, pp. 323–26.

17. *Unsung Voices*, chapter 5, "Wotan's Monologue and the Morality of Musical Narration," pp. 156–205. Subsequent references to Abbate in this chapter will be to her chapter on Wotan's monologue.

18. Letter to August Röckel of 25/26 January 1854. Richard Wagner, *Sämtliche Briefe*, vol. 6, *Januar 1854–Februar 1855*, ed. Hans-Joachim Bauer and Johannes Forner (Leipzig: VEB Deutscher Verlag für Musik, 1986), pp. 59–76 (here cited from p. 69).

19. Dahlhaus, *Richard Wagners Musikdramen*, pp. 119–21.

20. Dahlhaus, *Richard Wagners Musikdramen*, p. 111; Herbert Schnädelbach, " 'Ring' und Mythos," in *In den Trümmern der eignen Welt: Richard Wagners "Der Ring des Nibelungen"*, ed. Udo Bermbach, Hamburger Beiträge zur öffentlichen Wissenschaft, vol. 7 (Berlin: Dietrich Reimer, 1989), pp. 145–61 (here cited from pp. 158–59). See also: Kurt Hübner, *Die Wahrheit des Mythos* (Munich: C.H. Beck, 1985). Hübner's chapter on Wagner (pp. 386–402) is entitled "Richard Wagners Mythos vom Untergang des Mythos."

21. See: Cooke, pp. 277–81.

22. Cooke, pp. 316–17.

23. Peter Wapnewski, "Die Oper Richard Wagners als Dichtung," in *Richard-Wagner-Handbuch*, ed. Ulrich Müller and Peter Wapnewski (Stuttgart: Alfred Kröner, 1986), pp. 223–352 (here cited from p. 286).

24. Wapnewski, "Die Oper Richard Wagners als Dichtung," p. 288.

25. See: Cooke, pp. 313–16.

26. Cooke, p. 327.

27. Cooke, p. 327.

28. Norbert Bolz, "Entzauberung der Welt und Dialektik der Aufklärung," in *Macht des Mythos—Ohnmacht der Vernunft?*, ed. Peter Kemper (Frankfurt am Main: Fischer, 1989), pp. 223–41 (here cited from p. 236).

29. Dahlhaus, *Richard Wagners Musikdramen*, p. 121.

30. Tibor Kneif, "Wagner: eine Rekapitulation. Mythos und Geschichte im *Ring des Nibelungen*," in *Das Drama Richard Wagners als musikalisches Kunstwerk*, ed. Carl Dahlhaus, Studien zur Musikgeschichte des 19. Jahrhunderts, vol. 23 (Regensburg: Gustav Bosse, 1970), pp. 213–21 (here cited from p. 215).

31. Dahlhaus, *Wagners Konzeption des musikalischen Dramas*, p. 105.

32. Dahlhaus, *Wagners Konzeption des musikalischen Dramas*, p. 43.

33. Dahlhaus, *Wagners Konzeption des musikalischen Dramas*, p. 43.

34. Roland Barthes, *Mythologies*, trans. Annette Lavers (New York: Hill and Wang, 1972), p. 135.

35. The stage direction reads, "Wotans Gebärde geht aus dem Ausdruck des furchtbarsten Schmerzes zu dem der Verzweiflung über" (MD 616).

36. Franke, p. 310.

37. Cooke, pp. 25, 353.

38. My book on this subject is forthcoming, in which the concepts of Romantic irony and deconstruction are applied, as they are to the *Ring* in this book, to the other six Wagner dramas from *Holländer* to *Parsifal*. See: *Modern Myths and Wagnerian Deconstructions: Literary-Critical Approaches to Wagner's Music-Dramas*, forthcoming from Greenwood Press.

39. *Sämtliche Briefe*, vol. 6, p. 69.

40. Cooke, pp. 230–32.

41. *Sämtliche Briefe*, vol. 6, p. 68.

42. Dieter Borchmeyer, "Vom Anfang und Ende der Geschichte," in *Macht des Mythos—Ohnmacht der Vernunft?*, ed. Peter Kemper (Frankfurt am Main: Fischer, 1989), pp. 176–200 (here cited from p. 190); Hübner, p. 389. Hübner writes (p. 389), about this motive, "Dieses Motiv ist die Verheissung einer kommenden Welt, eines mythischen goldenen Zeitalters, wo der Einklang von Mensch, Natur und Göttern wiederhergestellt ist."

Conclusions: Wagnerian Deconstruction?

*N*o single extratextual system, be it political or psychological, the two extremes that I have chosen to present for the sake of argument, is adequate to interpret the *Ring*. Therefore, I have chosen to work from the premises that Wagner himself outlines in his theory, investigating how it functions as a work of art, and to this end bringing in tools as need be from modern literary criticism. Wagner's work represents a collision of mythological elements, literary influences, musical lines, historical consciousness, and philosophical currents of ideas, posing a perpetual challenge to scholars of various disciplines.

My approach, I would argue, suits a composer whose works defy classification, and, furthermore, have inherent contradictions due to their very artistic nature. They are works of art which have indirect practical purposes, as outlined in their aesthetic program, and Wagner obviously had a profound consciousness of the point in time at which these mythological dramas were written. The inherent paradoxes of his work make Wagner's musical-dramatic output especially susceptible to a post-structuralist analysis. When the topic is Wagner, interpretative eclecticism is not only tolerated, but sometimes it seems, rather, absolutely necessary.

To the interpretations of the *Ring* that have previously been advanced, I have added that of the tetralogy as a Romantic drama, thereby attempting to place the *Ring* and *Oper und Drama* more firmly within the German tradition. I have argued that the *Ring* portrays Romantic aesthetics, and it has an implicit Romantic irony that somehow permeates and fatefully controls the textual structure of the work. I have viewed Wotan as a human god, a mortal myth somehow embodied on the modern stage, and outlined some of the implications that the words/music dichotomy and the mythologically synthetic nature of the work actually have for the interpretation of the whole tetralogy.

Derrida names four precursors of deconstruction: Nietzsche, Freud, Heidegger, and Husserl. I have shown that Wagner can be included in this list as a forerunner of post-structuralism. The controversiality of my proposition can be countered by noting that one does not deconstruct the *Ring*; rather, as I have demonstrated, the *Ring* deconstructs itself. I have argued that the *Ring* is by its very nature and because of the theory that it exemplifies basically deconstructive. I hope to have shown how this deconstructive view of Wagner's work evolves naturally from the nature of the dramas under discussion. The *Ring* portrays itself and its own premises of mythological reconstruction. The world that the prelude to *Rheingold* evolves is, after all, destroyed in the finale of *Götterdämmerung*.

There is no doubt that at the time he wrote the *Ring* Wagner was a revolutionary in his art as well as his life. From his artistic creations and theoretical writings it is evident that he wanted to revise both verbal and nonverbal languages to form new means of communication. Hence the applicability, when discussing his works, of vocabulary taken from critical trends which have as their cornerstones the notion of the inadequacy of verbal means of communication. My deconstructive approach does justice to the work by pointing out this facet of its nature. When viewed in this light, Wagner's aesthetics do seem to have a definite affinity with the literary theory of Derrida.

Thus, analyzing Wagner's tetralogy using the tools of modern literary criticism, rather than being a willful dissection of a masterpiece, actually highlights the inherent contradictions despite or even because of which any great work of art functions. I hope the present study will prove to be a provocation to literary scholars and musicians alike to use new means and terms to discuss the problems that the *Ring* poses, and thus somehow inspire them to further illuminate and describe in a new way, with new terminology, the recesses and interpretative complexities of Wagner's huge cycle.

Selected Bibliography

Abbate, Carolyn. *Unsung Voices: Opera and Musical Narrative in the Nineteenth Century*. Princeton, NJ: Princeton University Press, 1991.

Aristotle. *Poetics*. Loeb Classical Library, vol. 199. Edited and translated by Stephen Halliwell. Also includes: Longinus, *On the Sublime*, and Demetrius, *On Style*. Cambridge, MA: Harvard University Press, 1995.

Baldick, Chris. *The Concise Oxford Dictionary of Literary Terms*. Oxford: Oxford University Press, 1990.

Barth, Herbert, ed. *Bayreuther Dramaturgie. "Der Ring des Nibelungen"*. Stuttgart: Belser, 1980. Includes: Martin Geck, "Wagners 'Ring'—Summe einer Lebensphilosophie," pp. 309–26.

Barthes, Roland. *Mythologies*. Translated by Annette Lavers. New York: Hill and Wang, 1972.

Beckson, Karl, and Arthur Ganz. *Literary Terms: A Dictionary*. 3d ed. New York: The Noonday Press, 1989.

Behler, Ernst. *Klassische Ironie, Romantische Ironie, Tragische Ironie. Zum Ursprung dieser Begriffe*. Darmstadt: Wissenschaftliche Buchgesellschaft, 1972.

——. *Frühromantik*. Sammlung Göschen 2807. Berlin: Walter de Gruyter, 1992.

Bermbach, Udo, ed. *In den Trümmern der eignen Welt: Richard Wagners "Der Ring des Nibelungen"*. Hamburger Beiträge zur öffentlichen Wissenschaft, vol. 7. Berlin: Dietrich Reimer, 1989. Includes: Udo Bermbach, "Die Destruktion der Institutionen. Zum politischen Gehalt des 'Ring' ," pp. 111–44; Herbert Schnädelbach, " 'Ring' und Mythos," pp. 145–61; Götz Friedrich, "Regieprobleme im 'Ring'," pp. 85–102.

Black, Max. *Models and Metaphors: Studies in Language and Philosophy*. Ithaca: Cornell University Press, 1962.

Blumenberg, Hans. *Arbeit am Mythos*. Frankfurt am Main: Suhrkamp, 1979.

Bohrer, Karl Heinz, ed. *Mythos und Moderne. Begriff und Bild einer Rekonstruktion.* Edition Suhrkamp, Neue Folge, vol. 144. Frankfurt am Main: Suhrkamp, 1983.

Bolz, Norbert. "Entzauberung der Welt und Dialektik der Aufklärung." In *Macht des Mythos—Ohnmacht der Vernunft?*, edited by Peter Kemper, pp. 223–41. Frankfurt am Main: Fischer, 1989.

Borchmeyer, Dieter. *Das Theater Richard Wagners: Idee, Dichtung, Wirkung.* Stuttgart: Reclam, 1982.

——, ed. *Wege des Mythos in der Moderne. Richard Wagner, "Der Ring des Nibelungen".* Munich: Deutscher Taschenbuch Verlag, 1987. Includes: Dieter Borchmeyer, " 'Faust' und 'Der Ring des Nibelungen'. Der Mythos des 19. Jahrhunderts in zwiefacher Gestalt," pp. 133–58; Wolfgang Frühwald, "Wandlungen eines Nationalmythos. Der Weg der Nibelungen ins 19. Jahrhundert," pp. 17–40; Dieter Bremer, "Vom Mythos zum Musikdrama. Wagner, Nietzsche und die griechische Tragödie," pp. 41–63; Carl Dahlhaus, "Musik als strukturale Analyse des Mythos. Claude Lévi-Strauss und 'Der Ring der Nibelungen'," pp. 64–74.

——. "Vom Anfang und Ende der Geschichte. Richard Wagners mythisches Drama. Idee und Inszenierung." In *Macht des Mythos—Ohnmacht der Vernunft?*, edited by Peter Kemper, pp. 176–200. Frankfurt am Main: Fischer, 1989.

Breig, Werner. "Das Schicksalskunde-Motiv im *Ring des Nibelungen.* Versuch einer harmonischen Analyse." In *Das Drama Richard Wagners als musikalisches Kunstwerk*, edited by Carl Dahlhaus, pp. 223–34. Studien zur Musikgeschichte des 19. Jahrhunderts, vol. 23. Regensburg: Gustav Bosse, 1970.

——. "Wagners kompositorisches Werk." In *Richard-Wagner-Handbuch*, edited by Ulrich Müller and Peter Wapnewski, pp. 353–470. Stuttgart: Alfred Kröner, 1986.

Bremer, Dieter. "Vom Mythos zum Musikdrama. Wagner, Nietzsche und die griechische Tragödie." In *Wege des Mythos in der Moderne. Richard Wagner, "Der Ring des Nibelungen"*, edited by Dieter Borchmeyer, pp. 41–63. Munich: Deutscher Taschenbuch Verlag, 1987.

Breuer, Rolf. *Tragische Handlungsstrukturen. Eine Theorie der Tragödie.* Munich: Wilhelm Fink, 1988.

Burkert, Walter. "Mythisches Denken. Versuch einer Definition an Hand des griechischen Befundes." In *Philosophie und Mythos. Ein Kolloquium*, edited by Hans Poser, pp. 16–39. Berlin: Walter de Gruyter, 1979.

Cicora, Mary A. " 'Eva im Paradies': An Approach to Wagner's *Meistersinger.*" *German Studies Review* 10, no. 2 (1987): pp. 321–33.

——. *"Parsifal" Reception in the "Bayreuther Blätter".* American University Studies, 55. New York: Peter Lang, 1987.

——. "From Metonymy to Metaphor: Wagner and Nietzsche on Language." *German Life and Letters* 42, no. 1 (1988): pp. 16–31.

——. "Wagner Parody in *Doktor Faustus.*" *Germanic Review* 63, no. 3 (1988): pp. 133–39.

——. "Beethoven, Shakespeare, and Wagner: Visual Music in *Doktor Faustus.*" *Deutsche Vierteljahrsschrift für Literaturwissenschaft und Geistesgeschichte* 63, no. 2 (1989): pp. 267–81.

——— . "Aesthetics and Politics at the Song Contest in Wagner's *Tannhäuser.*" *Germanic Review* 67, no. 2 (1992): pp. 50–58.

——— . *From History to Myth: Wagner's "Tannhäuser" and its Literary Sources.* Germanic Studies in America, 63. Bern: Peter Lang, 1992.

——— . "Music, Myth, and Metaphysics: Wagner Reception in Günter Grass' *Hundejahre.*" *German Studies Review* 16, no. 1 (1993): pp. 49–60.

——— . *Wagner's "Ring" and German Drama: Comparative Studies in Mythology and History in Drama.* Westport, CT: Greenwood Press, forthcoming.

——— . *Modern Myths and Wagnerian Deconstructions: Literary-Critical Approaches to Wagner's Music-Dramas.* Westport, CT: Greenwood Press, forthcoming.

Clément, Catherine. *Opera, or the Undoing of Women.* Translated by Betsy Wing. Minneapolis: University of Minnesota Press, 1988.

Cooke, Deryck. *I Saw the World End: A Study of Wagner's "Ring".* London: Oxford University Press, 1979.

Corse, Sandra. *Wagner and the New Consciousness: Language and Love in the "Ring".* Madison, NJ: Fairleigh Dickinson University Press, 1990.

Cowen, Roy C. *Das deutsche Drama im 19. Jahrhundert.* Sammlung Metzler, vol. 247. Stuttgart: Metzler, 1988.

Dahlhaus, Carl, ed. *Das Drama Richard Wagners als musikalisches Kunstwerk.* Studien zur Musikgeschichte des 19. Jahrhunderts, vol. 23. Regensburg: Gustav Bosse, 1970. Includes: Carl Dahlhaus, "Das unterbrochene Hauptwerk. Zu Wagners *Siegfried*," pp. 235–38; Tibor Kneif, "Wagner: eine Rekapitulation. Mythos und Geschichte im *Ring des Nibelungen*," pp. 213–21; Werner Breig, "Das Schicksalskunde-Motiv im *Ring des Nibelungen*. Versuch einer harmonischen Analyse," pp. 223–34.

——— , ed. *Richard Wagner: Werk und Wirkung.* Studien zur Musikgeschichte des 19. Jahrhunderts, vol. 26. Regensburg: Gustav Bosse, 1971. Includes: Dietrich Mack, "Zur Dramaturgie des *Ring*," pp. 53–63; Reinhold Brinkmann, "Szenische Epik. Marginalien zu Wagners Dramenkonzeption im *Ring des Nibelungen*," pp. 85–96; Carl Dahlhaus, "Über den Schluss der *Götterdämmerung*," pp. 97–115.

——— . *Richard Wagners Musikdramen.* Velber: Friedrich, 1971.

——— . *Wagners Konzeption des musikalischen Dramas.* Regensburg: Gustav Bosse, 1971.

——— . *Die Idee der absoluten Musik.* Munich: Deutscher Taschenbuch Verlag and Bärenreiter Verlag, 1978.

——— . "Die Musik." In *Richard-Wagner-Handbuch,* edited by Ulrich Müller and Peter Wapnewski, pp. 197–221. Stuttgart: Alfred Kröner, 1986.

——— . "Wagners Stellung in der Musikgeschichte." In *Richard-Wagner-Handbuch,* edited by Ulrich Müller and Peter Wapnewski, pp. 60–85. Stuttgart: Alfred Kröner, 1986.

——— . "Musik als strukturale Analyse des Mythos. Claude Lévi-Strauss und 'Der Ring des Nibelungen'." In *Wege des Mythos in der Moderne. Richard Wagner, "Der Ring des Nibelungen",* edited by Dieter Borchmeyer, pp. 64–74. Munich: Deutscher Taschenbuch Verlag, 1987.

Denkler, Horst. "Politische Dramaturgie. Zur Theorie des Dramas und des Theaters zwischen den Revolutionen von 1830 und 1848." In *Deutsche Dramentheorien.*

Beiträge zu einer historischen Poetik des Dramas in Deutschland, edited by Reinhold Grimm, vol. 2, pp. 345–73. Frankfurt am Main: Athenäum, 1971.

——. *Restauration und Revolution: Politische Tendenzen im deutschen Drama zwischen Wiener Kongress und Märzrevolution.* Munich: Wilhelm Fink, 1973.

Derrida, Jacques. *Of Grammatology.* Translated by Gayatri Chakravorty Spivak. Baltimore: The Johns Hopkins University Press, 1976.

Donington, Robert. *Wagner's "Ring" and its Symbols. The Music and the Myth.* London: Faber and Faber, 1963.

Eco, Umberto. *A Theory of Semiotics.* Bloomington: Indiana University Press, 1976.

——. *Semiotics and the Philosophy of Language.* Bloomington: Indiana University Press, 1984.

Ewans, Michael. *Wagner and Aeschylus: The "Ring" and the "Oresteia".* New York: Cambridge University Press, 1982.

Frank, Manfred. *Der kommende Gott. Vorlesungen über die Neue Mythologie.* Edition Suhrkamp 1142. Frankfurt am Main: Suhrkamp, 1982.

Franke, Rainer. *Richard Wagners Zürcher Kunstschriften: Politische und ästhetische Entwürfe auf seinem Weg zum "Ring des Nibelungen".* Hamburger Beiträge zur Musikwissenschaft, vol. 26. Hamburg: Verlag der Musikalienhandlung Karl Dieter Wagner, 1983.

Friedrich, Götz. "Die Bühne als Welttheater." In *Theaterarbeit an Wagners "Ring"*, edited by Dietrich Mack, pp. 104–10. Munich: Piper, 1978.

——. "Regieprobleme im 'Ring'." In *In den Trümmern der eignen Welt: Richard Wagners "Der Ring des Nibelungen"*, edited by Udo Bermbach, pp. 85–102. Hamburger Beiträge zur öffentlichen Wissenschaft, vol. 7. Berlin: Dietrich Reimer, 1989.

Fries, Othmar. *Richard Wagner und die deutsche Romantik: Versuch einer Einordnung.* Zurich: Atlantis, 1952.

Frye, Northrop. *Anatomy of Criticism: Four Essays.* Princeton, NJ: Princeton University Press, 1957; paperback, 1971.

Fuhrmann, Manfred, ed. *Terror und Spiel: Probleme der Mythenrezeption.* Poetik und Hermeneutik 4. Munich: Wilhelm Fink, 1971.

Gamm, Gerhard. "Wahrheit aus dem Unbewussten? Mythendichtung bei C.G. Jung und Sigmund Freud." In *Macht des Mythos—Ohnmacht der Vernunft?*, edited by Peter Kemper, pp. 148–75. Frankfurt am Main: Fischer, 1989.

Geck, Martin. "Wagners 'Ring'—Summe einer Lebensphilosophie." In *Bayreuther Dramaturgie. "Der Ring des Nibelungen"*, edited by Herbert Barth, pp. 309–26. Stuttgart: Belser, 1980.

Gockel, Heinz. "Mythologie als Ontologie: Zum Mythosbegriff im 19. Jahrhundert." In *Mythos und Mythologie in der Literatur des 19. Jahrhunderts*, edited by Helmut Koopmann, pp. 25–58. Studien zur Philosophie und Literatur des neunzehnten Jahrhunderts, vol. 36. Frankfurt am Main: Vittorio Klostermann, 1979.

Graevenitz, Gerhard von. *Mythos: Zur Geschichte einer Denkgewohnheit.* Stuttgart: Metzler, 1987.

Gregor-Dellin, Martin. *Wagner-Chronik. Daten zu Leben und Werk.* Munich: Carl Hanser, 1972. 2d ed., Munich: Deutscher Taschenbuch Verlag, and Kassel, Basel; London: Bärenreiter-Verlag Karl Vötterle, 1983.

————. *Richard Wagner—die Revolution als Oper*. Reihe Hanser, 129. Munich: Carl Hanser, 1973. Includes: "Beziehungen zum Sozialismus," pp. 20–41.

————. *Richard Wagner: Sein Leben, Sein Werk, Sein Jahrhundert*. Munich: Piper, 1980.

Grimm, Reinhold, ed. *Deutsche Dramentheorien. Beiträge zu einer historischen Poetik des Dramas in Deutschland*. 2 vols. Frankfurt am Main: Athenäum, 1971. Includes: Peter Schmidt, "Romantisches Drama: Zur Theorie eines Paradoxons," vol. 1, pp. 245–69; Horst Denkler, "Politische Dramaturgie. Zur Theorie des Dramas und des Theaters zwischen den Revolutionen von 1830 und 1848," vol. 2, pp. 345–73.

Groos, Arthur, and Roger Parker, eds. *Reading Opera*. Princeton, NJ: Princeton University Press, 1988.

Harris, Wendell V. *Dictionary of Concepts in Literary Criticism and Theory*. Westport, CT: Greenwood Press, 1992.

Hass, Hans-Egon, and Gustav-Adolf Mohrlüder, eds. *Ironie als literarisches Phänomen*. Cologne: Kiepenheuer und Witsch, 1973.

Heimrich, Bernhard. *Fiktion und Fiktionsironie in Theorie und Dichtung der deutschen Romantik*. Studien zur deutschen Literatur, vol. 9. Tübingen: Max Niemeyer, 1968.

Heinzle, Joachim, and Anneliese Waldschmidt, eds. *Die Nibelungen. Ein deutscher Wahn, ein deutscher Alptraum. Studien und Dokumente zur Rezeption des Nibelungenstoffs im 19. und 20. Jahrhundert*. Suhrkamp Taschenbuch 2110. Frankfurt am Main: Suhrkamp, 1991. Includes: Thomas Koebner, "Minne Macht. Zu Richard Wagners Bühnenwerk *Der Ring des Nibelungen*," pp. 309–32.

Hinck, Walter. *Theater der Hoffnung. Von der Aufklärung bis zur Gegenwart*. Suhrkamp Taschenbuch 1495. Frankfurt am Main: Suhrkamp, 1988.

————, ed. *Handbuch des deutschen Dramas*. Düsseldorf: August Bagel, 1980. Includes: Gerhard Kluge, "Das romantische Drama," pp. 186–99.

Hübner, Kurt. *Die Wahrheit des Mythos*. Munich: C.H. Beck, 1985.

Ingenhoff, Anette. *Drama oder Epos? Richard Wagners Gattungstheorie des musikalischen Dramas*. Untersuchungen zur deutschen Literaturgeschichte, vol. 41. Tübingen: Max Niemeyer, 1987.

Ingenschay-Goch, Dagmar. *Richard Wagners neu erfundener Mythos: Zur Rezeption und Reproduktion des germanischen Mythos in seinen Operntexten*. Abhandlungen zur Kunst-, Musik- und Literaturwissenschaft, vol. 311. Bonn: Bouvier Verlag Herbert Grundmann, 1982.

Japp, Uwe. *Theorie der Ironie*. Frankfurt am Main: Vittorio Klostermann, 1983.

Johnson, Mark, ed. *Philosophical Perspectives on Metaphor*. Minneapolis: University of Minnesota Press, 1981.

Kafitz, Dieter. *Grundzüge einer Geschichte des deutschen Dramas von Lessing bis zum Naturalismus*. Vol. 1. Königstein/Ts.: Athenäum, 1982.

Keller, Werner, ed. *Beiträge zur Poetik des Dramas*. Darmstadt: Wissenschaftliche Buchgesellschaft, 1976.

Kemper, Peter, ed. *Macht des Mythos—Ohnmacht der Vernunft?* Frankfurt am Main: Fischer, 1989. Includes: Dieter Borchmeyer, "Vom Anfang und Ende der Geschichte. Richard Wagners mythisches Drama. Idee und Inszenierung," pp. 176–200; Norbert Bolz, "Entzauberung der Welt und Dialektik der Aufklärung," pp. 223–41; Gerhard Gamm, "Wahrheit aus dem Unbewussten? Mythendichtung bei C.G. Jung und Sigmund Freud," pp 148–75.

Kleist, Heinrich von. *Sämtliche Werke und Briefe.* 2d ed. 2 vols. Edited by Helmut Sembdner. Munich: Carl Hanser, 1961.

Klotz, Volker. *Geschlossene und offene Form im Drama.* 4th ed. Munich: Carl Hanser, 1969.

Kluckhohn, Paul. "Die Arten des Dramas." *Deutsche Vierteljahrsschrift für Literaturwissenschaft und Geistesgeschichte* 19, no. 3 (1941): pp. 241–68.

Kluge, Gerhard. "Das romantische Drama." In *Handbuch des deutschen Dramas,* edited by Walter Hinck, pp. 186–99. Düsseldorf: August Bagel, 1980.

Kneif, Tibor. "Wagner: eine Rekapitulation. Mythos und Geschichte im *Ring des Nibelungen.*" In *Das Drama Richard Wagners als musikalisches Kunstwerk,* edited Carl Dahlhaus, pp. 213–21. Studien zur Musikgeschichte des 19. Jahrhunderts, vol. 23. Regensburg: Gustav Bosse, 1970.

Koebner, Thomas. "Minne Macht. Zu Richard Wagners Bühnenwerk *Der Ring des Nibelungen.*" In *Die Nibelungen. Ein deutscher Wahn, ein deutscher Alptraum. Studien und Dokumente zur Rezeption des Nibelungenstoffs im 19. und 20. Jahrhundert,* edited by Joachim Heinzle and Anneliese Waldschmidt, pp. 309–32. Suhrkamp Taschenbuch 2110. Frankfurt am Main: Suhrkamp, 1991.

Koopmann, Helmut, ed. *Mythos und Mythologie in der Literatur des 19. Jahrhunderts.* Studien zur Philosophie und Literatur des neunzehnten Jahrhunderts, vol. 36. Frankfurt am Main: Vittorio Klostermann, 1979. Includes: Heinz Gockel, "Mythologie als Ontologie: Zum Mythosbegriff im 19. Jahrhundert," pp. 25–58.

Korff, H.A. *Geist der Goethezeit. Versuch einer ideellen Entwicklung der klassisch-romantischen Literaturgeschichte.* Vol. 3: *Frühromantik.* 7th ed. Leipzig: Koehler & Amelang, 1966.

——— . *Geist der Goethezeit. Versuch einer ideellen Entwicklung der klassisch-romantischen Literaturgeschichte.* Vol. 4: *Hochromantik.* 7th ed. Leipzig: Koehler & Amelang, 1966.

Krohn, Rüdiger. "Richard Wagner und die Revolution von 1848/49." In *Richard-Wagner-Handbuch,* edited by Ulrich Müller and Peter Wapnewski, pp. 86–100. Stuttgart: Alfred Kröner, 1986.

Kröplin, Eckart. *Richard Wagner: Theatralisches Leben und lebendiges Theater.* Leipzig: VEB Deutscher Verlag für Musik, 1989.

Kunze, Stefan. *Der Kunstbegriff Richard Wagners: Voraussetzungen und Folgerungen.* Regensburg: Gustav Bosse, 1983.

Lakoff, George, and Mark Johnson. *Metaphors We Live By.* Chicago: University of Chicago Press, 1980.

Lévi-Strauss, Claude. *The Raw and the Cooked.* Translated by John and Doreen Weightman. New York: Harper and Row, 1969.

Levin, David J., ed. *Opera Through Other Eyes.* Stanford, CA: Stanford University Press, 1994.

Loos, Paul Arthur. *Richard Wagner: Vollendung und Tragik der deutschen Romantik.* Munich: Leo Lehnen, 1952.

McInnes, Edward. *Das deutsche Drama des 19. Jahrhunderts.* Grundlagen der Germanistik, 26. Berlin: Erich Schmidt, 1983.

Mack, Dietrich. *Ansichten zum Tragischen und zur Tragödie. Ein Kompendium der deutschen Theorie im 20. Jahrhundert.* Munich: Wilhelm Fink, 1970.

——, ed. *Theaterarbeit an Wagners "Ring".* Munich: Piper, 1978. Includes: Herta Elisabeth Renk, "Anmerkungen zur Beziehung zwischen Musiktheater und Semiotik," pp. 275–88; Götz Friedrich, "Die Bühne als Welttheater," pp. 104–110.

Magee, Bryan. *Aspects of Wagner.* Rev. ed. Oxford: Oxford University Press, 1988.

Magee, Elizabeth. *Richard Wagner and the Nibelungs.* New York: Oxford University Press, 1990.

Mann, Otto. *Geschichte des deutschen Dramas.* 3d ed. Kröners Taschenausgabe, vol. 296. Stuttgart: Alfred Kröner, 1969.

Martini, Fritz. *Deutsche Literatur im bürgerlichen Realismus 1848–1898.* 4th ed. Stuttgart: Metzler, 1981.

——. "Drama und Roman im 19. Jahrhundert: Perspektiven auf ein Thema der Formgeschichte." In *Literarische Form und Geschichte: Aufsätze zu Gattungstheorie und Gattungsentwicklung vom Sturm und Drang bis zum Erzählen heute,* pp. 48–80. Stuttgart: Metzler, 1984.

Mayer, Hans. *Anmerkungen zu Richard Wagner.* Edition Suhrkamp 189. Frankfurt am Main: Suhrkamp, 1966. 2d ed., 1977. Includes: "Zerstörung und Selbstzerstörung im 'Ring des Nibelungen'," pp. 91–99; "Wagners 'Ring' als bürgerliches Parabelspiel," pp. 100–111.

——. *Richard Wagner: Mitwelt und Nachwelt.* Stuttgart: Belser, 1978. Includes: "Der 'Ring' und die Zweideutigkeit des Wissens," pp. 230–35; "Siegfrieds Trauermarsch," pp. 236–41.

Meier, Helmut G. "Orte neuer Mythen. Von der Universalpoesie zum Gesamtkunstwerk." In *Philosophie und Mythos. Ein Kolloquium,* edited by Hans Poser, pp. 154–73. Berlin: Walter de Gruyter, 1979.

Michel, Laurence, and Richard B. Sewall, eds. *Tragedy: Modern Essays in Criticism.* Englewood Cliffs, NJ: Prentice-Hall, 1963.

Mork, Andrea. *Richard Wagner als politischer Schriftsteller: Weltanschauung und Wirkungsgeschichte.* Frankfurt: Campus, 1990.

Müller, Ulrich, and Peter Wapnewski, eds. *Richard-Wagner-Handbuch.* Stuttgart: Alfred Kröner, 1986. Includes: Werner Breig, "Wagners kompositorisches Werk," pp. 353–470; Peter Wapnewski, "Die Oper Richard Wagners als Dichtung," pp. 223–352; Carl Dahlhaus, "Die Musik," pp. 197–221; Ulrich Müller, "Richard Wagner und die Antike," pp. 7–18; Carl Dahlhaus, "Wagners Stellung in der Musikgeschichte," pp. 60–85; Rüdiger Krohn, "Richard Wagner und die Revolution von 1848/49," pp. 86–100.

Nattiez, Jean-Jacques. *Wagner Androgyne.* Translated by Stewart Spencer. Princeton, NJ: Princeton University Press, 1993.

Novalis. *Werke, Tagebücher und Briefe Friedrich von Hardenbergs.* Edited by Hans-Joachim Mähl and Richard Samuel. 2 vols. Munich and Vienna: Carl Hanser, 1978.

Poser, Hans, ed. *Philosophie und Mythos. Ein Kolloquium.* Berlin: Walter de Gruyter, 1979. Includes: Helmut G. Meier, "Orte neuer Mythen. Von der Universalpoesie zum Gesamtkunstwerk," pp. 154–73; Walter Burkert, "Mythisches Denken. Versuch einer Definition an Hand des griechischen Befundes," pp. 16–39.

Prang, Helmut. *Die Romantische Ironie*. Erträge der Forschung, vol. 12. Darmstadt: Wissenschaftliche Buchgesellschaft, 1972.

Rather, L.J. *The Dream of Self-Destruction: Wagner's "Ring" and the Modern World*. Baton Rouge: Louisiana State University Press, 1979.

Renk, Herta Elisabeth. "Anmerkungen zur Beziehung zwischen Musiktheater und Semiotik." In *Theaterarbeit an Wagners "Ring"*, edited by Dietrich Mack, pp. 275–88. Munich: Piper, 1978.

Richards. I.A. *The Philosophy of Rhetoric*. New York: Oxford University Press, 1936.

Ricoeur, Paul. *Interpretation Theory: Discourse and the Surplus of Meaning*. Fort Worth: Texas Christian University Press, 1976.

Schadewaldt, Wolfgang. "Richard Wagner und die Griechen." In *Richard Wagner und das neue Bayreuth*, edited by Wieland Wagner, pp. 149–74. Munich: Paul List, 1962.

———. *Antike und Gegenwart. Über die Tragödie*. Munich: Deutscher Taschenbuch Verlag, 1966.

Schaefer, Albert, ed. *Ironie und Dichtung*. Munich: C.H. Beck, 1970.

Schanze, Helmut. *Drama im Bürgerlichen Realismus (1850–1890): Theorie und Praxis*. Studien zur Philosophie und Literatur des neunzehnten Jahrhunderts, vol. 21. Frankfurt am Main: Vittorio Klostermann, 1973.

———, ed. *Friedrich Schlegel und die Kunsttheorie seiner Zeit*. Wege der Forschung, vol. 609. Darmstadt: Wissenschaftliche Buchgesellschaft, 1985.

Schlegel, Friedrich. *Charakteristiken und Kritiken I (1796–1801)*, edited by Hans Eichner. Vol. 2 of *Kritische Friedrich-Schlegel-Ausgabe*, edited by Ernst Behler et al. Munich, Paderborn, Vienna: Verlag Ferdinand Schöningh, 1967.

Schmidt, Peter. "Romantisches Drama: Zur Theorie eines Paradoxons." In *Deutsche Dramentheorien. Beiträge zu einer historischen Poetik des Dramas in Deutschland*, vol. 1, edited by Reinhold Grimm, pp. 245–69. Frankfurt am Main: Athenäum, 1971.

Schnädelbach, Herbert. " 'Ring' und Mythos." In *In den Trümmern der eignen Welt: Richard Wagners "Der Ring des Nibelungen"*, edited by Udo Bermbach, pp. 145–61. Hamburger Beiträge zur öffentlichen Wissenschaft, vol. 7. Berlin: Dietrich Reimer, 1989.

Schnell, Ralf. *Die verkehrte Welt. Literarische Ironie im 19. Jahrhundert*. Stuttgart: Metzler, 1989.

Schulte, Bettina. *Unmittelbarkeit und Vermittlung im Werk Heinrich von Kleists*. Göttingen: Vandenhoeck und Ruprecht, 1988.

Schweikle, Günther and Irmgard, eds. *Metzler Literatur Lexikon. Stichwörter zur Weltliteratur*. Stuttgart: Metzler, 1984.

Sengle, Friedrich. "Vom Absoluten in der Tragödie." *Deutsche Vierteljahrsschrift für Literaturwissenschaft und Geistesgeschichte* 20, no. 3 (1942): pp. 265–72.

Shaw, George Bernard. *The Perfect Wagnerite: A Commentary on the Niblung's Ring*. 4th ed. New York: Dover Publications, Inc., 1967. (Originally published 1898; 4th ed. originally published 1923.)

Siegel, Linda. "Wagner and the Romanticism of E.T.A. Hoffmann." *The Musical Quarterly* 51 (1965): pp. 597–613.

Steffen, Hans, ed. *Die Deutsche Romantik: Poetik, Formen, und Motive*. Göttingen: Vandenhoeck und Ruprecht, 1967. Includes: Ingrid Strohschneider-Kohrs, "Zur Poetik der deutschen Romantik II: Die romantische Ironie," pp. 75–97.

Steiner, George. *The Death of Tragedy*. New York: Alfred A. Knopf, 1961.

Strässner, Matthias. *Analytisches Drama*. Munich: Wilhelm Fink, 1980.

Strohschneider-Kohrs, Ingrid. "Zur Poetik der deutschen Romantik II: Die romantische Ironie." In *Die Deutsche Romantik: Poetik, Formen, und Motive*, edited by Hans Steffen, pp. 75–97. Göttingen: Vandenhoeck und Ruprecht, 1967.

——. *Die romantische Ironie in Theorie und Gestaltung*. Hermaea, Germanistische Forschungen, Neue Folge, vol. 6. 2d, rev. ed. Tübingen: Max Niemeyer, 1977.

Szondi, Peter. *Schriften I*. Edited by Wolfgang Fietkau. Frankfurt am Main: Suhrkamp, 1978. Includes: "Versuch über das Tragische," pp. 151–260.

——. *Schriften II*. Ed. Wolfgang Fietkau. Frankfurt am Main: Suhrkamp, 1978. Includes: "Friedrich Schlegel und die romantische Ironie," pp. 11–31.

Vaget, Hans Rudolf. "Erlösung durch Liebe: Wagners *Ring* und Goethes *Faust*." *"Götterdämmerung": Programmhefte der Bayreuther Festspiele* (1985), pp. 14–31.

Wagner, Cosima. Die Tagebücher. 4 vols. 2d ed. Edited by Martin Gregor-Dellin and Dietrich Mack. Munich: Piper, 1976, 1982. English translation by Geoffrey Skelton. *Diaries*. 2 vols. New York: Harcourt Brace Jovanovich, 1978/80.

Wagner, Richard. *Gesammelte Schriften und Dichtungen*. 10 vols. Leipzig: E. W. Fritzsch, 1887–88. Rpt. Steiger, 1976.

——. *Sämtliche Briefe*. Vol. 4: *Briefe der Jahre 1851–1852*. Edited by Gertrud Strobel and Werner Wolf. Leipzig: VEB Deutscher Verlag für Musik, 1979.

——. *Die Musikdramen*. Edited by Joachim Kaiser. Hamburg: Hoffmann und Campe, 1971; Munich: Deutscher Taschenbuch Verlag, 1978, 1981.

——. *Mein Leben*. Edited by Martin Gregor-Dellin. Munich: Paul List, 1963; Goldmann, 1983.

——. *Oper und Drama*. Edited by Klaus Kropfinger. Stuttgart: Reclam, 1984.

——. *Sämtliche Briefe*. Vol. 6: *Januar 1854–Februar 1855*. Edited by Hans-Joachim Bauer and Johannes Forner. Leipzig: VEB Deutscher Verlag für Musik, 1986.

——. *Sämtliche Briefe*. Vol. 5: *September 1852–Januar 1854*. Edited by Gertrud Strobel and Werner Wolf. Leipzig: Deutscher Verlag für Musik, 1993.

Wapnewski, Peter. *Richard Wagner—Die Szene und ihr Meister*. Beck'sche Schwarze Reihe, vol. 178. Munich: C.H. Beck, 1978.

——. *Tristan der Held Richard Wagners*. Berlin: Severin und Siedler, 1981.

——. *Der traurige Gott. Richard Wagner in seinen Helden*. Munich: C. H. Beck, 1978; Deutscher Taschenbuch Verlag, 1982.

——. "Gedanken zu Richard Wagner hundert Jahre nach seinem Tode." *"Die Meistersinger von Nürnberg": Programmhefte der Bayreuther Festspiele* (1983), pp. 2–17.

——. "Der Ring und sein Kreislauf. Überlegungen zum Textverständnis der 'Götterdämmerung'." *"Götterdämmerung": Programmhefte der Bayreuther Festspiele* (1984), pp. 25–50.

——. "Die Oper Richard Wagners als Dichtung." In *Richard-Wagner-Handbuch*, edited by Ulrich Müller and Peter Wapnewski, pp. 223–352. Stuttgart: Alfred Kröner, 1986.

Westernhagen, Curt von. *Richard Wagners Dresdener Bibliothek 1842 bis 1849. Neue Dokumente zur Geschichte seines Schaffens*. Wiesbaden: F.A. Brockhaus, 1966.

Wiese, Benno von. "Probleme der deutschen Tragödie im 19. Jahrhundert." *Wirkendes Wort* 1 (1950/51): pp. 32–38.

———— . *Die Deutsche Tragödie von Lessing bis Hebbel.* Hamburg: Hoffmann und Campe, 1948. 6th ed., 1964.

Index